Jasmine Birtles has a background in financial and business journalism as well as being a TV presenter and humorist. She writes for the *Mirror*, the *Independent on Sunday*, *Cosmo*, *Glamour* and *Essentials* and has a daily column in the *Express*.

Jasmine appears regularly as a financial expert on GMTV, *This Morning*, *The Wright Stuff*, BBC *Breakfast*, *Working Lunch*, *Tonight* and all the news channels. She also presents online for BBC RaW Money, helping with financial literacy and skills for everyday life.

the money magpie

'I can help you ditch your debts, make money and save £1000s'

JASMINE BIRTLES

1 3 5 7 9 10 8 6 4 2

Published in 2009 by Vermilion, an imprint of Ebury Publishing

Ebury Publishing is a Random House Group company

The Random House Group Limited Reg. No. 954009

Addresses for companies within the Random House Group can be found at www.rbooks.co.uk

A CIP catalogue record for this book is available from the British Library

The Random House Group Limited supports The Forest Stewardship Council (FSC), the leading international forest certification organisation. All our titles that are printed on Greenpeace approved FSC certified paper carry the FSC logo. Our paper procurement policy can be found at www.rbooks.co.uk/environment

Printed and bound in Great Britain by
CPI Cox & Wyman, Reading, RG1 8EX

ISBN 9780091929466

The information in this book is general in nature and not intended to constitute nor be relied on for specific financial or any other professional advice. The author and publishers disclaim, as far as the law allows, any liability arising directly or indirectly from the use or misuse of the information contained in this book.

This book is a work of non-fiction. The names of people in the case studies have been changed solely to protect the privacy of others.

To the Moneymagpie.com team. Thanks guys!

Contents

Acknowledgements

First, I must thank the Moneymagpies who kept things going while I was buried behind my computer writing this book. So big thanks to Alessia Horwich, Jo Robinson, Chiara Cavaglieri and Serena Cowdy for doing that for weeks on end.

I had superb research, editing and writing help from other Moneymagpies, particularly David Ryder, Mel Feisst and Mara Pattison-Sowden, and extra research from Moneymagpies Amy Smith, Sarah Squires and Nicky Peckham. Financial journalists Martin Fagan and Sarah Jagger also gave invaluable help, as did my friends John Byrne, Hamish Gordon and Richard Lacquiere who also contribute to Moneymagpie.com as cartoonist, blogger and writer respectively. Thanks, too, for important help and advice from my ever-helpful financial friends Cliff D'Arcy and Tom McPhail.

Naturally, my editors – the very professional Julia Kellaway and Clare Hulton – played an impressive part in the production of the book, and the whole process was made possible by the hard work of the Random House sales, marketing, PR, design and IT teams.

My literary agent, Euan Thorneycroft, did his usual great work, as did my managing agent, June Ford-Crush, who has supported the book throughout.

introduction

Why Do You Need This Book?

Welcome to the start of your new life as a Money Magpie! I launched Moneymagpie.com in April 2007 because I wanted to give people friendly, easy and fun information on making, saving and managing money. It's a free site about living a richer life – in all senses – and it's got lots of laughs in it!

I got into financial journalism because I realised that, actually, managing your money and getting rich are not difficult things. In fact, they're pretty straightforward if you have the basic knowledge and you're willing to take it gradually.

But that's the problem – most of us don't have that knowledge and we get taken in by promises of get-rich-quick schemes.

We get into debt and make very bad financial decisions because we haven't been taught about money at school, and most of us had parents who didn't know a lot about the subject either. It doesn't help that the way money is presented by most financial institutions (and much of the media) is so confusing and frightening that most people don't know where to start. So they don't.

I'm regularly asked on to television or radio to explain 'in simple terms' some new financial product or economic situation we're facing. I also often appear on television giving people new and different ideas for making money on the side or showing how they can get things for free or very cheap. You will find all these things in this book.

You will also find them on Moneymagpie.com. The site has information on hundreds of ways to earn a bit on the side and be clever with your money day to day. We add up-to-date information and advice every week so make sure you're signed up to the free weekly newsletter.

The other reason to sign up to the newsletter, and read the whole of this book, is because everyone needs a lot more financial knowledge now than they did just a couple of decades ago. We're in a new age economically. We've come out of the 'golden age' when we could depend on the State to provide for us. Our parents and grandparents took it for granted that the State would provide some sort of liveable pension, that they could get most of their healthcare free on the NHS and that education was free.

Not only that, but until the 1980s there weren't too many financial products that we Brits had to bother about. We had a current account, a bank manager who was cautious and would ask all sorts of questions if we wanted to borrow money, and we probably had some savings in a building society. Most of us had a job for life (or at least expected one) and those jobs often had pensions attached – sometimes nice, fat, final-salary pensions. Some of us who were a bit daring had some stock market investments but that sort of thing was mostly left to the 'professionals' in the City.

But that all changed in the 1980s – even though most of us didn't notice. We have only just started to notice now, and that's really only because of the financial turmoil of recent years.

In the 1980s many of the State provisions started to drain away – university and college education was starting to cost; we were encouraged to opt out of the State Second Pension and the main State Pension was already too low for most people to live on. At the same time, we had greater access to increasingly complex – and often financially dangerous – financial products. These included credit cards, bigger and more complex mortgages (such as endowment mortgages), stock market investments and new types of bonds and other odd-sounding investments.

What we didn't have was the knowledge and skill to use them properly.

We still don't. That's why most of us have money problems now. We've been like children playing with fire and we've been badly burned. It's also why the banks and other financial providers got away with behaving so selfishly for so long. We let them.

So we're in a whole new world economically and financially. The difference, now, is that we know we are – and it's upsetting us. That's where this book and the Moneymagpie.com website come in. The point of them both is to give you the knowledge, the power and the tools to make the most of the money you have, earn more if you want to and make your own future secure, whatever governments and financial institutions try to do.

This book will give you all the power you need. In fact, it will show you the power you already have – you just didn't know you had it. It will help you:

- *Get out of debt.*
- *Learn to spend and save cleverly.*
- *Find fun ways of making extra cash on the side.*
- *Understand how to invest in great products for a rich future.*

It will also, I hope, take away the fear and mystique from your finances. Money is not to be feared or revered. It's there to support your life and help you do what *you* want to do.

Think of money as something you sit on. That's where it should be in the grand scheme of things – under your control and in its place. Not over your head, pressing down on you. Not far away, escaping your clutches. Not in front of you as a golden statue to be bowed down to. It should be in its box, in its place, serving you and not dictating to you. The more we learn about money – how to use it, how not to abuse it and how to make it work for us – the more confidence we have and the smaller the 'Money Monster' will become.

Becoming a real Money Magpie and getting control over your finances is a step-by-step process. This book will take you through those steps. In a nutshell, you will:

- *Throw off old beliefs, limitations and indoctrinations from parents or your upbringing.*
- *Accept no limitations to your potential.*

- *Get a plan.*
- *Get out of debt.*
- *Plug the holes in your money machine by cutting out overpaying for essentials. See Chapters 5 and 6 for loads of ideas on how to be a really smart spender and never pay more than you have to for anything.*
- *Insulate yourself even more by cutting down on inessential spending.*
- *Get into the habit of shopping around and getting the best price for everything (not necessarily the cheapest, but definitely the best value).*
- *Set up methods of increasing your monthly income, either by increasing your salary or by adding to your income through extras.*
- *Build up solid foundations by getting the savings habit.*
- *Invest for now. Put money into assets like your home or other products that offer you a good return.*
- *Invest for the future. Invest regularly into simple, straightforward products. Spread your money across various 'asset classes' such as the stock market, pensions and property.*
- *Set up streams of income that will keep bringing in royalties, rent, dividends or interest for little effort for years to come.*
- *Live! Continue the habit of living well, not wasting money on junk but spending it on things you love. Keep an eye on your investments and on your spending here and there but don't become obsessed. Money is there to help your life; it is not something to live for.*

By the end of this book you will have the knowledge to be in control of your finances rather than letting them control you – I promise!

part one

GETTING THE BASICS RIGHT

chapter one

Quiz: What Money Type Are You?

Are you wondering how your financial situation compares to that of other people, particularly your friends and family? You might think you're a complete dunce when it comes to money, but I might have news for you. Take my quick money quiz and find out what state your finances are in. It will reveal whether you're a beginner, if you've got a handle on the basics or if you're ready for more of a challenge.

Quick Money Quiz

1. How would you describe your feelings about your money situation right now?

a. Scary. I can't bear to look at it but I know it's not in a good state.

b. Half and half. I'm pretty sure I've got some things covered, but there are big areas that I just don't understand.

c. Pretty solid actually. I don't know it all but I've got savings and investments and I like to think I'm fairly sensible about spending.

2. What did your parents teach you about money?

a. Nothing. They didn't have a clue. They just lurched from money crisis to money crisis. They're still having problems and I think I'll have to bail them out at some point.

b. The basics I suppose – how you shouldn't spend more than you earn. I haven't always followed it!

c. They showed me how to budget when I was a teenager. It was so obvious it made sense to me and I've done it ever since.

3. How are you with figures?

a. Terrible. I hate numbers. My eyes glaze over the moment I hear the word 'percentage'. I'm asleep by the time you mention a 'pension'.

b. Not great. I can do the basics but I prefer words.

c. Love them. I enjoy doing sums in my head and I don't understand why more people don't like maths. It must be that it's badly taught.

4. How do you deal with your bills?

a. I ignore them if I can, although I do manage to pay the essential ones eventually. It's frightening, though. I hate the red demands.

b. I pay them by direct debit. It's easier and I usually have enough in my account to cover them.

c. I pay by direct debit and I check once or twice a year that I'm getting the best deal. I always end up switching at least one of my utilities to a cheaper version.

5. Have you got any debts?

a. Have I?! Even my debts are in debt. I'm doing my best to juggle them but I'm losing sleep over it.

b. Mainly my mortgage, but I regularly go overdrawn and I sometimes struggle to pay my credit card bills.

c. My mortgage is the only debt I have/I have no debt.

6. Have you got any savings?

a. You're having a laugh, aren't you?

b. Yes, but I'm still wondering whether the money would be safer under the bed?!

c. Yes, it's spread about in different banks. I save regularly, and I intend to set up more investments.

7. Do you know what your monthly outgoings are?

a. No, I just know they're too much/what's an outgoing?

b. Not really. Just a vague idea. I cringe a bit if I catch a glance at my bank statement when it comes in.

c. Yes, on the whole. I check them about once a year.

8. Do you have a budget that you stick to?

a. Nope.

b. Not really. I know I should cut down on my spending, but I manage.

c. Oh yes. I don't understand how people cope without one.

9. Can you cook or do you rely on pre-prepared meals and takeaways?

a. I can cook a bit but usually I'm too tired when I come home. And microwave meals are so much more convenient.

b. Yes, but I probably have takeaways too often.

c. Yes, but I eat out quite a lot too.

10. Do you ever buy things on hire purchase or with in-house finance like you get in car dealerships?

a. Yes, and they're a real burden. I'm still paying for a sofa that broke last year!

b. No, but I signed up for some car finance that I wish I hadn't agreed to.

c. No. I would rather buy second-hand or do without than use a hire purchase agreement.

11. How are you investing for your future?

a. Bah! I can't even cope with paying for now, let alone the future.

b. I've got a bit of money in the company pension and then there's my cash ISAs. If I had the money I would invest in property.

c. I'm investing in various stocks and share funds although they haven't done so well recently. I would like to investigate the stock market properly once I have enough money.

12. What do you think about the stock market?

a. The what? I haven't got a clue.

b. Scary.

c. Interesting. I wish I could make money from it.

13. Do you like your job? Would you like to do something different?

a. I'd love to do something different. I'm waiting until my Lottery win.

b. It's all right but there are lots of other things I'd like to try.

c. Yes, but I have other plans for later.

14. If you won millions in the Lottery, what would you do with it?

a. Give up this life and move to a place in the sun.

b. I'd sort my family out, give some to friends and then live the life I want to.

c. I hate the Lottery. It's a tax on the poor and stupid. I never play it.

15. Do you have a five-year plan for yourself and/or your family?

a. You're kidding aren't you? I don't even have a five-week plan!

b. Not really. I have some ideas of what I'd like to do with my life and there are a few things I'd really like to do soon, but I don't know when.

c. Yes, I review it every year or so.

16. If you have children, have you invested for their education and their future?

a. No. Just getting by day to day takes up all, and more, of my money.
b. I have put a bit by, but I don't know if it's enough. We've got some children's savings bonds but universities are getting so expensive I don't know if they will cover the cost when it comes around.
c. Yes, I invest in stock market funds for them.

17. Do you own your own home? If you don't, would you like to?
a. No. I would like to but I don't see how I'm ever going to afford one.
b. Yes, and the mortgage payments are the bane of my life!
c. Yes, and I can cope with the mortgage payments easily.

18. How long could you keep going if you suddenly lost your income?
a. About a week, but mainly on credit cards.
b. Maybe a month or so. I'm not sure.
c. Six months. I have enough put by in savings to cover me in case I lose my job.

19. Have you made a will?
a. No. Why would I? It's too depressing and, anyway, I'm too young to think of that now.
b. I keep meaning to. I know I should but there are other things that are more pressing.
c. Yes, but I haven't updated it for a while. I am planning on doing it when the next 'Will Aid' month comes round.

20. What do you think are the economic prospects for our country?

a. Bad. You don't hear anything but doom and gloom on the telly. I don't think it's ever going to get better.

b. Not great. You hear so many different things from people who seem to know. I hope it will get better but it's not looking good.

c. I think it will get better but we've got some pain to get through first. We're being forced to change our ways and that's never pleasant.

HOW DID YOU GET ON?

Mostly 'a's: Beginner

Now, honestly, believe me when I say this: money is not frightening.

However bad your current financial situation is, or seems to be, you can get out of it and improve your lot. Even if you are horribly in debt and everything seems hopeless, there is *always* a way out and up. The first step is facing the 'Money Monster', which you have started to do by reading this book.

My advice is to read the whole book to the end of Chapter 9 and then go back and read it all again, soaking in the changes I suggest you start making. These include: facing your bills and statements; talking to your creditors; getting a friend to join in with you to give you support; and signing up to all the various money-saving ideas in those chapters.

Once you have made real progress on the basics, including properly managing your incomings and outgoings – and this might take six months to a year or more – then read the rest of the book. A little further on, I'll let you into all of the secrets about how to set yourself up for long-term wealth by investing and setting up passive streams of income. Oh yes, you can – don't stop yourself before you've even started. Take it 'baby step' by 'baby step' and one day you will find, to your surprise, that you're giving your friends tips and advice about their money.

Mostly 'b's: Basics Covered

You've made a start and you can do the basics, so some of the chapters in this book will be plain sailing for you. Skim through the first few chapters (stopping and making notes anywhere that fills a gap in your knowledge). It sounds like you're on the right track but you need to build a more solid foundation for your future, give some of your spending habits a kick and plug some holes in your 'money machine' where you're currently losing cash.

Don't be frightened or too blasé to start investing for yourself. The advice in the investing chapters is broken down into steps so it's easy to follow. I'll show you how you really can do it yourself – better than the suited, booted, slick-haired City types. Once you arm yourself with more knowledge, and therefore more confidence, you will be able to get really clever with your spending and even smarter with your investing. Just take it step by step and you will be amazed at how quickly you get the idea, and how easily you change from just getting by to having a surplus of money each month.

Mostly 'c's: Ready for a Challenge

All right clever clogs. You really are well on your way to secure finances. I'd suggest you read the chapters on switching, getting good deals on everything and the ones on investing, and making more money. There might be all sorts of tips and hints that could come in handy.

Don't forget, too, that even if you are good at budgeting, controlling your spending and keeping a lid on debt, there are infinite possibilities open to you for new and challenging goals.

Life is full of all kinds of possibilities for everyone – including any number of money-making possibilities. Take the blinkers off and who knows what you will be able to see and make use of! Because you're probably naturally at ease with money, you also have the opportunity to share those skills with others. Don't forget to pass this book on.

What to do now ...

- Use this book as a step-by-step guide to your financial life. Read through it and put each of the tips relevant to your stage into practice.
- Join the Moneymagpie.com weekly newsletter (at www.moneymagpie.com) to get exclusive ideas, tips and bargains sent straight to your inbox.

chapter two

Making Plans and Setting Goals

In this chapter I'm going to show you how to plan your financial life and set goals you can achieve. It will cover:

- *Setting a plan for long-term growth (see below).*
- *Setting achievable goals (page 22).*
- *How to change negative, old ways of thinking to new, more positive ones (page 25).*

Your Plan for Steady, Long-term Growth

This is not a 'get rich quick' book. It's about slow, steady and safe wealth creation. The majority of wealthy people – those who keep hold of their money for years – tend to be those who built up their wealth over time, not overnight.

Many books about getting rich talk only about the big picture. They make you feel good about taking great leaps and going for the big money. I certainly believe in thinking big, expecting big things and smashing through the limits that the world tries to impose on our expectations of life. However, I know that this way of thinking has to be balanced by looking after the small things day to day. It's about clever saving, only spending on things that improve the quality of your life, dodging cunning marketing tactics used by those who want to take our money off us, and steadily putting money away each month.

WHERE DO I START?

This is one of the most common questions I'm asked when chatting to people about how to make a meaningful difference to their money management; or, for that matter, about how to get out of debt or get rich.

And the answer? It's not to retrain or sell your second-hand stuff or rent out your driveway to strangers (although more on that later). It's: get a cuppa, sit down with your feet up, close your eyes and daydream ...

Daydream about what you fancy from your life for the next one, five or fifteen years. Daydream about what you want for yourself, for your family and even for generations to come. Really get into it, picturing what you want – perhaps a life free of money worries, or just a few extra pounds a month, perhaps a new home or a glamorous, jewel-encrusted retirement ...

Now, get up. Grab a pen and paper, and let's begin.

Simply writing down what you want and when you want it – in other words a basic plan – is one of the most important elements in getting on top of your money and creating wealth for yourself. It's so important that I'm dedicating this whole chapter to it.

I'm not talking about drawing up a spreadsheet with a rigid deadline that you have to achieve or else you're a failure. I mean a general idea, first, of what you would like to do in your life and, roughly, when you'd like to do it.

Let me give you some examples:

- *You would like to buy your own home some time in the next five years.*
- *You want to take a year off and travel round the world.*
- *You want to get together a savings account that will tide you over during tight months.*
- *You would like to be able to afford some really nice Christmas presents for the kids this year.*

If you don't make a conscious effort to work towards your goal, who will? We're all different and we all have our own dreams. Usually, though, those dreams need some sort of funding. It's easier to fund them using money you have already saved rather than trying to make money while you're doing them.

WHAT NEXT? SETTING GOALS

Now, first of all, don't be put off by the word 'goals'. We all set ourselves tasks, deadlines and goals. Some of them we don't keep, and that can be discouraging. The secret to meeting your goals is to make them achievable and to set mini-goals along the way. So, for example, if you want to lose two stone, you can set yourself the goal of losing two pounds a week and tick off each goal as you meet it. (For more on setting achievable goals, see page 22.)

The other secret to meeting goals is to get some good support along the way, particularly if it's a long-term aim like getting out of thousands of pounds of debt. Happily, you can get help with that on the Moneymagpie.com message-boards (www.moneymagpie.com/index.php?action=showMessageBoardHome). We have a thread there for goal-setters so you can talk to others who are trying to complete projects and get their lives back on track.

Look at your list of the things you want to do with your life. Now put these things in order of importance to you. Would you like to go round the world as soon as possible? Do you need to get money for a car pretty quickly? Do you want to start your own business sooner rather than later? Setting goals is about taking charge of your life and deciding where you want to go next. It's a way of ensuring you get what you want instead of letting life just happen haphazardly.

CASE STUDY

Last year, Sarah – a single mother of three – was at her wits' end trying to pay her rent and bills. She had spent the past five years struggling from one income support payment to the next. After hitting rock bottom and having to borrow money from her parents for the third time in a year, she resolved to make a change.

After a good think about it (and some long hours chatting to her most supportive and wise friends for advice) she pinpointed that she wanted to finish her education and get some training in the next year, so she could have a secure job in floristry within three years.

Once the goal was clear, Sarah could plan what needed to be done to get there. The plan included a number of steps for her to work through one at a time:

- Earn extra money for childcare by getting a lodger or taking up part-time weekend work with local florists.
- Sign up for night classes to get better reading, writing and maths skills. This could be easier with a class buddy or friend acting as a part-time tutor/homework helper/support person.
- Create a budget for the family for the next year (reviewing it every three months) to free up money for skills training and childcare.
- Speak to local florists about training that will immediately increase chances of being paid better and investigate study grants for people on benefits.
- Complete a short course in floristry, which is recognised in the industry and is useful to prospective employers.
- Write a basic CV emphasising new skills and work experience to get permanent work (as much as possible around school hours so family time doesn't suffer).
- Kiss goodbye to dependence on income support and asking family for handouts. Major celebration!

HOW TO SET REALLY ACHIEVABLE GOALS

Once you've got a list with a rough idea of where you want to go next, it's much easier to see the steps that need to be taken to get there (like in the example above). Not everyone is going to have a concrete financial or career goal, but there are lots of things you can work on to create a more fulfilling life. What about reducing your working hours to spend more time with the family? Or perhaps you'd like to buy a house abroad? Working through the following steps will point you in the right direction.

- *Ask supportive friends and family members to help you set your goals. Choose these people carefully – some people can be too negative and will put you off before you've started.*
- *Pick three or four ideas from your list to take further. These could be short-term goals such as saving for a milestone birthday party or bigger, long-term goals like paying off your mortgage.*
- *Write each goal down in a sentence then commit to seeing it through. If you have goals that you are all working towards as a family, then put them up on your fridge so you can all be reminded of what you're working for. If it's just you, then put the list somewhere private that you look at a lot, like in your purse or diary.*
- *Make sure they're SMART goals: **S**pecific, **M**easurable, **A**ttainable, **R**ealistic and **T**imely.*
    - **Specific.** Concentrate on nailing what it is you want to achieve. 'To lose 10kg of weight in a year' is much more effective than 'lose a bit round the tummy'.
    - **Measurable.** If you can't measure it, you can't manage

it. Adding some numbers to your goal statement can help you track your progress. For example, 'I want to travel to 10 new countries before I'm 50'.

- **Attainable.** Goals should challenge you, but not be beyond your grasp. It's great to throw in a bit of 'blue sky thinking' – letting your imagination run wild – but these are supposed to be things you can work towards. With each step forward, no matter how small, you can feel like you've achieved something.
- **Realistic.** Let's face it, if you love to shop, saving all of your disposable income (the money left after rent, food and so on) is just going to seem like a punishment. It's much better to save half your leftover income, which will be a push, but it will let you go wild with the other half.
- **Timely.** Set a timeframe for your goals so you get to work immediately. This could be within the next year, before you retire or before your wedding next month. Set yourself mini-goals along the way to help you get there.

- *Next, work out how you are going to achieve each goal. Get a piece of paper for each goal and write a list of steps you are going to take to achieve it (like the example above). Keep it handy for quick reference and concentrate on working on one step at a time. It's really satisfying to cross one off.*

Ideally, you should have about three goals with three steps for each so you don't get overwhelmed with things to do. Here's an example:

Save £10,000 for our wedding – for clothes, transport, venue, food and drink – within three years.

- *Make £200 extra each month using ideas in this book.*
- *Cut back on spending – save at least £100 a month.*
- *Put savings into a high-interest account. Look on a comparison site to find the best one – set it up by this weekend.*

Set some goals

- Now that you have seen how you can plan for your future and set goals, give yourself some time over the next couple of weeks to set these goals.
- Go back to them during the next fortnight and refine and update them until they look achievable.

GOAL EXAMPLES

- Save £20 a month throughout the year towards Christmas spending.
- Pay off your credit card in six months.
- Save for a new car over the next 12 months.
- Pay off your mortgage in 15 years instead of 25.
- Increase your income by £500 in the next year to put into investments.
- Save £1,000 for an overseas trip next year.
- Maintain a retirement income equal to 70 per cent of your working income.
- Teach your children basic money skills so that they learn to be self-sufficient when they move out.

Challenge Old Habits and Old Ways of Thinking about Money

Like any other area of our lives, the way we run our finances is very much connected to our expectations, the things we love and fear, and the belief systems we have picked up from parents, friends and the media. There are lots of money myths – the kind of things that your own 'Money Monster' might be saying to you. Here are just a few:

- *Money Monster says: Money is scarce.*
  - Money Magpie says: Money comes from all over the place and is constantly moving around, being created by different economies. There's no reason why you shouldn't have more of it.
- *Money Monster says: If you don't have cash, you can't get 'things'.*
  - Money Magpie says: Think of how many goods and services you can get for free by swapping, bartering with friends and neighbours or applying for grants or bursaries.
- *Money Monster says: Buying 'things' – fast cars, electronics, clothes and handbags – makes you happy.*
  - Money Magpie says: In short: it doesn't. Bhutan is one of the happiest nations in the world (according to a study by the University of Leicester), despite the average wage being as low as £1.20 a day.
- *Money Monster says: There's a finite amount of good in the world.*
  - Money Magpie says: On the contrary, there are infinite

possibilities and ideas, any one or more of which could do you good.

- *Money Monster says: Other people are lucky – I'm just not.*
    - Money Magpie says: It really isn't about luck or some being 'destined' for good things while others are not. Certainly some people have more work to do to get somewhere than others but there is no law to say that you can't have access to all the good there is. As Thomas Jefferson put it, 'I find that the harder I work the more luck I seem to have.'

Help yourself

- Sign up to the Moneymagpie.com newsletter to get practical and inspirational ideas each week on how to make and save more money.
- Hang out with positive and successful people. Get into their way of thinking – not the negative patterns of thought that so many carry around with them.

chapter three

Facing Facts and Budgeting

This is where you start your plan for a secure and wealthy future. Follow these steps and you will be well on your way to creating solid foundations for yourself and your family. In this chapter I will be covering:

- *How to get your paperwork in order and finding out the financial facts (page 30).*
- *How to keep a secret spending diary (page 36).*
- *How to do a brilliantly simple budget (page 39).*

It really is true that if you look after the pennies the pounds will look after themselves. Getting to your big goals and creating ongoing serious wealth does start with small, basic steps.

Getting Your Statements Out and Facing Facts

The very first thing you need to know is how much money is coming in and how much is going out each month. This is so that you can take control of your money and make it serve you, rather than the other way round. Once you know how much money is coming in then you can work out what you are able to spend, and also how much more, ideally, you need to make. When you know how much money is going out then you will have the incentive to bring your costs down where you can and plug gaps in your money chest!

You need to start with the basics – getting your statements out and facing the facts. This will enable you to be clear about your income and your debt situation, and how much money you have or haven't got at the end of the month. I will then show you how to turn your income into a surplus that you will invest regularly for your future.

Think of yourself and your household finances as a very simple and easy-to-manage business. What we're going to do is improve your profits. Just as with businesses, the aim is to keep your costs down and increase your income so that the overall profits go up. With individuals and families the ideal is to cut down your outgoings (such as food, bills, transport, and so on) and increase your income so that you have more money to invest in yourself.

First, get your bank statements and credit card bills out. Go on! You know you want to. They're in that drawer, still in their envelopes and your Money Monster is taunting you with the likelihood of their contents. Be strong – open the drawer, open the envelopes and find out what you owe and to whom. It's very simple and very, very necessary. You *need* to do this because:

a) This simple step is a massive leap towards taming your Money Monster.

b) You will get a pretty good idea of where your money is going just by reading these statements.

c) If you haven't looked at them for a year or more it's *highly* likely that you can effectively *make* money doing this. Banks are notorious for making mistakes with our accounts and you won't know they're losing money for you unless you look.

d) This is the only way to protect your money against criminals who are trying to steal it with identity fraud. Someone could be taking money out of your account right now which you won't know about unless you look. Who knows what direct debits or standing orders might still be going out for goods and services you don't use any more? Once you find out, you can stop them and immediately save money.

Get your statements into date order and put them into a file. You may need a few files to sort out your various financial papers – perhaps a few lever-arch files with dividers (see box, overleaf). Your statements are there to be used as reference material and as the basis for your budgeting and financial planning.

Next, grab your other bills from the last month or quarter, including:

- *gas and electricity*
- *rent or mortgage*
- *phone*

and any other receipts you have from the last month, such as:

- *supermarket*
- *train tickets*
- *restaurants*
- *clothes shops*

Get out your payslips, tax credits and benefit statements, investment information and any other paperwork to do with your income.

TAME THE PAPER TIGER

To get on top of your finances you need to set up a filing system for all your statements, bills and receipts. Everyone works in a different way so you should decide for yourself how you would like to organise your papers – whether it's lever-arch files, a filing cabinet or just a series of big coloured envelopes. However you arrange it, make sure you:

- Keep, and file, all your bank, credit card and loan statements and utility, phone and council tax bills.
- At the end of each year (or the end of your financial year if you're self-employed) put all your bills and statements in a storage box and store them away with the other things you don't look at often.
- Receipts for major items should be kept where you can lay your hands on them quickly. If you have the receipt then it's much easier to claim your rights if the thing goes wrong. Keep the receipts for six years (or as long as the item lasts) because you can still get redress in that time under the Sale of Goods Act 1979. (For more on this, visit the Department of Trade and Industry's website at www.dti.gov.uk.)

DO A MONEY MENU

Armed with this information you can take the next step towards financial control of your life. This is to do a Money Menu (also known as a 'Statement of Affairs'). You can do this online at Moneymagpie.com (search for 'statement of affairs'), or just fill in the boxes below.

Working out Your Income

First, using your statements, payslips and official documents, work out how much money comes into your household each month. This will include things like your salary, investment income, tax credits and benefits. Fill in the box overleaf and add up the total. Don't forget to put in a percentage of money that comes in less frequently such as payments that come in once or twice a year. So, for example, if you get money from investments twice a year, add that up then divide it by 12. If you get, say, £60 twice a year, that's £60 + £60 = £120, divided by 12 gives £10 a month. Therefore you put £10 down for your monthly investment income (get a calculator out if you need to). Put that amount in the box for the monthly amount.

If you are freelance and you have an erratic income then, again, take the annual amount you usually make and divide it by 12. Put that in the income column.

MONEY MENU: MONTHLY INCOME

Income	Amount (£)
Salary	
Freelance income	
Benefits	
Tax Credits	
Investment income	
Child support payments	
Other	
TOTAL:	

Working out Your Outgoings

So that's the pleasant table to fill in. Now comes the harder one – the outgoings. In the table opposite you need to write down your monthly outgoings including essentials and non-essentials. Get your bills and receipts together, including annual payments, and fill in the amount you pay (put in an average if necessary) for your utilities (gas, electricity, phone), travel, food, entertainment, debt repayments, pension and other investments, clothes and so on.

I've put a list of possible expenditure in the table opposite (and in the online one) so just put the amounts in the empty boxes. Add some rows for yourself if I've missed anything out!

MONEY MENU: MONTHLY OUTGOINGS

Outgoings	Amount (£)
Mortgage/rent	
Gas	
Electricity	
Council tax	
Heating oil	
Water	
Credit card payments	
Loan payments	
Bank interest	
Telephone	
Mobile phone	
TV licence	
TV package	
Internet/broadband	
Buildings/contents insurance	
Life insurance	
Car insurance	
Car maintenance	
Other insurance	
Travel	
Petrol	
Groceries	
Eating out/takeaways	
Clothing	
Entertainment	

Childcare/nursery
Other child-related costs
Medical/dental expenses
Presents
Holiday costs
Pet costs
Child support payments
Cleaning
Laundry
Domestic wages (such as cleaner)
Emergencies/repairs
Other
TOTAL:

Once you have come up with the total for both tables, subtract the 'Outgoings' total from the 'Incomings' total and you will see how much you have left over (or not!) at the end of each month.

Are You Left with a Surplus?

Well done! Not many people are. However, there are still more steps you can take to improve your financial situation:

1. Do you have a surplus simply because you are not putting away regular amounts of money into short-term savings and long-term investments for your future? If so, now is the time to look at the chapters on saving (Chapter 9) and investing (Chapters 10–13). You need to start putting money away for short-term spending, such as covering

yourself for emergencies and saving for holidays, and other big expenses. You also need to set up standing orders into investment products to create a rich retirement for yourself.

2. Stop any wastage. Even if you have some money left over at the end of the month, you could have more. Go to Chapters 5 and 6 to find out how to save more money by switching your bills, shopping around and generally cutting down on the amount you spend on essentials. After all, why pay more than you have to for gas, electricity, phones and the like?
3. Keep a spending diary (see overleaf) to see where you're wasting money day to day. Even if you are managing to live within your means, there's no point wasting money on things you don't need or want. This is money that could be invested to make even more for you later on.

Are You Left with a Minus Figure?

Well, it probably won't surprise you to learn that you are living beyond your means – spending more than you are earning. You may be having difficulty paying some bills and you will probably be dealing with various debts too, possibly a mix of credit cards, an overdraft and at least one loan. So, what you need to do now is:

1. Go to the next chapter to find out how to get out of debt. Even if you feel like you're drowning in debt, you can get out of it in time if you follow the rules.
2. Go to Chapters 4 and 5 to find out how to cut down on your fixed costs drastically by switching your utility and

other providers, changing banks, moving your loans and credit card debts to cheaper versions, finding cheaper insurance and other essentials.

3. Also find out in these chapters how to save money on other things we have to spend on, including food, travel, clothes and entertainment.
4. Visit Moneymagpie.com for even more ideas on saving money in all aspects of day-to-day living so that you can bring your costs down.
5. Cut out some of your spending. You might think that you don't spend much at all and you can't understand how this money is going out of your account every month. If so, do a spending diary (see below) and you will find out over just a few days where the money is going and what you can cut out.
6. See how you can increase your incomings. Look at Chapters 14 and 15 for ways to make money on the side. We could all do with making extra cash here and there but if you are finding it hard to make ends meet – and certainly if you are struggling with debt – it's really important to make extra money where you can. Also check out the 'Making Money' section of Moneymagpie.com for even more cash-generating ideas to help you out.

Keep a Monthly Spending Diary

Whether you've got wads of cash or you're struggling with everyday expenses, it's important that everyone keeps a one-month spending diary at least once every two or three years. This is simply a notebook that you take around with you every day for a month in which you write down *everything* you spend every day. It doesn't matter how small or embarrassing that purchase is – you write it down! If you buy a latte on the way to work, write it down. If you buy a round of drinks afterwards and get a bus home, write both of those purchases down. Also write down your bills on the day you pay them (or when they go out by direct debit). Everything you spend has to go in your diary.

So, for example, your first three days' writing in your spending diary might look like this:

Monday 6 April	
Bus ticket	£1.10
Coffee	£2.40
Magazine	£2.80
Lunch	£5.60
Tea and cake	£3.60
Bus ticket	£1.10
Takeaway	£6.00
Total	**£22.60**
Tuesday 7 April	
Bus ticket	£1.10
Coffee	£2.40
Present for Sophie	£15.00
Lunch	£4.80
Bus ticket	£1.10
Drinks with Sophie	£12.00
Total	**£36.40**

Wednesday 8 April	
Council tax	£90.50
Phone bill	£24.00
Bus ticket	£1.10
Coffee	£2.40
Lunch	£6.20
Bus ticket	£1.10
Chocolate bar	£0.45
Total	**£125.75**

You see how quickly the numbers add up? It's quite startling how these little bits of spending can add up to a horrible, Money Monster figure by the end of the day. By writing everything down every day you get to work out quite quickly why it is that the £30 you took out of the cash machine in the morning has disappeared by the time you get home.

In fact, in my experience, the simple act of keeping this diary will cut your spending down after just a few days. On day four you might think twice about that morning coffee and decide to take a flask instead. You might also bring a salad into work and even walk home rather than spend on another bus ticket. It's so embarrassing to yourself to write down, yet again, 'tea and cake, £3.60' that you go without half the time!

If you are married, or have a financial relationship with a partner or family member then try and do this exercise together. Share the bills between your two diaries but otherwise each of you must write down everything you spend each day. This will be a test of the honesty in your relationship apart from anything else! Will you be able to own up to that £120 pair of shoes or the night out that cost you £90?

However upsetting (or just tedious) it may seem to keep a spending diary, you must keep the exercise going for a whole month. At the end of that month you will be able to put more accurate figures in your Money Menu (see page 31). More importantly, you will be able to see areas in your spending (and that of your partner) that can be cut back.

Everyone is different so for one person it could be that they need to cut back on takeaways and lunches out. For another they should stop buying so many newspapers and magazines and read them online or get books from the library instead. It may be that you keep taking taxis everywhere and that is eating into your money supply.

Do a Budget

A budget can transform your financial life, almost like magic! Doing a budget actually sets the foundations for a wealthy future. It helps you tame the Money Monster and become master or mistress of your money. It's that powerful.

It doesn't have to be rigid or depressing either. You can leave room for manoeuvre and have fun with it too. Fun? Yes, really. You can have fun by challenging yourself to improve your money-saving each month; to get for free things you currently spend on; to haggle with suppliers so that you bring down some of your essential spending to free up more money for fun stuff. See, it doesn't have to be boring!

THE GUIDE TO EASY BUDGETING

Right, go back to the tables above (or search for 'budgeting' on www.moneymapie.com). Divide your outgoing payments section into two columns: 'flexible' and 'not flexible'. The 'not flexible' column should include payments vital to the running of your home that you can't cut out, such as your mortgage or rent (although you can remortgage and sometimes negotiate on mortgages for a payment break), council tax and any child support payments.

The 'flexible' column should include all payments you can cut back on, or withhold for a short period of time. These include utility bills, which can be reduced, food, clothes, a television package, entertainment bills, travel and so on. You can also reduce the money paid out to banks, credit card companies and loan companies. These do need to be paid but they are a lot less important than your mortgage payments and council tax.

Now, see where you could make savings. Switch your utility suppliers to get better deals; shop around to get a better insurance quote; change your credit cards and loans (if possible) to cheaper or even free versions (like 0 per cent balance transfers – see Chapters 4 and 5 for instructions). Once you have done that you will have different amounts (lower, I hope!) to put in the 'Outgoings' table.

Now that you have reduced your outgoings, where possible, add them up again and subtract this figure from the total in the 'Incomings' table. What is left over? Nothing? See Part 4 on making money, so you can increase your incomings. Also, check Entitledto.co.uk to see if you could get more benefits or other State help. If things are really bad then now is the time to change something fundamental about your lifestyle like moving to a cheaper property or selling your car.

Do you have something left over? Write that figure down. This is where you make your decision. How do you want to allocate this money?

- *If you have debts to pay, you should now decide to spend as little as you possibly can on everything else – really give yourself a survival budget with basic food, barely any new clothes, no holidays and so on. If you're serious about getting out of debt you have to cut down on everything in order to free up that money (see Chapter 4). And don't think I don't know what it's like; I've been in debt myself and I did exactly this for over a year to pay it off.*
- *If you don't have debts to pay you can be a little more generous with yourself but remember to keep costs down where you can.*
- *Ideally, you need to be at the point where you have a good chunk of cash left over each month to put into your savings and investments. You should then be setting up standing orders from your bank account into a savings account for your emergency savings (see Chapter 9) and for big things you want to save up for (such as holidays, a new sofa or a car). You should also have regular amounts of money going into long-term investments (see Chapter 13).*

TIPS FOR STICKING TO YOUR BUDGET

- Keep your goals and rewards in mind. If necessary, write them on a piece of paper and take it around with you.
- Start training yourself to think long term; think about the bigger picture rather than being swayed by immediate potential purchases.
- Have fun beating retailers at their own game. So, they want you to spend, do they? Well, you can see how much better you are at not spending! Don't be manipulated by them. Be your own person.
- Get into the habit of asking yourself whether you really need something or if you just want it. If you've got the money and you want it badly then go ahead, but make sure it's genuinely something that will improve your life, not just something you're being persuaded to buy.
- Give yourself the odd treat here and there. Controlling your money is about balance. You don't have to deny yourself everything. If possible, see if you can get that treat for free (like having a meal out through mystery shopping, page 120).

What now?

- Are you in debt? Move straight to the next chapter and keep reading.
- If you are not in debt, move to Chapters 5 and 6 where you can find out more about smart spending, getting the most out of your money and becoming a true Money Magpie.

chapter four

Free Yourself from the Debt Trap

So you're in debt. Maybe you're just annoyingly in debt so that you owe a couple of thousand on your credit cards and you can't quite pay it all off in one go? Or maybe you are really worryingly in debt so that you fear the postman coming and you can't sleep at night? This chapter will help you get out of the debt trap whatever your situation. I'll cover:

- *Facing up to the situation (see below).*
- *A step-by-step guide to getting out of debt (page 45).*
- *What to do if things have gone too far – and how to get free help (page 66).*

Facing up to Debt

If you are in any sort of debt, you are not alone. There are millions of people out there in the same position as you. Lying awake worrying will not solve the problem; neither will ignoring it and living in denial. It's important to accept that you have the debt, and that now is a great time to give yourself a good kick to do something about it. Handily, there are hundreds of free organisations that exist specifically to help you get out of debt. There are also websites, forums, government-backed initiatives and church-based support groups that can help you. So you are not alone with your debt problem in any sense.

Admitting that you need help can be the hardest part of getting out of debt. Talk to your friends and family and listen to their suggestions. It's highly likely that you know someone who's been badly in debt and they might be able to give you some decent advice. Be willing to listen to other people, and set yourself debt-busting targets to work towards. Be aware of the fact that all your problems won't be solved overnight – and things might even seem to get worse before they get better – but, ultimately, your life will be of a much higher quality once it's all over and you are back in the black again.

THE FIRST QUESTION YOU MUST ASK YOURSELF

'How bad is it?' If you have done the Money Menu and the budget in the previous chapter (pages 31–36 and 39–42) and you have realised that you can at least start to pay off some of your debt, then you should be able to manage to get out of this hole on your own. Keep reading this chapter, follow the recommended steps and you will be out of debt in due course.

If, however, having done the exercise in the last chapter, you've found that your debts are totally overwhelming your income, then you need help fast. Certainly read all of this chapter, but I suggest you look at the steps below and follow these first. There is good, free, professional advice all over the country and you can make the most of it.

If things are bad but not quite that bad – perhaps the red demands are coming through the door and you are being harassed by creditors on the phone – then something still needs to be done sooner rather than later. Don't panic though. Keep reading and follow the steps below.

Getting out of Debt –Step by Step

STEP 1: MAKE A PLAN

A plan is essential in the breakdown of your debt. This might take up a real wedge of your time but without it you're facing a much worse situation. If you haven't already done a Money Menu, do one now (see Chapter 3 for instructions), either with pen and paper or online at Moneymagpie.com (search 'money menu'). At this point, don't worry if your monthly outgoing payments exceed your incoming cash – it's a common money management problem, and one that I'm going to help you fix.

STEP 2: OPEN YOUR BILLS AND BANK STATEMENTS AND KEEP THEM ORGANISED

We looked at this in Chapter 3 (pages 27–30). It's not that scary! If there are any mistakes in the statements then call up the bank or lender to get them to rectify them as soon as possible. Cancel any direct debits and standing orders for items and services you no longer use. You'd be surprised at how much you can save by doing this.

Once you have a filing system in place, it will make keeping on top of your finances much easier. This way, you won't be able to pretend you've forgotten a bill. A simple system could work wonders for you.

STEP 3: CUT THE COST OF YOUR CREDIT CARDS, LOANS AND OTHER BORROWING

Borrowing more money to pay off your debts is a slippery slope – don't go there. However, you do need to check that you are getting the best deals for your existing borrowing – that way you pay less interest and can shift your debts faster.

Credit Cards

If you've been borrowing on credit cards or store cards, you can cut back on your monthly interest by transferring the balance to a card with lower interest rates. If you can find a credit card with a deal such as 0 per cent interest for the first few months then it might be worth transferring your balance for the interest-free period to give yourself an interest payment break. Meanwhile you can concentrate on steadily repaying the actual balance. For information on how to switch your credit card debt to a 0 per cent deal see Chapter 5. Also look at the independent comparison table on Moneymagpie.com for the latest and best credit card deals.

WHAT IS A 0 PER CENT CREDIT CARD?

There are two main types of 0 per cent offers on credit cards – 0 per cent on balance transfers or 0 per cent on purchases. With 0 per cent balance transfers you can switch your debt from another credit card to this one and for a few months you won't have to pay interest on your debt (although you will have to keep paying the debt!) It's nice and cheap, although you might have to pay a fee for moving the money (probably about 2.5 per cent) and at the end of the 0 per cent period you will have to pay their usual interest rate or switch to a better deal. With 0 per cent deals on purchases, you get to buy things and you don't pay interest for a few months if you can't pay the full amount off immediately.

However, switching to a 0 per cent credit card may not be the cheapest way to pay off your debt. When you transfer your existing debt you may have to pay a fee, and the costs can mount up if you do this every six months. Also, you may not be able to get a 0 per cent deal because of your credit rating (see box, pages 53–54). You could be better off with a 'low lifetime balance transfer' card. This is a credit card that will give you a low rate of interest on your transferred balance until you pay the whole lot off, however long that takes.

WHAT IS APR?

APR stands for 'annual percentage rate'. When it comes to borrowing, it shows you how much your loan, credit card or mortgage will cost you per year including any charges. For savings it is the rate that is normally quoted showing how much you should make each year on your savings.

Remember to look at the APR for each product you are comparing rather than getting confused by other figures that may be advertised, such as the amount you will pay each month. This way you can compare all products on the same basis and work out how much they would cost you or earn you over the same amount of time.

(See also page 183 for an explanation of the difference between AER and APR.)

Loans

After the best credit card deals, a personal loan is usually the next cheapest way to borrow money. You have to make regular repayments over a fixed amount of time.

How to Get an Unsecured Loan

An unsecured loan is one that is not 'secured' against an asset, such as your house or your car. It's just a loan, plain and simple.

Your main concern when taking out an unsecured loan should be to find the cheapest possible. This usually means getting the cheapest APR (annual percentage rate), although it's not the only consideration. If you think you might be able to pay the loan off fairly quickly then it is best to go for a *flexible* deal that you can pay off early without a penalty (these often have a slightly higher APR than the less flexible loans). The quicker you pay off a loan, the cheaper it is in the long run. Otherwise just choose the cheapest APR rate.

Here are some other important things about unsecured loans:

- *Borrow for the least amount of time – the longer you take to pay off a debt the more expensive it will be. For example, if you borrow £5,000 at 5 per cent interest (APR) and take five years to pay it off, you will end up paying back £5,661.37 altogether. If you take 10 years to pay it back, you will have to pay £6,363.93 altogether. It may seem like just numbers, but would you walk past the difference – £702.56 – if it were lying on the street?*
- *Don't just concentrate on how much the debt will cost you each month. You need to know the TAR (total amount repayable) – that's how much the debt will cost you to pay off altogether. So, if you look at the example above, borrowing £5,000 for five years means you have to pay it back at £94.36 per month. If you borrow it over 10 years you will only pay £53.03 a month. Even though it looks cheaper each month, the total amount you will pay back is £700 more than the five-year deal.*
- *Make sure you understand the terms and conditions whenever you borrow (if you're unsure of what any of the words and phrases mean, search for information on Moneymagpie.com). For example, with some 0 per cent finance deals on offer*

in shops, if you are late with any payments or miss one month they insist you pay all the rest of the money immediately and they slap on all the interest you would have paid during the 0 per cent period. Nice!

BEWARE OF PAYMENT PROTECTION INSURANCE HARD SELLS

Don't be pressurised into taking out PPI (payment protection insurance) when you get a loan. Loans companies make a good profit from the commission on selling this kind of insurance so they're very keen for you to buy it. It can be useful for some people as it is supposed to pay some of your loan payments if you can't earn for a while because of redundancy or illness, but there are a lot of downsides:

- It tends to be expensive and will add to the amount you have to pay each month and to the total amount you pay overall.
- You could get better and cheaper cover elsewhere by shopping around on insurance comparison websites.
- The payments don't start until at least a month after you stop being able to earn. Sometimes it takes at least three months (depending on the insurer) and they often only last for 12–24 months (again, depending on the insurer).
- This insurance will only cover you if you are employed. If you are self-employed or unemployed when you take out the PPI it won't cover you at all and it will be a waste of money.

The key to getting the best deal is to shop around using loan comparison tables. Moneymagpie.com has some tables that will help you find the best loan for your needs. Just look at www.moneymagpie.com/bestbuys/insurance.

The Dangers of a Secured Loan

Secured loans are primarily available to people who own their own home although you can get a loan secured against a car, for example, or another major, fixed asset. The majority of secured loans, however, are secured against a person's home. That's how they work – the loan is 'secured' against your property so that if you default the lender can take your home. I usually advise against taking out a secured loan, although it may be worth looking at if you absolutely trust yourself to make the repayments (this is really, really important!)

For some borrowers, a secured loan can make sense. If:

- *You are clear about the dangers of not repaying the loan.*
- *You are in control of your finances and are not overspending.*
- *You are not just taking out the loan to spend on a holiday, car or other inessentials (it's not worth endangering your home for these things).*
- *You really have to have the money and you cannot get an unsecured loan.*

Although there are some honest companies that provide secured loans, it's an area where you have to be very careful. There is a lot of money to be made from loans (have you ever wondered how they afford those expensive television ads that run through the day?) Some companies purposely attract the wrong people – those who are already deep in debt.

Secured loan companies use very aggressive sales tactics. Although their salespeople might seem like they are being nice to you, in fact they are often fleecing you and tying you into the worst possible deals. If you fail to pay they can take your home!

These loans often run over a much longer time than other types of loan – sometimes as long as your mortgage. The longer it takes to pay off a loan the more expensive it will be because when you borrow money, really it's like *renting* it. The more months and years you rent that money, the more expensive it will be overall.

Not only that, but interest rates on these kinds of loan can vary, which means they could go up or down at any time after you have taken the loan out. Make sure you can comfortably afford to pay it each month, even if the interest rate were to increase by 1 or 2 per cent.

Managing Your Mortgage

How long have you had your mortgage? If the fixed rate or introductory period has expired, the chances are you're shelling out far more than you need to. As mortgage payments are likely to be your single biggest expense, it's definitely worth keeping on top of them.

Before you try to remortgage it's a good idea to contact your existing lender to make them aware of the fact you're considering making a switch. They might even offer you cheaper rates there and then if you're lucky (although, unfortunately, that's not as likely as it used to be) but shop around elsewhere as well to make sure you are getting the best deal possible. Check whether you will be charged an exit fee if you move your mortgage because the saving might be outweighed by the fee.

It's then a case of tracking down the cheapest deal you

can get. Start by researching on the internet. We have independent comparisons on Moneymagpie.com but you can also look at Moneysupermarket.com, Charcolonline.co.uk and Moneyextra.co.uk. Remember to take into account any exit fees from your old lender, and entry fees for your new lender, to get the true amount you will pay or save by switching.

Using Your Mortgage to Clear Other Debts

It may seem tempting to get a bigger mortgage and use some of the cash to pay off your existing debts. But beware – this is not a decision to be taken lightly and should only be carried out if it's ultimately going to save you money. Remember that adding all your unsecured debts (credit cards, loans and so on) to your mortgage increases the risk of losing your home. Read the Moneymagpie.com article about remortgaging your home to pay off your debts to help you make a better-informed decision (search 'remortgaging' on Moneymagpie.com).

To find out everything you ever need to know about mortgages, have a look at Chapter 8.

TAME YOUR CREDIT RATING

Any time you apply for some sort of loan – including a mortgage – the bank or lender will check your credit history to see if you're a good bet. Two of the main agencies they turn to are **Experian** and **Equifax**, which you can contact at any time to get a copy of your credit report. Between them the two agencies hold details on some 44 million people in the UK – and I mean *details*. Each file includes information about your credit cards, your mortgage and your bank accounts as well as facts and figures on any unpaid bills, failure to pay hire-purchase debts and County Court Judgements (CCJs).

All sorts of things can affect your ability to get a loan or set up a credit agreement (such as a mobile phone contract):

- If you have applied for several new loans or credit or loan payments.
- If you don't pay your phone bills for a few months – this is considered a big black mark.
- If you are not on the electoral roll.

Still, though, all lenders are different and you might be surprised who will lend to you and who won't. Some lenders like students with lots of debt, for example. Others won't touch them and will only go for people in established jobs with, ideally, their own homes. Amazingly, if you've never borrowed in your life, never owed money and don't own any credit cards, many lenders will view you with immense suspicion. Sometimes it seems that you just can't win!

To improve your credit record:

- *Make sure you are on the electoral roll.*
- *Make your payments on time. If you can't do this, contact the lender as soon as possible to try and arrange easier payment terms.*
- *If you have paid a fine imposed by a county court judgement,*

make sure it is shown as being settled on your credit record. If not, contact the court.

- *If a bankruptcy order has ended or been withdrawn and this is not shown on your credit report, send a copy of your certificate of discharge or annulment to all credit reference agencies and ask for your report to be updated.*
- *If you have paid off a credit account but your report doesn't show it, contact the lender and ask them to make the necessary changes. Or contact one of the debt charities, such as the Citizens Advice Bureau or the Consumer Credit Counselling Service (see Resources), and they will help you put it right.*

Avoid credit repair companies. If information on your credit report can be removed or altered, the credit rating agencies will do it for free.

If you are wondering how high (or low) your credit score is you can get a printout of your credit report for just £2 by applying to either Experian (www.experian.co.uk) or Equifax (www.equifax.co.uk). Either that or, if you go to the special online ebook on Moneymagpie.com for readers of this book, you can get access to your credit report for *free* for a whole month. Go to Moneymagpie.com/bookgift and look for the free credit report link.

STEP 4: SNOWBALL YOUR DEBTS

The quickest and cheapest way to get those debts paid is to 'snowball' them which means paying them off faster and faster as you go on. The way to do this is to:

1. First move as many as possible of your expensive credit and store card debts to 0 per cent deals (see pages 46–47 for information on how to do this).
2. Once you know you can't get any of your debts any cheaper (without taking out a nasty consolidation loan, see page 69), list your debts from the most expensive (the highest interest rate) downwards. It doesn't matter what the size of the debt is, just the interest rate or APR (Annual Percentage Rate). Ask the bank what the rates are if you can't find them on your statements.
3. Use any money you have each month to pay off as much of the most expensive debt as possible. Just pay the minimum on all the others.
4. Once you have paid off the most expensive debt, do the same to the next most expensive (i.e. put as much as you can in each month), still paying just the minimum on the others.
5. Continue like this with the rest of the debts until they're all paid off. You will find that it gets quicker as you go down the list because you will have more money to throw at them as the first debts are paid off. This is why it's called 'snowballing'!

STEP 5: CUT YOUR OTHER COSTS

Go back to your plan (Step 1). Once you have your flexible column sorted, sit down and brainstorm every possible idea for cutting down. Use advice from friends and family, information on Moneymagpie.com (there's loads!) and original ideas you come up with yourself. For example, get into buying supermarket own-brand products rather than brand names, hunting down bargains in charity shops and sales and setting limits for spending on a night out. You could even ditch the car and cycle to work or take the bus.

Whatever you can do to cut back, write it into your plan and stick to it. Be proactive in your decisions and try not to leave it till tomorrow, otherwise your plan might turn into the diet that you've been starting every Monday for the past six years. Have a look at Chapter 6 to find ways of cutting your costs and being a really smart spender in order to free up more money.

Don't be depressed though. You don't have to do without totally. You may be able to find a cheap or free alternative. For example:

- *Have a go at joining some mystery shopping companies so that you can get free trips to restaurants, hotels and bars (see Resources for a list of the main agencies).*
- *Go through your wardrobe and see what you can alter, dye, cut down or mend.*
- *Use air miles that you may have forgotten about or get free flights by being a courier (www.courier.org).*
- *Consider house swaps for a cheap or free holiday (try www.holswop.com, www.homeexchange.com, www.digsville.com, www.echangeimmo.com).*
- *Use eBay, Amazon and local second-hand shops to sell old books, CDs and DVDs.*
- *Barter with friends to get services done that you don't like doing yourself. For example, offer one evening's babysitting for two hours of ironing by a friend who enjoys doing it.*

- *Have a girls' night in where you give each other facials and manicures.*
- *Swap power tools with neighbours instead of buying your own.*
- *Have a swap shop with friends where you swap clothes, books and so on that you don't want and probably couldn't sell for much.*
- *Call in favours and loans from family members and friends. Let them know, politely, why you're doing it. Most people understand what it's like to be up against it financially.*

Whatever you do, cut down your spending as drastically as you are able to. It's up to you but remember: the less you spend, the more you'll save, therefore the more you'll have to put in to your debts, the quicker and cheaper it will be to pay them off and the sooner you'll be free and able to start building your wealth. Certainly give yourself occasional little treats as a reward for achieving goals to keep yourself going – as you might if you were dieting – but don't make it a daily habit.

STEP 6: KEEP YOUR CREDITORS ON YOUR SIDE

If you're still struggling to make your repayments, the worst thing you can do is stick your head in the sand. Believe it or not, most lenders don't want to see you in debt. Reclaiming property and possessions is really costly, as is going through the courts, so most creditors will use these options as very last resorts. Rather than hiding away from your debts, call everyone you owe money to and explain your situation.

Give them details of your plan to cut back so they know that you're doing all you can to pay them. Some banks and loan providers can be sympathetic in particular circumstances and in some special cases they may offer a short payment holiday until you're back on your feet. You're not going to be punished for calling them to make them aware of your situation – however, bad things *can* happen when you ignore the situation.

If you hate confrontation, and can't bear the thought of having to talk it through with your creditors, then there are organisations that can help. Providing you have serious debts, the CAB (Citizens Advice Bureau) or the CCCS (Consumer Credit Counselling Service) will speak with your creditors on your behalf. (For contact details, see page 398.)

One of the most miserable aspects of being *seriously* in debt is the nasty calls, letters and even visits that you get from increasingly irate creditors and bailiffs. That's a big reason why a lot of people pay money to debt management companies, just so that they'll make the 'nasty men go away'. But why pay money you don't have, to do something that you could do (yes, really, you could) for nothing? It's just a question of knowing how to deal with these people. So, here we go:

- *Firstly, realise that credit card companies, banks and loan companies can actually do comparatively little to harm you in the short term. What they are good at is making your life miserable by threatening you. As most people think they do have power, this often works for them. Frankly, given that there are many people in the world who don't pay because they don't want to, not because they can't, this is not always a bad thing. It's just miserable if you mean to pay but you're genuinely having problems.*

- *The worst thing you can do with creditors is to ignore them. Horrible (even terrifying) though it is, the best, least painful and cheapest way to deal with them is to keep communicating, be polite and respectful and keep them abreast of your situation and everything you are doing to pay the money back.*
- *Learn how to speak their language. As in so many areas of business, if you know how the other side are thinking, and the words that press their buttons, you will get on much better. The Motley Fool website (www.fool.co.uk) has sample letters to creditors written by an actual debt collector, which are really worth using if you need to.*
- *Contact your creditors before they contact you. If you send a letter explaining your situation and showing how much you are doing to pay off your various debts, many (though not all) will accept your terms and be reasonable.*
- *Remember there are some debts that take precedence over others – mortgage, rent, council tax, utilities and so on – although even with these you can often arrange to pay smaller amounts for a longer time if necessary.*
- *As long as you show that you're honestly trying to sort things out as best you can, many creditors will accept an offer of much smaller payments and may even suspend the interest charges.*
- *Some companies are more aggressive and unreasonable than others so remember that you do have a right, established by the Office of Fair Trading (OFT), to be treated fairly. Don't be intimidated by demands for payments that you can't afford or threats to send the bailiffs round. They can't do anything without a court order and that includes coming into your home to take away your possessions. They know this but they're counting on your not knowing it to intimidate you. If they get*

really nasty you could mention that they're not treating you fairly according to the OFT's rules (you can find these on their website at www.oft.gov.uk). That'll shut them up for a bit.

CREDIT CARD AND LOAN COMPANIES

Contrary to popular belief, these companies don't have as much power to force you to pay as they make out unless the loan is secured against your property. Bailiffs, in particular, have far fewer powers than they like to make you think, particularly if you don't physically let them into your home. In fact, just for your reference:

- If County Court bailiffs come to your home, you don't have to let them in and the very best thing is not to let them in at all.
- They can't force their way in on their first visit, but they can enter through an open window or an unlocked door. Forced entry includes pushing past you once you have opened the door to them or leaving their foot in the door to prevent you closing it. Such action would make the whole process illegal.
- Bailiffs trying to recover money you owe the HMRC are allowed to break into your home, provided they have a magistrates' warrant. Bailiffs recovering unpaid magistrates' court fines, however, do not have the power to force entry.
- Bailiffs can't take essentials such as clothing, bedding, cookers, fridges, most furniture and the 'tools of your trade' (for example, a computer you use for work).
- They can take non-essential items such as your television. They can also take possessions kept outside your home or in unlocked sheds or garages (for example, your car or garden equipment).

However, do not be misled into thinking you can ignore these debts. Prioritise your payments. Talk to your creditors and explain the situation, but let them know that your first priority will be the essential bills.

STEP 7: GET A DEBT-BUSTING BUDDY

You'd be surprised at how many people you know are in some form of debt or financial trouble. Ask one or more friends to help you work out your plan and allow you to cry on their shoulder. Offer the same service in return, share tips on saving money and text each other money-saving deals whenever you're out and about.

There is a strong link between debt and depression. Having someone around to help you can really lift your spirits. Think up plans to make money together, like job sharing or a cake stall, and set yourselves targets each month. Like trying to lose weight, it's always easier when you do it with others. Don't panic when sometimes you don't achieve your targets. Getting out of debt can be a slow process and there's always next month to start over.

If you don't feel comfortable discussing your debt problems with friends, do make use of the debt forums on the internet. Moneymagpie.com has one on its message boards (search 'debt demons'). It's a great way to get support from others while keeping your anonymity. You will find hundreds of people on these boards who are going through, or have been through, the same problems as you. They can be incredibly helpful and supportive. Use them!

Sign up to the Moneymagpie debt-busting emails. This is a free series of articles that we email you over a period of a couple of months to give you ideas, hints, tips and encouragement to help you get out of debt. It's totally free and anyone can sign up for it so do it now and tell your friends! There's a link to it in the free online resource that is free to readers of this book. Just go to www.moneymagpie.com/bookgift.

STICK YOUR CREDIT CARDS IN THE FREEZER!

Really, the best way to help yourself get and stay out of debt is to cut up all your existing credit cards – particularly any wicked, they-don't-deserve-to-live store cards that you possess. Once you manage to pay any cards off – or you transfer the debt to a 0 per cent card – make sure they're closed down too. Just cutting up the card won't sort it completely; the account itself has to be shut down too.

Keep one credit card in case of emergencies though (the one with the lowest interest rate). However, if you're scared that you might use it for non-essentials, put it in a bowl of water and stick that bowl in the freezer. The freezing water won't harm the card but microwaving it would. So if you suddenly get a desperate urge to use it to buy something you don't need, you will have to take the bowl out and wait for it to thaw.

This means that you will have a couple of hours in which to consider whether you really, *really* need that fabulous, jewel-encrusted wok-polishing kit that you've just seen on QVC. After a couple of hours the desperate urge to own it will probably have faded and you will have saved yourself another crazy spend session. Cool huh?

STEP 8: INCREASE YOUR INCOME EASILY

'What?' you cry. 'That's impossible!' It's not, and it's a lot easier than it sounds. There are loads of things you can do on top of your full-time job (or instead of a job) which can help boost your income, and most of them are really enjoyable too. Think about what skills you have. Think about what you enjoy doing. Then think about how you can turn these things into a money-making opportunity. Check out Chapters 14 and 15 for loads of ideas on making extra cash. Also scour the money-making ideas on Moneymagpie.com. There's no shame in doing everything you can to get yourself out of the debt trap, and you never know what kind of interesting people you'll meet along the way!

If your household income is below a certain amount you may be entitled to benefits or tax credits, particularly if you have children. Even if you don't think you're eligible it's worth taking a look on Entitledto.co.uk, a free benefits calculator, to work out if you should be getting any extra money from the government. If you want professional advice about what you're entitled to then you can pop into your local Job Centre and they'll tell you what you need to know.

STEP 9: DON'T MAKE THINGS WORSE

Remember, whatever you do, don't borrow more money to pay off your debts. If you do this you dig yourself in deeper and deeper, and interest will keep rising until you're in way over your head. There are no benefits at all to paying off debts with credit cards and more loans.

REMIND YOURSELF

- Face the demon now: the quicker you tackle the debt, the quicker – and cheaper – it will be to pay it off.
- Get out of the credit trap. Any time you see the word 'credit' in shops or banks, mentally replace it with the word 'debt', because that's what it is. Suddenly, then, even 'interest-free debt' doesn't sound quite so appealing.
- Don't be afraid to tell your friends that you can't afford things because you're paying off your debt. You need their support and, anyway, they may be grateful that they don't have to spend either.
- If you don't want to keep yo-yoing between debt and solvency all the time, change your whole approach to money for good, not just until the debt goes. Read the whole of this book and your attitude will change naturally.

Follow the steps and get support

- Even if your debts are large, if you follow the step-by-step instructions above, and keep to them, you will get out of your debt situation. Read the steps again several times if you need to and stick with them.
- Get moral support from friends. Go on the Moneymagpie.com message boards to share your situation and get inspiration from others.

If Things Have Gone Too Far ...

Don't panic if you feel your debts are getting out of control. There are several excellent, free organisations that exist to help us get out of debt as painlessly as possible. These include the National Debtline, Citizens Advice Bureau (CAB) and the Consumer Credit Counselling Service (CCCS). (For contact details, see Resources, page 398.)

If things are really bad and you don't think you can deal with it on your own, get in touch with one or more of these organisations *as soon as possible*. Don't leave it another day. The earlier these specialists get to deal with your problems, the better able they are to help you. This is particularly true if you think you may be in danger of losing your home. If you think there's any possibility that your home might get repossessed in the near future, get in touch with Shelter or the CAB right now.

DON'T TURN TO DEBT MANAGEMENT COMPANIES

There are a lot of debt management companies around. Many advertise debt solutions in the form of debt consolidation (they say they can turn all your debts into one easy monthly payment) or IVAs (individual voluntary arrangements, see opposite). Other companies will talk to your creditors and organise a debt repayment plan for you. All of these companies charge you for this service. If you are facing serious debt problems then you really can't afford to pay for a service that you could get for free from one of the organisations mentioned above.

Not only that but many of these companies will make your situation worse. Some claim that they can halve your debts thanks to a 'government loophole'. What they mean is they will sell you (yes, sell you – it costs) an IVA. IVAs can be a good solution for some but they're certainly not right for everyone. Also, they need to be set up by someone who is properly qualified, and not all of the people working for these debt companies have the right qualifications. It's best to speak to the CCCS, National Debtline or the CAB to find out if this is the right solution for you.

Companies that offer debt consolidation will often tie you into a much worse situation than you have now by selling you loans that last for decades and can end up making you lose your home.

What the Advisers Might Suggest ...

Here are some options you can consider if things are *really* bad, but watch out for the downsides. Really, if you are going to take any of the drastic steps below it must *only* be because you've been advised to do so by one of the debt advice charities mentioned above. Debt management companies might suggest these too but you should check with the free, charitable agencies to see if they are genuinely useful to you.

IVAs

These are effectively glorified debt management plans designed to give creditors a better return than they would get if you went bankrupt. Essentially you come to an agreement with your creditors about how to pay off part of your various debts. It's done under the supervision of a licensed

Insolvency Practitioner (usually an accountant or lawyer) who sorts it all out for you. In some circumstances, an IVA is the best option because it's a way of avoiding full bankruptcy and sometimes it can help people keep their homes.

> Only ever take out an IVA through the advice of a professional independent organisation such as the Consumer Credit Counselling Service (CCCS). Never go to a company advertised on television or anywhere else. The CCCS now offers an IVA service so they are worth talking to. See also Insolvency.gov.uk, which is a site run by the Department of Trade and Industry.

The good thing about an IVA is that it stops your creditors from knocking at your door and it gives you more control over how your assets are dealt with than you would get with bankruptcy. So long as you keep up the payments under the IVA, your creditors are bound by the agreement. This means they cannot petition for your bankruptcy or bring any other kind of court action against you in respect of the debt you owe them. It also means you don't have to pay off the full amount of your debt.

However, the very bad thing about IVAs is that it all costs money. In fact, it's likely to cost a few thousand – money that could be spent paying off your debts. IVA providers can charge big, front-loaded fees (i.e. you pay *them* before you pay your creditors). These are paid within the arrangement which means that a lot of the money you're paying in at the beginning is actually going into paying their fees rather than the debt itself.

Also, they don't always work. Many times IVAs break down a year or so into the scheme and the debtor has to find another way of dealing with things. If you default on making payments as per the agreement, your Insolvency Practitioner has to petition for your bankruptcy.

Debt Consolidation Loans

This involves combining all your existing debts into one big loan. As with an IVA, you should use this option only if you've been advised to do so by a not-for-profit debt counsellor at one of the debt charities. If you can find a loan with a cheaper interest rate than you already have, which isn't secured against your home, it might be worth considering. Once again, avoid the companies that advertise on television.

By taking out a consolidation loan, you'll ultimately be paying out more money, even if it is in lesser amounts over a longer period of time. Also, in my experience, a lot of people who take on consolidation loans (or who remortgage to cover their debts) often keep on spending on their old credit cards after taking out the loan. This means their overall debt gets even bigger.

There are some circumstances in which you could consider a consolidation loan:

- *Once you have closed down all your other credit cards, loans and overdrafts so that you won't use them.*
- *Once you have started to live – and spend – more sensibly.*

- *If you can't transfer your debts to one or more 0 per cent credit cards.*
- *If you have a loan that is flexible – you can pay it off early if possible and not be fined.*
- *If the loan is not 'secured' on your home.*

The problem with most people who take out consolidation loans is that they do not usually meet the above criteria. It might look like a good idea on paper but for a lot of people they can make their lives much worse. Beware.

BANKRUPTCY

Bankruptcy (known in Scotland as 'sequestration') can turn your life upside down, although, thanks to recent laws, the disruption doesn't last as long as it used to. In fact, most bankrupts are now automatically discharged after just one year. Although you're still liable for your debts for three years after being made bankrupt, after that the debts that remain are written off and you're cleared to borrow money and set up businesses again.

Once you're declared bankrupt, the majority of your assets are handed over to a trustee to control them. To start with, you will deal with the official receiver who needs to find out as much as possible about what you own and what you owe. You are then protected from your creditors, who can no longer pursue you for money. You might have to pay part of your debts each month, but that will be based on what you can afford.

If your debts exceed your assets the only things you'll be allowed to keep are some basic household items and any tools you need in order to work. If you own your home, the official receiver can sell it off to go towards paying your debts. If you have a mortgage and can't meet the payments, the lender may repossess your home. If you have any income over and above what's necessary to live on, you'll have to hand that over too for the next three years. If you want to have a bank account, you have to tell the bank you're a bankrupt – which means you might not get one at all.

The Downsides of Bankruptcy

- *You will probably lose all of your assets of any value including your home and cards.*
- *You can't get credit for more than £500 without first telling the lender you're bankrupt.*
- *You can't use most bank or building society accounts or credit cards.*
- *You can't practise as a chartered accountant or lawyer.*
- *You can't be a Justice of the Peace (JP), a Member of Parliament, a local councillor or a company director. In fact, you can't form, manage or promote a limited company without the permission of the court.*
- *You can't trade in any business under any other name unless you inform all the people affected by each transaction of your bankruptcy.*

Most importantly, bankruptcy is not the 'quick fix' or 'short sharp shock' it is often made out to be. A record of your bankruptcy is kept on your credit file for the next six years, which will make getting loans, bank accounts or mortgages difficult and expensive. You can sour relationships with business contacts. If you're found to be dishonest, reckless or blameworthy, many of the restrictions imposed by your bankruptcy could, in effect, continue for up to 15 years.

For really useful bankruptcy advice ...

Get in touch with the Bankruptcy Advisory Service at www.bankruptcyadvisoryservice.co.uk. This is a very cheap service run by mother and daughter team Gill and Jo Hankey. They charge a subscription of just £25.00 for all their advice.

REPOSSESSION

If you think your home might be repossessed, first off, before you think of doing anything, get in touch with Shelter or the Citizens Advice Bureau (see Resources, page 398, for contact details). Both are free and have a lot of experience in helping people with housing-related problems.

Both organisations say they have often come across cases where they could have helped a lot more, including staving off repossession, if the person in question had come to them much earlier. So don't leave it till it's too late. The moment you feel worried about keeping the roof over your head, go to see one of these groups and get proper help.

Banks and building societies can be quite sympathetic to customers who have money troubles so if you have just missed one payment you'll probably get a friendly phone call, just in case they have made a mistake. After missing two payments, you'll get a letter – if you haven't already told your lender that you are having troubles.

A third missed payment, on the other hand, may trigger legal action. The bank will have to get a court order before they can take your home away. This is why it is really important to speak to your bank as soon as you know you are having difficulties, and why it is also really important to speak to one of the free advice agencies mentioned above very early on in the process. Don't suffer in silence and don't suffer alone. You don't have to. Remember, lenders do not really want to have to repossess your home. After all, it costs them money to go to court so always speak to them, even if you don't want to.

What to Do if You Can't Afford Your Mortgage

1. Check whether your repayments are covered by an insurance policy. Some types of medical insurance will pay out if the reason you can't afford your mortgage is because you had to take time off work due to illness.
2. Tell your mortgage lender you are having trouble or contact the CAB to do this for you. Some lenders will allow you to keep paying a smaller portion of your mortgage; if you are out of work, for example, and are likely to find a new job soon your lender might be prepared to accept a smaller but regular amount.
3. See if you are entitled to any benefits that could help with repayments, such as tax credits or unemployment benefit.

Get advice NOW

- If your debts are really serious, speak to one or more of the free debt advice agencies. They are busy so you might have to wait but it's worth it.
- Don't suffer alone. Get moral support and help from others on the Moneymagpie.com message boards (www.moneymagpie.com/index.php?action=show MessageBoardHome). Remember, you will get out of this.

part two

SMART SPENDING

chapter five

Switch Your Bills and Save a Bundle

In this chapter I will explain how to switch all your bills so that you get everything cheaper. You will find out:

- *How to get cheaper gas, electricity, broadband and phone bills (page 78).*
- *How to switch to a better bank account (page 80).*
- *How to shop around for the best insurance deals (page 83).*
- *How to find a better mortgage deal (page 91).*
- *How to find the best value loans and credit cards (pages 93 and 95).*

Switch the Basics

You've probably heard people say quite a few times that you should switch your bills regularly to get the best price and save on your monthly outgoings. But have you heard it enough to galvanise you into action?

Probably not. Only about half of Brits have taken up the

opportunity to grab some really good savings and spend a lot less each month on boring stuff like gas, phones and bank accounts, freeing up money for living a great lifestyle.

So, as I mentioned in Chapter 3, your mission – should you choose to accept it – is to get on that computer now and decide that you're going to *make* yourself a load of money by *saving* it on your bills. Yes, I know, it's not *actually* making money but it has the same effect (and you don't have to pay tax on it).

> The average household could save around £1,000 in a year just by switching all their bills (including insurance, utilities, loans and other household stuff).

If you think that you're 'earning' rather than saving an extra £1,000, you might get more excited about it. In fact, you're actually saving/earning over £1,200 because if you're *really* earning then you have to make around £1,240 *before* tax to come home with £1,000. So you're really quids in when you *save* money!

Or, imagine how you would feel if someone told you that you could make £1,000 in a day just by playing on your computer? You'd race to do it. Well, that's what you can do if you spend a day, or, say, a couple of evenings going through all your bills and switching providers. And after you've done it once, it's easy to do it again (or bargain with the kids to do it for you).

So, get your bills together, including credit card statements, bank statements and the like, and get on the internet to save money. Here's how you do it.

GAS, ELECTRICITY, BROADBAND, HOME AND MOBILE PHONES

Around half of us are still with the original gas, electricity and phone companies we started with when we moved into our homes. That means that around half of us are probably paying too much for these services! What's the point of that?

Even if you are tied into a contract it can still be worth switching now. Sometimes getting out of a bad contract can cost you less than seeing it through to the end. It's a good idea to check at least once a year that you're not over-paying for these boring but essential utilities. This is what you should do:

Step 1: Get Your Paperwork Together

Grab some of your latest bills. Look at the price they charge per unit and see how much you use, on average, per month.

Step 2: Go on the Internet

Use a comparison service like the one at Moneymagpie.com (search for 'energy comparison'). Here you will have to type in a few details about your current supplier and how much your annual bill comes to. Click 'continue' and up will come a list of the cheapest suppliers for your needs, with details of how much you can save. To get the most accurate information for gas and electricity, enter the amount of energy you've used (in Kwh) on this page – the total will be on your last bill – rather than just the amount you've spent.

Have a look at buying your phone and broadband services all in the same bundle because you may be able to pay a lot less than having them all separate.

Step 3: Shop around Even More

You can either make the switch right away or, if you want to be extra-sure you've got the best possible price, try a number of other comparison websites. It's worth checking out as many as you can before you commit, to make sure you get the best deal.

Try some of these sites:

- *Moneysupermarket (Moneysupermarket.com)*
- *Energyhelpline (Energyhelpline.com)*
- *Consumer Choices (Consumerchoices.co.uk)*
- *SwitchwithWhich (Switchwithwhich.co.uk)*

Step 4: Do the Paperwork

When you've chosen a deal, give your original supplier a call and see if they will match it. If not, go ahead with your new deal; the website will ask you to click on it and then fill in the online application. This will include all your personal details, and if you wish to pay by direct debit (usually cheaper this way) you'll have to fill in your bank details. This is so they can pass them on to the provider you've chosen, so the direct debit can be set up.

Step 5: Change Suppliers

Once you've filled out the application form, the website will pass on all the details to your new supplier, who will then contact your old supplier and organise a transfer date. It is on this date that you should take your final readings for the meter, broadband usage and so on. Then give it to your new supplier so they can organise your final bill (with your old supplier) for you. Remember, it's only after you've paid the final bill that you can cancel your direct debit with your old supplier.

SAVE EVEN MORE ON YOUR BILLS

Once you've switched suppliers you can save even more by being green at home. Plug up all the draughty gaps around doors and windows; turn the heating down and wear warmer clothes; switch lights and all electrical appliances off when you're not in the room and unplug chargers when you're not using them. Over the year you can save loads just by these simple kinds of steps. Don't believe me? Just try it.

YOUR BANK ACCOUNT

Four simple facts about bank accounts:

1. We're more likely to get divorced than change our bank.
2. You might not think you're losing money through your bank account, but if you're with one of the big high street names you could easily be.
3. If you're mostly in credit, you could be earning more interest on your cash in an account which rewards you for saving.
4. If you're regularly overdrawn you could be paying *less* interest on your debt in another bank.

So you really could save (or make) money by switching your account. Some of the best options to be had are with the newer internet and phone banks. Not only that, but some of them will do all the work of moving your direct debits and standing orders for you if you switch to them.

However, money-saving shouldn't be your only consideration. There are a few things you should consider when choosing the right bank account for you:

- *Service – it's really important to have quick and efficient help from your bank when you have a query or a problem. For many people it's worth paying more to be able to speak to someone helpful rather than putting up with people at a call centre thousands of miles away. So find out the number of the service centre and call it a couple of times at peak time (early evening) and see if they pick up quickly and can answer some test questions.*
- *Good online banking – some banks have better, more efficient websites for their customers to use than others. If you bank by internet a lot, your bank needs to have a good one.*
- *Accessibility – if you need to bank cheques regularly or make other transactions then it's important to have easy access to a branch of your bank. If there are few branches in your area then don't bother.*

So, to find the best account for you, follow these steps:

Step 1: Shop Around

Have a look at the comparison tables on Moneymagpie.com to see which bank accounts are offering the best savings rates when you're in credit. If you want one that gives cheap overdrafts, check out the Moneymagpie article on bank accounts that give the best overdrafts for the latest best deals (www.moneymagpie.com/article/current-accounts-with-bonuses/3).

Step 2: Look at the Bank Websites

When you've found the banks that offer the best rates, the next step is to visit their websites. Here you can check out their services and see if they meet your criteria for accessibility, online banking and so on.

Step 3: Make a Decision

Decide whether one of the banks really is better than the one you're currently with. Your decision should be personal – based on your requirements from a bank such as service, online banking and accessibility (as mentioned above).

Step 4: Apply to Join

If you are happy that another bank offers a better deal and service, contact the new bank and apply to join. If they accept you then either a) get them to move your direct debits and standing orders for you, if they offer that service, or b) contact the various companies you pay regularly so that they can change their direct debit instructions. In fact, while you're doing this, make sure you don't have any unnecessary direct debits going out.

Step 5: Keep Your Old Account Open for Six Months

You never know, you might find that this new bank isn't as good as you expected and you want to go back. Also, you may have forgotten companies that are paying into your old account, or some direct debits may have slipped your mind. Keeping the old account open will help scoop these up.

(For information about savings accounts, see Chapter 9.)

INSURANCE

Insurance is very much a product where cheap isn't necessarily cheerful. Naturally, you need to find the best price for each insurance product you use, but you also have to be careful that the policy you get covers all your needs. Sometimes (though certainly not always) the cheapest policies are able to be so because they don't cover you for much, as you can find out to your horror if you have to claim after an accident or disaster.

However, like most other companies, insurers bank on us just sticking with them without shopping around when we renew our policies, and that's how they manage to overcharge us each year. So it is definitely worth shopping around whenever you have to renew your car, home, travel or other types of insurance. Just make sure that the policy you go for is *good value* as opposed to just cheap, that is, it actually covers everything you need and does it at the lowest rate.

Car Insurance

Step 1: Decide which Level of Insurance You Need

Do you need (and can you afford):

- *fully comprehensive;*
- *third party, fire and theft;*
- *or just third party insurance?*

The last one is likely to be the cheapest type of insurance but it does mean that in an accident you would have to cover the cost of all repairs, legal fees and so on.

Step 2: Shop Around

Shop around on the comparison sites again and save yourself a load of cash. Internet sales have fewer overheads so companies can pass on savings to the buyers. The Moneymagpie.com car insurance comparison will get you a good cheap deal but don't just try that – compare comparison services. See how Compare the Market (Comparethemarket.com) does, or Go Compare (Gocompare.com) or Kwik-fit (Kwik-fitinsurance.com).

Step 3: Decide on Your Excess Policy

You can bring the price of your insurance down by agreeing to pay a higher amount if you ever do have to claim. If you're pretty confident that you won't have an accident (or you have the money to cover it if you did) then go for it. Otherwise, though, be cautious as it could cost you later on if you have an accident.

Home Insurance

Step 1: Shop Around

Look at internet comparison sites for buildings and home contents insurance. Try the Moneymagpie.com comparison service (www.moneymagpie.com/bestbuys/insurance) and others like Moneysupermarket (Moneysupermarket.com) and Kwit-Fit (Kwit-fitinsurance.com). Check to see if it would be cheaper to buy both home and contents insurance together.

Step 2: Make Sure You're Getting the Right Type of Cover

For buildings insurance you need to insure yourself against the cost of actually rebuilding your home, not the current value of your property. Work out how much it could cost to rebuild it exactly as it is now. Insurers you contact may be able to help you work that out. Other elements that affect the cost of buildings insurance are the land on which your home is built and the structure of the building you live in. If there is a history of subsidence in your home, for example, the buildings insurance will be higher. Similarly, if it is very old and was built before certain building standards were enforced, your insurers might see the property as more of a risk and charge you higher premiums.

For home contents insurance, make sure that you don't underestimate the value of your property. A wardrobe full of clothes, for example, could cost thousands to replace. Also, think about very valuable single items; most home contents insurance policies have a section that you can fill in that insures individual items separately. They can even be insured when they are out of the house. So, for example, if you have some bits of expensive jewellery that you wear regularly, or even prescription glasses, you should insure them individually so that if you lose them in the street you can get the money back.

It's worth noting that if you insure your things for less than the total value of your contents, the insurance company will 'average down' the compensation payment if you make a claim. In other words, they will divide the total amount you have insured by the items that you have and use that figure to pay you back for each thing lost. So don't underinsure.

Step 3: Switch to a New Insurer

This is where you go on the comparison service at Moneymagpie.com (go into the 'Comparisons' section and click on 'insurance') and see which gives you the best deal for your needs. You will need to fill in details about yourself, your home and your contents which can take a while, but persevere as it's worth it in the end!

HOW TO CUT HOME INSURANCE COSTS

- Try to pay for the insurance once a year rather than in monthly instalments if you can manage it. Some insurers charge interest on the instalments, which makes the whole thing more expensive.
- Fit anti-crime devices. Do all you can to make things difficult for burglars. If you live on the ground floor, grow hedges and prickly shrubbery outside the windows. Fences, gates and doors should be properly maintained. Bars on windows are also essential for most basement and ground-floor flats, particularly in cities.
- Keep your roof well-maintained and the guttering clear (particularly in autumn) so that you reduce the chance of damp and flooding, which would increase your premiums.
- Installing a sprinkler system massively reduces the chance of a fire in your home. It costs quite a lot to put in but can potentially save you thousands.

Travel Insurance

Step 1: Decide on the Level of Cover You Need

Do you need annual insurance cover or are you just making a single trip? If you will travel twice or more in the year then an annual travel insurance policy will be the best value for you. If you travel very rarely, just go for a single trip option each time (bearing in mind that you have to remember to buy insurance each time).

Step 2: Check Your Existing Insurance Policies

Look carefully at any policies you're already paying for, like your home contents insurance and car insurance. You may find that these policies already cover you for certain things like driving abroad and loss of belongings outside of the home. This way you can work out what you do and don't need to have covered by your travel insurance and it may mean that you can pay lower premiums. Also, check your bank account as you might be getting travel insurance for free with it.

Step 3: Shop Around

Go to the Moneymagpie.com comparison service and search for the best policy for you. Other good websites to try for travel insurance are Moneysupermarket.com and Insurancewide.com. Make sure your policy covers what you need, such as winter sports, travel around the world (not just Europe) and enough medical cover. Also, if you're particularly attached to your belongings, make sure the deal covers your bag (take note of special clauses for carrying jewellery on your person and so on). If you're in a couple, you might also be able to get a discount on the normal price of two separate policies.

Life Insurance

Life insurance promises (in an insurance kind of a way, that is, with conditions) that if you die, a sizeable chunk of change will be given to your family. This will give you the peace of mind of knowing that your loved ones will be covered financially if you go. As a possible drawback (or a plus if you're into Agatha Christie novels), you may find that in purely financial terms, you're worth a lot more to your family dead than you are alive.

Life insurance is rather more complicated than other types of insurance. There are several different types of life insurance, so consider which type would make the most sense for your situation. Also, different policies cover different things so you'll need to think about your lifestyle (your job, hobbies and health) when choosing the right one for you.

Here are the steps that you can take to get a better deal:

Step 1: Ask Yourself if You Really Need Life Insurance

If you have no dependants (that is no children at home and no elderly or infirm relatives who depend on you for their care) then you don't need life insurance. Check, though, to see if you have life insurance from your employer already. Some employers include that as a benefit.

However, if you have a family or anyone who would suffer if you were not around to provide for them, then you do need it. Unless, of course, you have already paid off the mortgage and have serious investments set aside that could keep them going for years if you were suddenly not around. This is the case with a few people, but not many are in that happy position. For most, life insurance is the way to go.

Step 2: Choose the Type You Need

This is the jolly bit (not!) There are several types. Here is what you have to choose from:

- *Level Term Insurance – This is generally the cheapest and simplest option. It's sometimes called 'protection only' insurance and guarantees to pay out a set amount if you die within a certain time. You pay a set amount each month, too, which is handy. However, it doesn't pay out anything if you live after the term agreed. If you do, then you'll have to negotiate another deal at that point. Be warned though, it could be a lot more expensive at that stage.*
- *Increasing Term Insurance – With this one, the cover increases over the years without the need for a medical. However, the amount you pay also rises.*
- *Decreasing Term Insurance – The cover decreases over the years at a flat, fixed rate. You pay less, as well.*
- *Mortgage Protection Insurance – Pretty obviously, this is insurance connected to your mortgage. It reduces over time as the amount you still owe on the mortgage goes down; and, if you die before the end of the term, it will pay off the mortgage.*
- *Renewable Term Insurance – This is a short-term policy that can be renewed at the end of the term without a medical. It is cheaper than most others because it lasts for a shorter time.*
- *Family Income Benefit – This pays a tax-free annual income to your family or other dependants if you die. This is instead of a one-off lump sum. The annual income lasts for a fixed period set by you.*

Step 3: Work out How Much You Should Insure Yourself for
The amount for which you insure yourself (and your partner/spouse) depends on how much you think the family would need without you. Ask yourself:

- *Will I need to cover them for school bills, university fees, child-care costs and other expenses?*
- *Will the mortgage be paid off by another policy if I die, or does it need to be paid?*
- *Would my spouse be able to fund much of it through their income?*
- *What other policies and investments would they benefit from if I died (pensions, death-in-service benefit, personal investments and so on)?*
- *What can I actually afford to pay into a policy now, each month?*

Do a 'back of an envelope' calculation yourself or create your own spreadsheet on the computer to work out the figures.

Step 4: Shop Around
It's really important to go for the one that covers your needs most and is the best value, rather than the cheapest you can get. It may be that the cheapest is the best for you but it's important to read the policy document and check that you are covered for what you really need.

Have a look at the personalised comparison service on Moneymagpie.com (www.moneymagpie.com/bestbuys/insurance) and also check out other services to see if you can find better elsewhere. Try Moneysupermarket.com, Moneyextra.co.uk or the Motley Fool (Fool.co.uk).

YOUR MORTGAGE

This section is about how to remortgage. I cover everything about getting a new mortgage in Chapter 8.

Step 1: Start Looking Straight Away

You can arrange a remortgage up to six months before the end of your fixed term period. And, because the good deals are snapped up so quickly at the moment, arranging it early is the best thing to do. If you find a better deal later on it's fairly easy to cancel one that you've agreed to before the money has been transferred over. Just be aware of the upfront mortgage set-up fees that you might have to pay. If you switch to another, better deal you will probably lose the money you spent on those so remember to factor that in when looking at better deals.

> If you find a good mortgage deal, grab it quick smart; you can always get out of it later on.

Step 2: Get a Broker

Not just anyone but a good – and, importantly, free – one. A good *independent* mortgage broker will look at the whole of the market for you (not just a few companies they are tied to) and will be able to get you the best deals on offer. As I mention in my free mortgage guide (see www.moneymagpie.com/downloadPDF/The_Friendly_Mortgage_Guide_from_Moneymagpie), companies like London &

Country (www.lcplc.co.uk) are fee-free, independent and cover the whole of the mortgage market. Other places to look are Charcol (Charcolonline.co.uk) and Moneysupermarket (Moneysupermarket.com).

If your broker finds you a great offer, you should also consider having a chat with your current provider to see if they will match it. They won't always be able to, but if they do, you can avoid the (often excessive) exit fees that are involved with changing your mortgage provider, and you may get cheaper arrangement fees.

Step 3: Start Budgeting

As soon as you start looking, you should also begin budgeting for your new mortgage. Depending on the current economic climate, your new mortgage deal might be more expensive than your current payments. If that's the case you should add increased mortgage payments into your monthly expenditure budget (don't have one? See Chapter 3). This way, when you do start repaying your new mortgage, it won't come as such a shock. Also, if you realise now that you can't afford to make the repayments then you can do something about it before your home is put at risk.

Things you'll have to fork out for straight away are the arrangement fees for the new mortgage and the exit penalties on your current one. These vary a lot across different banks and mortgages, but can be between £100 and £3,000. (Go to Chapter 8 to find out more about arrangement fees and other joys when you get a new mortgage.)

WATCH OUT FOR ARRANGEMENT FEES

Be warned. Recently, arrangement fees have become a tool to manipulate mortgage comparison tables. By offering a lower rate of interest a mortgage provider can get up high on comparison tables. They then make the money back by hiking up arrangement fees.

This can work to your advantage: if your mortgage is more than £200,000 you'll probably save money by paying a higher arrangement fee and then lower interest. However, less than £200,000 it's probably better to go for a slightly higher interest rate to save on arrangement fees.

LOANS

I don't like loans, unless they are for investment purposes (such as a mortgage to help you buy a house or a 'career' loan to help you pay for a course that will get you a better job). However, there are times when it is cheaper to have a loan than overdrafts and credit cards.

Ideally, if you have credit card debt, you should look to switch it to a 0 per cent deal (see pages 46–47 and 95–96 for instructions). However, if you can't get one of these, or a low lifetime balance on another credit card, then a cheap loan is often the next best thing. So if you *really* need to get a loan, and you are not able to use any of the alternatives above, then follow these steps to get the best value:

Step 1: Check Your Credit Record

See page 53 for information on what a credit record is and how to find out what score you have. Essentially, the higher your score, the more likely you are to get really good interest rates on your loan. If your credit score is really high then you can go ahead and apply for a low-interest loan. If it is medium to low then you will have to be careful because you may be offered a lousy APR (interest rate), which will make your debt much higher.

Step 2: Decide what Type of Loan You Will Go For

If you think you could pay the full amount off fairly early then only go for a flexible loan that will not penalise you for doing so. If you're not sure that you could pay it off early then go for a fixed loan as they tend to have cheaper rates than flexible ones.

Also, decide whether you want a secured loan or an unsecured loan. As I mentioned in the last chapter (see page 48), I would always go for an unsecured loan if possible because they are safer. Secured loans are 'secured' on your property. In other words, the lender says that if you don't pay that loan back they could potentially force you to sell your home in order to do so. Not good! Because these loans are secure for the lender (not for you) they tend to be cheaper than unsecured loans. Only consider such a loan if you are *absolutely* certain that you can pay it off and you really want to go for the cheapest offer. However, if you're a bit unsure, go for an unsecured loan. They may be a little more expensive (though not always) but at least you won't lose your home because of them.

Step 3: Shop Around

Look on comparison services like Moneymagpie.com, Moneyfacts (Moneyfacts.co.uk) and Moneyextra (Moneyextra.co.uk) to see which companies are offering the cheapest loans at the moment. If you are confident of your credit score then apply directly. However, if you are not confident that you would be accepted, phone them up and ask them to give you a quote for a loan. Explain that you don't want to apply immediately (as every time you apply and are rejected, this counts against you on your credit record). The quote may change when you actually apply, but it will give you an initial indication about what you can get – and whether you would actually be accepted if you formally applied.

Step 4: Pay It Off

If you get a flexible loan, do your best to pay it off as fast as possible. Remember, when you borrow money you really 'rent' it (see page 52), so the longer you have it, the more you will pay in the long run.

CREDIT CARDS

Credit cards are just a fancy way of putting off paying for things for a few weeks. There's a catch, however: if you don't pay it off in time, the lender will charge you a fee. The fees – or interest rates – on credit cards are one of the most expensive ways to borrow money there is. Before I tell you to switch your credit card to find a cheaper fee (interest rate), you should be clear about the choices available:

0 per cent Balance Transfer

The first credit card you need to consider is the 0 per cent balance transfer card. This means if you have several debts elsewhere you can combine them on a 0 per cent balance card and they will let you pay it off, without any interest, over a certain number of months.

Low Lifetime Balance Transfer

If you don't think you can pay off your balance within the time limit, you should consider getting a low lifetime balance transfer credit card. You will be able to transfer your debts to a new card and pay it off at a low rate for as long as it takes.

0 per cent on Purchases

If you will use your card for shopping more than for transferring balances then go for a card that offers 0 per cent interest on purchases. To make the most of these cards, you should aim to pay the whole thing off before the 0 per cent period finishes (often three, six or twelve months) so that you clear the debt before you need to pay any interest on it.

Credit Cards with Rewards

If you have no debts and you are able to pay off your credit card every month on time (nearly two in three Britons do this), then you could consider getting a credit card with rewards. These are cards that will give you cash back, points or air miles when you use them. Now is the time to demand rewards for your spending.

THINGS TO LOOK AT WHEN CHOOSING A CREDIT CARD

- The APR (annual percentage rate) which shows you, essentially, how much your loan will cost you per year, including any charges.
- Whether there is a one-off fee you have to pay to transfer your balance from another card.
- How long you have to pay off an entire balance transfer at 0 per cent and what the percentage will be when that period ends.
- Whether you have to pay a fee each year just to have the card.

You can consider these details and more with Moneymagpie's credit card comparison pages at www.moneymagpie.com (search for 'credit card comparison').

So, there we go; that wasn't too hard, was it? Give yourself a big pat on the back if you managed to trawl through even half of the list in this chapter. If you're all done now, go on to the next chapter for some more ideas about smart spending.

chapter six

Secrets of Smart Spending

In this chapter you will find out:

- *How to live more on less (see opposite).*
- *How to get all kinds of great things cheaply or even for free (page 120).*
- *How to shop smartly online and on the high street (pages 99 and 112).*

One of the secrets of being a true Money Magpie is to be really clever about your spending. This isn't about not spending at all – it's about spending in a smart way. There are loads of ways you can spend your money more wisely, and the more you do it, the more money you will have to spend on things you really love.

In fact, that's one of my key messages: 'Spend on things you love and save on things that aren't important to you.' Indeed, even when it comes to spending on what you love, there's no reason to spend more than you need. Here are lots of ways that you can save on pretty much everything and become a true Money Magpie.

Shopping Around – How to Sniff out the Best Deals

It has always been a good idea to shop around for the best prices on everything, but now that we have the internet it's a hundred times easier. You can look at prices for the same thing in shops and sites around the country and even abroad. Before you buy anything you should research it on the internet to see if you can:

- *find the cheapest version*
- *get a voucher to get even more money off (see page 111)*
- *get cashback on it if you buy it through a cashback site (see page 109)*
- *get it for free (not so likely but still worth a look) on a freebie site (see page 123)*

HOUSEHOLD GOODS

Electronics, kitchen appliances, toys and household goods can be bought for much less than high-street prices through specialist websites. First, compare prices on one of the comparison sites like Pricerunner (pricerunner.co.uk) or Shopping.com. Once you have found the best price, look on one of the cashback sites (see page 110) to see if you can get it at that price with cashback added. If you can't, or it's something you would like to buy from a shop anyway, print out the best price you can find on the internet and take that into the shop with you. Waving that about in front of the assistant should help you get a significant discount.

FOOD

The website Mysupermarket.com can help you save a packet on supermarket shopping. You select your chosen supermarket (from Asda, Tesco, Sainsbury's and Ocado) and do your online shopping through the easy-to-use site. While you shop, the website will keep a running tab of how much it would cost you at the three other major supermarkets. If you find at the end that you'd like to switch supermarkets you can do this at the click of a button. The great thing is that Mysupermarket's technology happily takes your order, and then with another simple click, fires it over to the supermarket of your choice.

Don't Be Bullied by the Supermarkets

We have all felt the effects of the economic downturn, and food shopping is making a significant dent in our hard-earned cash. With the supermarkets struggling, they're up to all kinds of tricks to get us to spend more money. What better time to learn their tricks and out-smart them?

To avoid unnecessary trips to the supermarket, always keep a good supply of canned, frozen and dried foods you know everyone in your household will eat. That way, even when your fridge is looking a little sad, you'll still have options and won't have to rush out for extras.

WHAT A WASTE

According to the excellent Love Food Hate Waste website (www.lovefoodhatewaste.com) a shocking one-third of the food we buy in the UK gets thrown away. They explain that it's largely related to dishing up portions that are too large. You can check out their portion planner to avoid this.

Obviously, you can't avoid the supermarket for ever (though wouldn't it be nice!) You can, however, be aware of all their marketing ploys and save some serious money on your shopping trip while helping your health and the environment. Also, why not get friendly with your local street market. Prices in open-air markets tend to be around 30 per cent cheaper than supermarkets.

Money-wasting Sweets and Goodies Near the Checkout

Supermarkets love to prey on tired, hungry and irritable shoppers, but don't get caught out. Never go shopping when you're hungry. It might sound obvious, but you'll end up buying things you don't need, and more often than not they'll be unhealthy and expensive.

Pretty Packaging

Ooh, the Tesco Finest Cheddar cheese looks delicious ... but wait a second. It's all about what's on the outside. The reason we tend not to buy a supermarket's own brand produce is partly because they purposely package it to appear bland and unappealing. However, own basic or mid-range brands offer better value for money than Tesco Finest or Sainsbury's Taste the Difference. Often, they are equally tasty. Why not test a few out on your family and see if they can tell the difference?

Special Offers

We all love a special offer. Big writing and colourful signs make us feel like we are winning and the supermarket is giving us something for free. This is NEVER true. They do it to get you to buy, not because they love you! The reason supermarkets run offers is to get you to buy things you wouldn't normally buy.

The only offer that is genuinely useful in the supermarket is buy one get one free – and then ONLY if you were going to buy the product (and that brand) anyway. Buy two for £X can be good too, but always remember to look at how much the item costs individually. Then, if the saving when buying two is significant, it's probably worth getting the deal. Only if you needed the item in the first place though (or if you could freeze one of them to use later)! If there isn't much saving, ask yourself if you really need two, particularly if there's a danger that you might end up throwing one away.

Deals that offer 50 per cent (or another percentage) extra for the same price can seem appealing. However, these offers often tempt you to buy a brand you wouldn't normally get. If this is the case, always look at the price per kg or per 100g. This will allow you to compare exactly how much you are paying for the amount of product. You'll often find that even though you get more with the brand on offer, you are actually paying more per kg or 100g.

There is an easy way to avoid these tempting offers – make a shopping list and stick to it. If it isn't something you use often, or something you were planning on buying anyway, don't be tempted!

Genuine Bargains

Supermarket stock that doesn't shift gets reduced – we've all seen it. These are not like the special offers supermarkets brag about; these are genuine bargains. Take advantage of them by finding out when your local supermarket gets rid of its stock (usually later in the evenings or on Sundays). Much more produce will be sold at bargain prices as it reaches its use-by date, and you'll be able to freeze many of the things you buy so you won't have to use them straight away.

Dirty Display Tricks

Did you know that supermarkets stack their shelves tactically? They put the most expensive items right in your eye-line. Look above and below and you can often get better deals. This also works on your kids in the trolley. Items are positioned so they reach out and grab the top-of-the-range products.

Get around this by looking at the whole range and comparing prices. Don't grab and run. You can also avoid your kids setting their heart on the most expensive item by leaving them at home – whenever possible.

SNEAKY SUPERMARKETS

To show just how sneaky supermarket displays are I did a little research at my local supermarket.

	Biscuits	Butter	Bread	Crisps	Cereal	Toilet Roll
Top shelf	65p	£1.29	61p	30p	85p	£1.96
Above middle	£1.28	£1.31	99p	46p		
Middle shelf	£2.54	£1.92	£1.19	51p	£2.32	£2.05
Below middle	71p	£1.65	£1.14	40p	£2.12	
Bottom shelf	26p		72p	28p	£1.53	£1.99
Maximum saving	**£2.28**	**63p**	**58p**	**23p**	**£1.47**	**9p**

This table clearly shows just how much more expensive the product in the middle of the shelf (in most people's eye-line) is. So give your neck some exercise and shop around on the shelf.

Cunning Store Layout

Believe it or not, all supermarkets follow a similar overall layout. Fresh produce, fruit, vegetables, meat and dairy are all stocked around the outer limits of the store, whereas pre-packed, processed and frozen foods are placed in the centre. They do this on purpose. It means that to get to the stuff you need, you have to look at all the stuff you don't need. Then, as you work your way through the aisles, you buy stuff you don't need. You therefore spend more and they make more. Cunning isn't it?

You can beat them at their own game. Help your health and your wallet – stick to the perimeter. If you have to go into the middle, use the aisle signs to find the product you need. Then you won't be looking at things you don't need.

'Convenient' Bags and Packets

When you're whizzing round the supermarket thinking about 10 other things at the same time, it's easy to opt for pre-packed items. However, buying items loose, such as fruit and vegetables, is cheaper than buying them in bags or packets. This is because the supermarket has to pay someone to pack them. Do the packaging yourself and you'll almost certainly save yourself some money (check the price per kg to make sure). You'll also help the environment by saving on packaging and producing less waste.

The power of price per kg

- Supermarkets have to give the price per weight or volume of each item. It's written underneath the price in much smaller writing. This is great for shoppers as it means we can look at how much the item costs per 100g or kg. This way we can easily see how much we are really paying for an item.
- However, to trip you up, supermarkets might show the price per unit in different amounts for similar products. For example, they might mark own-brand orange juice as 52p per litre. Then they'll mark Delmonte orange juice as 8p per

100ml. This is meant to confuse you and stop you being able to price compare.

- As soon as you see two similar items being priced according to different weight measurements like this then an alarm bell should be going off in your head. Luckily, it's easy to beat them if you know your metric measurements. A litre is 1,000ml so that means that a litre of Delmonte at 8p per 100ml costs 10 times 8p, or 80p per litre. This is actually more than the own brand, but it seems like it's less when you just look at it because of the smaller unit measurement. Don't let them fool you. Get clued up and get the most for your money.

SMART SUPERMARKET SHOPPING

Here are a few extra tips to help you save as much as you possibly can:

- Before you go shopping have a look on Mysupermarket (www.mysupermarket.com). You can compare prices of any items at all the major supermarkets, so you'll be well prepared when you reach the shops.
- Try not to visit the supermarket when all you need is a couple of pints of milk – you'll just end up buying things you don't need, and waste time and petrol. Plan ahead and use the freezer to the max (you can freeze milk and bread).
- Try eating one or two vegetarian meals a week and you'll be able to cut back on the meat you buy and save a small fortune!

- Buy fruit and vegetables that are in season. Not only is this better for the environment, but it'll help your wallet too! Produce shipped from overseas generally incurs more transport costs and is therefore almost always more expensive.
- It's not always cheaper to buy in bulk if you end up throwing lots of food away. However, you can buy staples (like rice and pasta) in bulk since they work out cheaper, last for ages and you know you'll always use them. It's worth checking out street markets and the bargain basement supermarkets such as Aldi, Lidl and Netto for these kind of products as well as for things like salt, sugar and flour.
- Buy from your local street market when you can. It's usually cheaper and there are often fantastic deals towards the end of the day.

CDS, DVDS AND BOOKS

Most of the best deals on books, CDs, DVDs, games and so on are to be found online. Again, use price comparison sites like Pricerunner.com and check cashback sites to see if you can get money back as well (see page 109).

Amazon (Amazon.co.uk) is a regular winner for books, electronics and games. Now you can qualify for their free 'Super Saver Delivery' by spending just £5. So even if you just want one album, you won't have to fork out extra for the delivery. Also look at Pricecutreview.com/UK/, a handy website that lists all of the current Amazon products that are selling at half price or less.

CDWow (www.cdwow.com) is a great place to get CD and DVD bargains. Play.com and HMV.com both offer great prices and free delivery on absolutely everything. Also, keep checking the 'Bag a Bargain' article on Moneymagpie.com (www.moneymagpie.com/article/bag-a-bargain-on-us) for new offers on DVDs particularly. We find that a lot of websites and supermarkets regularly have special sales of those, so we mention them in that article or in our newsletter (sign up now if you haven't already!)

ENTERTAINMENT AND GOING OUT

I never book a restaurant now unless it's offering a money-off deal. Why? Why not? There are so many to choose from. I suggest registering with:

- *Toptable.co.uk. It regularly has offers on restaurants around the country (and sometimes abroad) including two for one, 50 per cent off and special menus with free drinks thrown in. With Toptable you can earn points every time you book through them, which you can turn into a completely free meal when you've eaten out a couple of times.*
- *5pm.co.uk. This is another restaurant-booking site with lots of good deals around the country, particularly if you are looking at the last minute and willing to eat early on. Many restaurants don't get full until around 8pm so they are keen to get punters in earlier. 5pm.co.uk also has a loyalty points scheme which you can redeem for free dinners or spa days and beauty treatments.*

When it comes to going out to shows, there are other websites that also have special deals:

- *Lastminute.com is a good place to look for tickets for big musicals and plays as well as restaurant and theatre deals and the obvious travel offers.*
- *Get cheaper tickets for shows and sporting events through sites like Seatwave (www.seatwave.com), Viagogo (www.viagogo.co.uk) or Scarletmist (www.scarletmist.com) who are devoted to reselling tickets for all kinds of events.*
- *Check out TixDaq (www.tixdaq.com) where you can compare prices of tickets for all kinds of shows, gigs and sports games to find the cheapest available.*

Cashback Sites

Warning: DON'T buy things you don't need and DON'T use cashback if you're not disciplined in your spending.

There are loads of websites around that will give you money back if you buy things through them exclusively. They can be worthwhile, but only if you use them properly. This is what you do:

Step 1: Look on comparison sites first to find the best product for your needs.

Step 2: Choose a cashback site – or several. There are plenty around. Start with the sites that give you instant cash just by signing up such as Rpoints (Rpoints.com) which gives you £5, Cashback Shopper (Cashbackshopper.co.uk) which gives you £5, and Ecashback (Ecashback.co.uk) which gives you

£2.50 immediately. The catch is you can't take this money out straight away. They credit your account with this cash and you get your hands on it once you have used the site once or twice and been credited again.

Step 3: Look at the retailers. Have a look at the retailers on each cashback site to see if they have the product and brand you are looking for. If they all have it, see which sites give the most money for what you want.

Step 4: Make sure that you are getting the best deal. Getting 5 per cent cashback on a £100 hi-fi system is not a good deal if you can get the same hi-fi system for £50 somewhere else.

Step 5: Make more money. Many cashback sites reward you for getting friends to use the site too. This is an easy way to make extra money while helping your friends save cash. If you know that one of your friends wants to buy something big soon, get them on to these sites and make some extra money for yourself.

- *Top Cashback (www.topcashback.co.uk)*
- *We Promise To (www.wepromiseto.co.uk)*
- *Free Fivers (www.freefivers.co.uk)*
- *Give or Take (www.giveortake.com)*
- *Rpoints (www.rpoints.com)*
- *My Shopping Rewards (www.myshoppingrewards.com)*
- *Reward Circle (www.rewardcircle.com)*
- *Cashinco (www.cashinco.co.uk)*
- *Greasy Palm (www.greasypalm.co.uk)*

- *Mrscashback (www.mrscashback.com)*
- *eDealsUK (www.edealsuk.com)*
- *Trolleycash (www.trolleycash.co.uk)*
- *Cashback Junction (www.cashbackjunction.com)*
- *Moneyback Madness (www.moneybackmadness.co.uk)*
- *Cashback Shopper (www.cashbackshopper.co.uk)*

Voucher Sites

Voucher sites can be useful for getting money off things you were going to buy anyway. They're really marketing sites with codes and downloadable tokens that will give you money off things that companies are trying to push.

They're useful if you are disciplined. But don't allow them to persuade you to buy something you wouldn't normally go for. Also, give them a secondary email 'unsubscribing' when you register as they will send loads of spam out and you don't want it clogging your inbox.

The ones I recommend on Moneymagpie.com for discounts, free postage and vouchers are:

- *Send Me Cashback (www.sendmecashback.co.uk)*
- *Online Voucher (www.onlinevoucher.co.uk)*
- *My Voucher Codes (www.myvouchercodes.co.uk)*

These can also be good:

- *Wow Coupons (www.wow-coupons.co.uk)*
- *Shopping Bargains (www.shopping-bargains.co.uk)*
- *Voucher Codes (www.vouchercodes.com)*
- *Latest Discount Vouchers (www.latestdiscountvouchers.co.uk)*

- *Voucher Heaven (www.voucherheaven.com)*
- *Discount Voucher Codes (www.discountvouchercodes.co.uk)*

Also, keep checking the 'Bag a Bargain' article on Moneymagpie.com (www.moneymagpie.com/article/bag-a-bargain-on-us). It is updated each week with new vouchers, special offers and discounts.

GET THE BEST PRICE ON THE HIGH STREET

Did you know that you can get money off even in high-street shops just by negotiating? It's true. I have friends who simply assume that they should get a discount or a freebie thrown in or something else of value any time they buy anything. So they ask for it. It doesn't work every time but you'd be surprised at how often it does. If you don't ask you don't get.

Bargaining doesn't come naturally to me but I've been learning. I've been quite surprised at the discounts I've managed to get! Here are my tips (from my own experience) on how to get money off in shops:

- *Do some research before you go in to buy. Have a look on the internet for the thing you want to buy and see what price you can get it for. Print off the pages to show the assistant in the shop. Point out that you could get it for cheaper elsewhere and wouldn't they like to match that price? They may agree, in which case, buy it there. This tactic is good for things like sofas and electronics.*
- *Cash is king. Even when times aren't so hard, most businesses value money now rather than later when the credit card has*

cleared. Also, it saves them paying the credit card company 1–5 per cent commission on the sale. So ask them to split that difference with you by giving you a discount for cash. Many will.

- *Pick your salesperson. You need to speak to someone with the authority and power to do a deal. In large stores, target the assistant manager or floor supervisor. In a smaller shop ask to speak to the manager. Also, try to pick on shops where the salespeople have sales targets to meet. They're going to want sales at any cost and are more likely to meet you halfway. You can usually spot these assistants because they're the ones who come up to you the moment you've walked in the shop and try to help. You could also just boldly ask (nicely) if they work on commission.*
- *Remember the extras. If a shop isn't going to offer you money off, try getting more extras added on instead. For example, ask for free delivery, or ask them to throw in a couple of accessories. Try saying, 'Of course, you'll throw in these for free, won't you?' In sales speak this is called an 'assumptive close' so you'll be turning the tables on the salespeople!*
- *Pick the right time. If you want to do some bargaining, don't go in when they're really busy on a Saturday afternoon. Pick a Tuesday or Wednesday morning when it's quieter and calmer.*
- *Be nice. It's always better to do these things with a smile. Be assertive but not aggressive. Being friendly and polite will always get you further. Try to make the salesperson feel like they've won. One thing that can help is to mention that if you're happy with this deal, you'll be back for more. By asking for a better deal today and promising more custom further down the line, you could swing the odds in your favour.*

The Value of Second-hand

Thanks to eBay, some of the stigma of buying second-hand goods has gone away. There's something about buying on eBay (and other auction sites like eBid) that is kind of cool and makes you look like you're a good bargain-hunter. Buying second-hand is not only often much better value than buying new but is also a green way of living – recycling things that might have been thrown away. (For more on eBay, see pages 119 and 303–306.)

USED CARS

Cars are generally far better value second-hand. If you buy a brand new one you lose about 20 per cent of its sale price as you drive it off the forecourt. Buying a car that is around two years old with low mileage is often the smartest option. You don't have the VAT to pay, the parts are not usually very worn and, if it has been kept well by the first owner, you should have little trouble with it (ask for a full service history). However, you do have to be careful.

Whether you buy from a dealer, an auction or small ads, make sure you have a friend with you who is an expert in cars or, better still, pay for a vehicle inspector from the AA (www.the-aa.com) or the RAC (www.rac.co.uk) to check out the car you have fallen in love with. The AA charges £122–£165 for a qualified inspector to go over it for you. The RAC charges £125–£379 for their inspections. These are definitely worth forking out for if you're serious about the car you like. Paying this money can save you thousands in the long term.

FURNITURE

Second-hand furniture is often much cheaper than new stuff, but compare like with like and take into account the wear and tear. You can pick up some quality furniture at auctions around the country. Try these websites to find local ones:

- *www.auctionhammer.co.uk (good because you can search by speciality and region)*
- *www.ukauctionguides.co.uk (you can search only by region, not speciality)*
- *www.ukauctioneers.com (you need to register to use the search feature but registration is free)*

There are also online furniture auctions you could try such as:

- *www.cityfurnitureauction.co.uk (hotel furniture clearance)*
- *www.global-furniture.uk.com*

Did you know you can furnish your home for less than £250? Actually, £250 was the budget I gave myself, but I managed to fully furnish a fictional house with all the trimmings for a grand total of £242.82 (check out the article we wrote about it on Moneymagpie.com). I should mention here that while your home will be furnished, you should leave your WAG aspirations at the door now. I am not talking about getting three designer pieces and sitting on the floor. This house is furnished with every last detail that you would need to live comfortably, even down to a clock radio, extension cables and pretty wall paintings. It isn't all old, used or ugly either.

So, if you want to furnish your home for less, here's where you need to begin.

Step 1: Hunt for Freebies

All great furniture hunts should begin at Snaffleup.co.uk (see below), Gumtree.com (on their free stuff pages) and Freecycle.org.uk. They're great places to start when looking for free stuff. Yup, free! You can snatch up dining room tables, beds, futons, sofas – basically anything and everything can be found on this site, all for just the inconvenience of having to pick up the items yourself. If you don't have a car this may be a bit tricky but still well worth the effort if you can get a friend to help with transport.

Make sure that you see the articles before carrying them home, and definitely don't part with money before you have the goods in your possession. Try to commit to picking up only items that you've already seen a picture of online. Most postings do have a picture so avoid the dodgy ones.

Why do people give away their stuff for free? Simple. Most people just want the stuff out of their house without having the cost or hassle of disposing of it themselves. So you come along, take it off their hands and keep it.

Want more freebies? Join your local Freecycle group (www.freecycle.org.uk). This is a collection of local communities that joins together people who have free things to give away with people who want free stuff. The idea is that by swapping and sharing we aren't filling landfills up with unwanted items.

The newest free site on the block is Snaffleup.co.uk. It works in the same way as Freecycle except it's easier to get started as you don't have to sign up to browse around. The search engine shows postcodes so you can pick items that are close to you. At Moneymagpie.com we like it better than the other freebie sites.

Swap It Shop (www.swapitshop.com) is another great place to get free or cheap things, but you have to have something to swap first. Swapz (www.swapz.co.uk) is the largest and most established swapping website so give that a try, too.

Step 2: Hunt for the Cheapies

While on Gumtree look up the house clearance section where you will find loads of people desperate to sell off the things they no longer want. Buy a double bed with mattress for £25 or a 24-inch widescreen television for £15!

Some stores also offer great deals on household items. My virtual 'house' on Moneymagpie.com has been completely decked out with furniture from Ikea and Argos. While the stuff may be rather basic, when pulled together correctly it really does create a very polished and clean look. (Want to see the list of all the furnishings for my fictional house? See www.moneymagpie.com/showPage/furnish-your-entire-house-for-under-250-2.)

Have a look on Offer of the Day (www.offeroftheday.co.uk) where they search out all the best discount deals from hundreds of retailers. There are thousands of products listed from white goods to clothes, and you can easily look for exactly what you want all in one place.

WASTE NOT, WANT NOT

If you want to get rid of furniture yourself, there are other ways to do it. Visit your council website. Some, like the City of Edinburgh, offer free furniture removal that is also part of a recycling scheme. Contact Furniture Re-use Network (www.frn.org.uk) to have your used furniture donated to poor families who could otherwise not furnish their homes. The donation centres are spread out across all of the UK. If you are in Ireland go to Homeless Northern Ireland (www.homelessni.org) for details on how you can help. In Scotland visit Four Square (www.foursquare.org) for your local opportunities.

Other ways to save on furniture:

- *Host a swap party with your friends and neighbours.*
- *Stop and shop at garage sales and car boot sales.*
- *Shop at second-hand shops like Oxfam.*
- *Shop online for used goods at eBay.*
- *Traditional classified ads offer great deals.*
- *Shop at auctions, including Clearance Comet (www.clearance- comet.co.uk) for great cheap appliances.*

Don't buy into some ridiculous idea that you have to spend a fortune for your place to look great. Shop smartly and your digs will look classic while you have extra cash.

THE JOY OF EBAY – HOW TO GET BEST VALUE IN AUCTION SITES

I'm going to cover selling on eBay in Chapter 14, but of course it's a great place to buy too. Moneymagpie.com's eBay blogger, Nicky Peckham, offers these tips for safe and money-saving buying on eBay:

- *Check the feedback of the seller and only buy from someone with high feedback – at least 98 per cent. This is very important!*
- *Check out the other things the seller is offering. Do they have lots of the same item for sale? That should probably ring alarm bells unless you're buying from an eBay shop and are looking to purchase fairly standard items such as envelopes or light bulbs.*
- *Do some research and check out similar items to the one you want to buy. For this you can use eBay's completed auctions function (http://search-completed.ebay.co.uk). Is there a wide price range? Would it make more sense to 'buy it now' rather than go in for an auction? Is the seller charging excessive postage?*
- *If it's a large item you can search for the ones nearest to you in terms of miles, though it's always worth asking a buyer if you can collect in person.*
- *Ask the seller as many questions as you like, requesting additional photographs to be emailed if necessary.*
- *Be wary of buying from overseas and, in particular, anything 'from China'. You have very limited recourse if anything goes wrong.*
- *Always purchase through PayPal as it offers some protection.*
- *Just use your common sense! If it looks too good to be true at that knock-down price, it probably is (particularly when it comes to designer accessories).*

Live for Free

There are loads of things and experiences you can get for free if you know where to look. Moneymagpie.com has constantly updated articles with links to free sites, free offers and plenty of ideas for ways to live for free, so keep checking the site. Here are a few ideas for getting things for free regularly:

MYSTERY SHOPPING

You can get free meals, free drinks and even free nights in hotels by being a mystery shopper. You simply have to go along, maybe eating a meal in a restaurant or having drinks in a pub, and then afterwards answer questions about it on an online form. There are a few good mystery shopping agencies in this country but watch out for dodgy ones that pretend to be proper agencies, but actually aren't. Have a look at the article on Moneymagpie.com for a list of the agencies that we have checked out. Some of the longest-established reputable names in this market are:

- *TNS Global (www.tns-global.com)*
- *Performance in People (www.performanceinpeople.co.uk)*
- *GF Knop (www.gfknop.com)*

All you need to do is to register with an agency, giving them your bank details so that they can pay you, and then make yourself available for any jobs that come in.

FORAGING

There are lots of places you can go to pick up tasty, free food. Try foraging in hedgerows, woods and on the seashore, with one warning: you need to have a good understanding of what you are looking for. There are a number of books out there to help you identify everything from nuts and herbs to fruits, leafy vegetables and shellfish. Richard Mabey's book *Food for Free*, which has been around for over 20 years, is a great source of information, but there are many others out there just as helpful. Many also include recipes. Have a look at Wild Man Food (wildmanfood.com) and Naturali (naturali.co.uk) for more info, and on Moneymagpie.com, where 'food and family' blogger, Sarah Lockett, shares some useful recipes using free food (www.moneymagpie.com/blogs/food-and-family).

SWAPPING

Have a swap shop with your friends every few months. Get everyone round with their clothes, accessories, bric-a-brac and so on, and just swap with each other. That way you can pick up a new wardrobe and things for the house for nothing, *and* get rid of some of your junk in the process! (See page 397 for details of swapping websites.)

FREE ENTERTAINMENT

Learn to Freeload

There are lots of parties, launches and other free events that 'those in the know' attend. Free food, drink and entertainment are all there for those with enough front to blag their way in. Get yourself on the lists of local art galleries, museums and restaurant chains so that you get invited to launches, private viewings and tastings. Just visit their websites and look for the supporters clubs, networking events and similar. Ring them up and just ask to be put on their invitation list – you'd be surprised how often that works!

Set up a Reviewing Blog

If you love books, film or something similar, why not set up a blog that simply reviews these things (see pages 328 and 334)? Get in touch with the press officers at publishers or film companies (you can find them by searching online or through your local library) and let them know that you are a reviewer. Get them to put you on their press lists for review copies of books, CDs, DVDs or film premieres.

Get Free Holidays by House-swapping

It's a great idea, not only because it's more homely than impersonal hotels, but also because you get more space (good for children). You do have to pay for travel and subsistence while you're there, but you can cut out all hotel bills by swapping your home with someone else anywhere in the world. There are lots of websites that help you do this now such as Hol Swop (Holswop.com), Digsville (Digsville.com) and Home Exchange (Homeexchange.com). Register with these and then you can search their databases to find a home you would like to live in for your holiday!

If you have a campervan, like my friend Ken from New Zealand, you can always swap that too, saving a bomb! He swaps his with some lucky Brit each year to travel round over here. In return, they get to use his to tour New Zealand for a few weeks … complete with tips for all the best places to stop.

Join the Moneymagpie.com Newsletter

We have new entertainment freebies coming along all the time. Join up at Moneymagpie.com and you'll be in the know before anyone else.

FREEBIE SITES

Like voucher websites (see page 111), freebie sites are full of marketing programmes where they try to lure you in with free offers in order to get you to buy or give them your details so that they can spam you. Register with a secondary email (one from Hotmail or Yahoo) so that your main email address doesn't get tonnes of spam. Don't believe the hype for things that sound too good to be true, and don't get conned into signing up for something you will have to pay for later on.

There is a lot of rubbish on these sites, but there are a few really good free things hidden among the other bits. Be clever about which ones you apply for and don't give too much away about yourself. If they ask for a phone number, give a false one and maybe even give a false name. At least that way you will cut down on nuisance calls and emails and you will be able to tell what is junk mail when it comes through your door because it will be addressed to your pseudonym.

The sites we like are:

- *Freebie Town (www.freebietown.co.uk)*
- *British Freebies (www.britishfreebies.co.uk)*
- *Free Stuff Junction (www.freestuffjunction.co.uk)*
- *Free Stuff (www.free-stuff.co.uk)*

You could also look at:

- *Freebieholics (www.freebieholics.co.uk)*
- *Bob's Free Stuff Forum (www.bobsfreestuffforum.co.uk)*

Most of these sites are updated quite regularly so they're worth checking up on every month or so. Also, keep looking at the Free Stuff article on Moneymagpie.com, where we often have special free deals exclusive to the site (www.moneymagpie.com/article/freebie-deals-for-you/32). We have other exclusive free deals for our newsletter subscribers, so get yourself on there, too …

GET YOUR OWN BACK – GO ON, IT'S FUN

When you're having a bad money day, why not get your own back on the financial companies who call you up to try to sell you more stuff you don't need or want? Here are some handy little tips for sales calls or junk mail.

For cold-callers. Try these three little words: 'Hold on, please …' Saying this, while putting down your phone and walking off (instead of hanging up immediately), would make each telemarketing call so much more time-consuming that double glazing sales would grind to a halt (we can only hope). Then, when you eventually hear a 'beep-beep-beep' tone, you know it's time to go back and hang up your handset. You have efficiently completed your task.

For even more annoying, computerised calls. Do you ever get those annoying phone calls with no one on the other end? This is a telemarketing technique where a machine makes phone calls and records the time of day when a person answers the phone. This is then used to determine the best time of day for a 'real' salesperson to call back and get someone at home. After answering, if you notice there is no one there, immediately start hitting your # button on the phone, six or seven times, as quickly as possible. This confuses the machine that dialled the call and it kicks your number out of their system. Try it – it's better than just swearing.

N.B. Do listen to the first few words of the message, though. Some credit card providers are now contacting their customers this way if they suspect that someone is using their card fraudulently. If this is your bank or credit card provider, don't hang up. Do make sure it's genuine, though, as fraudsters will quickly be catching on to this and will start setting up dodgy computerised calls purporting to be from your bank. Typical!

For wasteful, forest-destroying, 'pre-approved' letters from financial companies. When you get these do not throw away the return envelope. Most of them come with postage-prepaid return envelopes and it costs them more than the regular postage if they are returned. It costs them nothing, though, if you throw them away. So, why not get rid of some of your other junk mail and put it in these return envelopes? If you want to remain anonymous, just make sure your name isn't on anything you return. You can even send the envelope back empty if you just want to keep them guessing!

chapter seven

The Cost of Living Together

Now you're feeling on top of your personal finances, it's time to consider your living arrangements. I find that so many people lose money by having expensive home lives (and expensive partners!) that I have put together a whole chapter on it. Here you will find out about:

- *Sharing a home with various different people (see overleaf).*
- *Sharing a home with a partner (page 131).*
- *Your financial rights in cohabitation and marriage (page 133).*
- *Making a will – why it's important and how to do it (page 138).*

Getting the Basics Right

A lot of people fall into the trap of spending money they can't afford and end up living beyond their means. Being in debt is miserable for the individuals and families but this doesn't have to happen to you. Find the section that applies to your living arrangements and learn how to make the most of your cash.

Sharing a Home

SHARING WITH HOUSEMATES

Sharing your home with friends or housemates has the potential to be one of the most fun and rewarding experiences of your formative years (or even your later years). If not managed properly, however, it also has the potential to ruin your health, affect your work and generally drive you up the wall. Here are some tips for dealing with the financial issues that will crop up when sharing with housemates.

Agree How to Pay the Bills

Set up a dedicated joint account for bill and rent payments. Get everyone to organise automatic payments from their existing bank accounts into the dedicated account. Then set up direct debit payments from that dedicated account to pay those bills. That way, no one person has to be in charge of great wads of cash and you can exploit the savings to be made from paying bills by direct debit. Make sure you set up the account so that no one person can withdraw money (withdrawals must be signed by at least two people).

Agree on an amount to deposit into the dedicated account each month in advance for bills (this should include enough to cover gas and electricity, telephone, water, television licence and any subscriptions plus any other shared bills). This means there will be no arguments about finding money to pay bills when they come in.

Get a Kitty

Set up a cash 'kitty' in a safe place, perhaps 'managed' by a trusted housemate. Each put in £5–£10 a month for an agreed set of house things, such as loo paper and soap, washing-up liquid and cooking oil.

Have Rules about Visitors

It's also a good idea to agree on basic rules for friends, girlfriends and boyfriends sleeping over. Do this even if everyone is single as these things can change pretty quickly. If anyone stays more than three nights a week, or 12 nights a month, then the person or host can be asked to contribute an extra, say, £5, per night to cover the extra cost. That might sound a lot but it's probably far short of the actual expense.

Sort out the Cooking

Will you share the cooking? This can be a great idea if everyone eats largely the same things and enjoys cooking (or doing the dishes). Just make sure you pool the money in advance (more money into the kitty), or tally up the money somewhere, so one person is not left always covering the cost. Alternatively, you can even things out at the end of the month.

Now you've got all those things in place, you can get on with having a great time … Toga party anyone?

What you should know about sharing

- Your credit rating will be affected if you have a financial link or 'association' with someone you're living with. This association is created when two or more people open a bank account or apply for credit together (such as a mortgage or loan). It used to be the case that sharing an address was enough to affect your rating, but now living together won't affect you unless you are financially associated.
- Before you link yourself financially with someone, you need to consider how their financial past will affect your credit rating. If you don't you could find yourself being refused credit even though your own financial history is good.
- It's a good idea for both you and whoever you are sharing with to get credit reports before you become financially linked. That way you know exactly what you are letting yourself in for. You can get a FREE credit report from the online book resource that goes with this book at www.moneymagpie.com/bookgift.

When you receive your credit report it will list the people (if any) you are associated with financially. Remember that this association will remain on your record until you or the other people tell the credit reference agency that you are no longer financially linked.

If you don't get a credit report, at the very least you should have a detailed discussion about your financial histories and your attitude to debt and credit.

SHARING A HOME WITH A PARTNER OR SPOUSE

As with sharing with friends or housemates, sharing with a partner or spouse – particularly when you pool money – can be fraught with difficulty. If you're considering moving in with a significant other, I suggest you work through the points raised above first. Then, there are a few other things you'll need to sort out, particularly if you pool money. Even if you don't have a joint bank account, you may want to work together to save for a special event, such as a holiday, or to save for your children.

It's very important to get the money side of things sorted in a relationship early on. Communication is the key. Talk about your attitudes to money and how you will manage it together. If your current arrangement isn't working, then you need to change it together. There's no one way that works for all couples. But you do need to work something out that is acceptable to both of you. The best thing is to talk it through as calmly as you can manage.

Be specific when it comes to shared expenses and savings. Make some notes that you can refer to later if any problems come up. Ideally, you should discuss the following:

- *Your individual attitudes to money, such as whether you're a spender or a saver.*

- *Discuss the financial tips you picked up from your parents. Do you copy any of their spending patterns? If so, are these positive or negative?*
- *How you both think your money should be managed, and which of you would be best at it. You may have to do it together if neither of you has the confidence to do it alone. Really, the best way to manage money is to follow the advice in this book. If your partner isn't prepared to go with that then you will need to be very careful and make sure that their ideas are workable.*
- *How much you earn.. If one of you is earning more than the other, should you both contribute equal amounts to the joint expenses or work out a percentage based on your individual earning power?*
- *What should be considered a joint household expense, such as the roof over your head, the gas, electricity and council tax, and what should be considered individual expenses?*
- *What about things like clothes, CDs and books? Is he going to get angry if you regularly spend a fortune on fashion items when you know the boiler needs replacing? Is she going to be annoyed if you have a passion for collecting DVDs when you know she has no interest in them? It's best to have a joint account (like the one suggested on page 128) which you both pay into and which is dedicated to paying household bills and essentials. Everything else you could keep separate if you want to.*
- *Savings: do you both have Individual Savings Accounts (ISAs) and pensions that you regularly pay into? Should these be considered joint expenses that will enable you to enjoy financial independence when you retire?*

If you can work out what your agreed joint monthly outgoings are and who's going to contribute what, then it's a good idea to open a joint household account and make sure your agreed contributions are automatically paid into it through a standing order. Ensure that all bills are paid from the joint account (use standing orders or direct debits to cut costs and avoid time-wasting). Then keep personal accounts for yourselves for your own money so that you can at least have a bit of privacy and independence.

Cohabitation Agreements

If you are serious about living together without the contract of marriage, it's important to draw up some sort of cohabitation, or living together, agreement. This is not recognised by law, but it could be used in court if there were a dispute after a separation. Think of it as a pre-nup without the 'nup'.

The reason a cohabitation agreement is so important is because you have almost no rights over any property or assets that you don't have your name on if you break up. It might come as a surprise, but **there is no such thing as a common law marriage**. It's one of the biggest money myths around. That means, even if you've lived together for years, have a couple of kids and own a home together, should you split up, you may not both be entitled to a share of the family home or anything in it, unless you can prove you bought it.

Former cohabitees Barry Stack and Dehra Dowden found this out to their cost when they split. The couple were forced to go to court in 2007 over their £750,000 home, despite the fact they had lived together for 18 years and had four children. The couple could not agree on how much of the property each was entitled to. In the end the court decided that Barry's share was worth 35 per cent because Carol was felt to have made a larger contribution to the mortgage during the time they were together. Every case is different, of course, but the point is that it was a difficult and expensive process to work out who deserved what because there was no marriage certificate.

Like a pre-nuptial agreement, a cohabitation agreement is a statement of the things you take into the relationship, the way you want your living arrangements to work between the two of you, and your expectations for living together. You can write one at the start of your relationship, or even if you've been living together for 15 years. AdviceNow (www.advice-now.org.uk) has an excellent, detailed template, which I highly recommend you follow.

If you would like to know more about cohabitation agreements, you can get free legal advice from the Citizens Advice Bureau (www.citizensadvice.org.uk), (www.cas.org.uk if you live in Scotland). You might also like to try Community Legal Advice (www.communitylegaladvice.org.uk) and One Plus One (www.oneplusone.org.uk).

Declaration of Trust

If you are buying a home with your loved one and you aren't married, or even if you're buying with a relative or a friend, you need to go to a solicitor and get a Declaration (or Deed) of Trust drawn up. This deals very specifically with buying a home together. It may not be exactly romantic, but it could spare unmarried couples a lot of pain if they ever split up.

A Declaration of Trust can be drawn up at the same time as title deeds when a property is bought. Like the deeds of the house, it is a legally binding document. It also allows you to formalise details of who should get what should you split. For example, if one person puts down a 55 per cent deposit and the other takes out a mortgage for the remaining 45 per cent, the one who put more down could end up losing out. It also prevents nasty disputes, which in some of the worst cases have forced bickering couples to carry on living together in a property until they can agree on the terms of a sale.

A Declaration of Trust can also state what happens if one of you dies. It can include how much notice must be given for a partner to buy out the other's share at the property's open market value. Lastly, having both names on the deed gives both people rights as tenants in common, which is again a legally binding agreement.

CASE STUDY: 'I DIDN'T KNOW I NEEDED A SEPARATE AGREEMENT'

Simon* bought a flat with his girlfriend Sandy* two years ago. They've just split up after 10 years together. He says: 'We've had to get lawyers because we own a flat together and we're arguing about who's entitled to what. I wish we'd drawn up some kind of agreement but because we'd been together for some time I didn't really think about it. I assumed we had the same rights as a married couple. When we bought the flat together we weren't told anything about having to make a separate agreement. All the solicitor did was draw up something that meant if one of us died the other one would automatically own the flat. I put down a £10,000 deposit and she didn't put down anything. I guess this means that in effect I own more of the flat than her, but the courts will have to decide that now.

** Names have been changed.*

SHARING A HOME WHEN YOU HAVE CHILDREN

In an ideal world, couples would have the time (and the motivation) to talk through their finances as part of the process of planning a family. However, in reality, pregnancy often comes as a surprise, and emotional upheaval can push out the chance to talk about the important money aspect of things. One thing is certain – the birth of a child means a lot of change. That alone makes it a good time to have a talk about new priorities and money:

- *Do you or your partner qualify for maternity or paternity leave through your work?*
- *Will one partner give up work for a period? Which one?*
- *How will you share one person's income?*
- *What extra costs will you have?*
- *Are you eligible for any child-related government benefits?*
- *How will you make use of your Child Trust Fund to plan for your child's future?*

All the financial aspects of running a family work equally for married couples and cohabiting couples. However, there are some key differences you need to be aware of if you have children and are unmarried.

Unmarried Dads

Unmarried fathers are required to pay maintenance for their children but they don't have the same rights over their children as married (or divorced) fathers do. For legal advice on your rights go to Advice Now at www.adviceguide.org.uk (for all of the UK) or www.advicenow.org.uk/living-together (England and Wales only).

An unmarried father without Parental Responsibility has no right to act on the child's behalf with regards to anything unless it's an emergency. However, an unmarried father who jointly signed the birth register with the mother from 1 December 2003 now has Parental Responsibility automatically. Otherwise, you will need to obtain a legally binding Parental Responsibility Agreement (with the mother's consent) or a Parental Responsibility Order (if she won't play fair).

Unmarried Mums

An unmarried woman who has lived with a man for many years and given birth to his children has no right to the house or any of his property if they split up unless her name is on the deeds. The children do have some rights, though, and, even if the property is in her ex's name, the mother can remain in the home till the last one turns 18. Then the child is on his or her own.

- If you're cohabiting, make sure you have a written agreement between you as to who owns what and what would happen if you split up.

Making a Will

I've mentioned it before and it needs mentioning regularly – as soon as you have any sort of property or investments, and certainly as soon as you enter into some kind of long-term relationship or have children, **you must make a will.**

It's not hard. More than half of us die 'intestate', that is, without a will, and even more do nothing about avoiding inheritance tax before shuffling off this mortal coil. This causes a load of nuisance – and potential expense – to the loved ones who survive us and it means they can lose out on a lot of the money they might have inherited. Even worse, if you don't specify who should get what when you go, the authorities divvy out your cash and belongings according to their rules. This can mean that your hated ex who went off with your best friend *and* your boxed set of ABBA CDs could potentially end up with your money, too.

The tax office love people who leave no will because they pour billions into their coffers each year. If you die intestate they take 40 per cent of your worth before anyone else gets a sniff of it. Now, however much you might love and admire the Inland Revenue (and, given the amount of tax money we give them each year, you'd think we adore them), surely you don't want to give them all that cash?

Making a will doesn't have to take long and can be pretty painless. At least you can take pleasure in mentally giving things to people you love – or sticking it to those you don't. You can make your own will using a will pack from WH Smith, Tesco or Office World (about £15) or one of the many on the internet. See these sites:

- *Ten Minute Will (www.tenminutewill.co.uk)*
- *Law Pack (www.lawpack.co.uk)*

If you prefer – and certainly if you have a vast set of possessions or a complicated family situation – you can get a solicitor to draw one up for you. Go to:

- *Solicitors Online (www.solicitors-online.com) for a list of local lawyers, or*
- *Search Will (www.searchwill.co.uk) for a qualified will writer in your area.*

Also, you could contact the Society of Trust and Estate Practitioners (STEP) for will-writing specialists (www.step.org or phone 020 7838 48850).

Or do it for charity. Once a year the Law Society of England and Wales runs a Make a Will Week, when solicitors write wills for a one-off donation to charity. Another scheme is Will Aid, where thousands of solicitors donate the fees they make for will writing to charity for one month. Keep an eye on the media and on Moneymagpie.com for when these events come up in the year.

- *Before you write the will, work out who should inherit what you own, how much each should get and at what age they should have it.*
- *If you're married, don't think that everything you own will go to your spouse. It depends on the total value of what you own, what it is, how you own it and which other relatives also survive you. Make sure you remember your spouse in the will!*
- *If you just cohabit – whether your relationship is heterosexual or same-sex – you certainly have to name your partner in your will, otherwise they could get nothing.*
- *You will also need to say who will deal with your affairs after you've gone – who will be your executors.*
- *Don't forget charities you'd like to give to.*
- *You can give instructions for the kind of funeral you would like.*
- *Don't forget your debts. Most people have debts, at least during their working life, and, on your death, creditors have to be paid before any money can be distributed. If your debts are bigger than your assets, consider taking out a life-insurance policy to ensure that your family at least gets something.*
- *With mortgages held under joint tenancy (which is the norm with married couples) and any loans in both names, the surviving spouse will be liable for paying off the debt. If you have only cohabited you won't be liable for any debts your former partner incurred unless they were taken out in both your names.*

So, to recap: if you are in any sort of financial relationship, make sure that you communicate. Talk about how you will manage your joint finances from the start, and keep talking. Don't just muddle along because that's how problems and misunderstandings happen.

chapter eight

Buying a Home

This chapter covers everything you need to know about buying a home:

- *Owning versus renting – the pros and cons (see overleaf).*
- *Mortgage brokers and different types of mortgages (pages 148 and 150).*
- *Getting a deposit (page 162).*
- *Property hunting (page 165).*

If you've bought your own home already and are not looking to reduce your mortgage payments through remortgaging, then you can skip this chapter. You already know the joy and pain of buying and running a home. However, if you are looking to remortgage, wanting to move house or simply need a refresher on how the house-buying process works, it would be worth scanning through these pages as things may have changed quite a lot in the mortgage market since you last did a deal with your lender. For a start, you may find that it is harder to get another mortgage, even though you have been paying yours faithfully for a few years. Also, lenders are now demanding that you have a greater amount of equity in your property. In other words, they want to see that the value of your home is at least a quarter (25 per cent) more than the mortgage you want to have. So if the home you want is worth £100,000, you'll be able to borrow up to £75,000. If it isn't then it could be difficult to get a mortgage.

I'll talk about property as an investment in Chapter 13 but here I'm going to concentrate on buying the roof over your head.

Why Buy?

Good question. There's no law to say that everyone should own their own home. It's certainly not the norm in many European countries where millions are happy renting for their whole lives.

There are many good reasons to rent:

- *Freedom. You can live where you want (if you can afford the rent) and you can leave when you want to (once you have given the necessary period of notice).*
- *Cost-saving. There are all sorts of invisible costs to running a home that you don't have to cover when you rent. You don't have to maintain the boiler, fix the roof, paint the place or replace the washing machine when it goes wrong. All of that expense and headache is your landlord's.*
- *Potentially low monthly outgoings. Depending on where you live and what the economy is doing, rents can often be lower than a mortgage for the particular place you are living in.*

There are also many good reasons to buy:

- *You are investing in a major asset that could be used later on to help fund your retirement or simply be passed on.*

- *If you own your own home and you pay off the mortgage early then your housing costs will drop significantly, particularly when you are retired.*
- *If you always rent then you will always have to rent and find that money every month, even when you are retired.*

So think about it seriously. Do you really want to buy a whole property? Are you ready for that step? Or are you happy being a tenant? You may decide that buying will be the right step for you at some stage but perhaps not just yet. Now might be the time when you want the freedom to go travelling, try out different jobs, or just give yourself space to sort out your finances before saving seriously for a deposit to enable you to buy a home. On the other hand, you may be thinking that now is the right time to buy if you have a regular income, you don't expect to move from your current area, and you can afford to take on the commitment. In which case, read on ...

All about Mortgages

Unless you are independently wealthy or the 'Bank of Mum and Dad' is stumping up a big wad of cash for you, you are probably going to have to get a mortgage to help you buy a place of your own. Until very recently it was really quite easy – far too easy in some cases – to get a mortgage. In fact, you could even get one to cover the entire price of the property you wanted to buy ... and some more.

Mortgage companies have gone back to *very* strict and quite limited lending. In other words, they're not dishing out anything like as much money to anywhere near as many people as they were before. So if you want to borrow money to buy a property you are going to have to make sure you have a good chunk of cash saved that can be used as a deposit (see page 162). You'll also have to prove you have a decent, regular income that will comfortably enable you to pay the mortgage each month. As a consequence you may find you have less disposable income and may have to cut back on some spending.

WHAT IS A MORTGAGE?

Basically, a mortgage is one big, fat loan that is secured to your home.

'Secured' means that if you don't maintain the payments then the bank or lender has the 'security' of being able to take your house from you – so it's secure for the lender, NOT for you.

This 'security' for the lenders means that they tend to charge you less interest on mortgages than on other loans because it's less risky for them.

HOW MUCH CAN YOU AFFORD TO BORROW?

Mortgage companies base their lending on the amount you earn, either on your own or as a couple. So before you start applying for loans or contacting any banks or brokers, you need to calculate how much money you make each year. That's straightforward if you're single and on a salary with no other sources of income, but if you're part of a couple or in a complicated financial situation, it could be more complex.

When you do your sums, remember to add in any extra cash that comes in regularly (like investments or child support payments). If you're self-employed, you'll need to calculate your net profit from the last three years. If you don't have three years' worth of accounts it will be harder to get a mortgage, but not impossible.

Generally speaking, in the current climate, a single income applicant can borrow about three-and-a-half to four times their salary. Couples are able to borrow about two-and-three-quarters to three times their joint income.

Use the Moneymagpie.com mortgage calculator (put 'mortgage calculator' into the search box) to give you an idea of how much your monthly mortgage repayments are likely to be. This can help you estimate the size of mortgage you can afford at a particular interest rate – and, importantly, see if you can still afford the payments if the interest rate goes up. Interest rates can go up very quickly for reasons way beyond your control. If you get a variable rate or tracker mortgage (see pages 157–159) your payments could go up a lot over just a few months. Even if you get a cheap fixed rate deal for a few years (see page 155), you could find that interest rates have shot up just before the fixed price deal you have finishes and you need to negotiate a new deal.

If things get really bad and you can't pay your mortgage, the lender can legally take your home away. They don't call it 'let's go and kick them while they're down'; instead they call it repossession. Once your home is repossessed they can then sell it and recoup their mortgage and legal fees.

So it's really important to make sure that you could pay your mortgage even if costs went up. Budget for your mortgage by listing your monthly income and outgoings so you can see how much disposable cash you have each month (see Chapter 3). Remember to include any increase in living costs as a result of the move, such as a rise in council tax or larger heating bills. Also, ensure you can afford the costs associated with the purchase (see page 169) as well as the ongoing maintenance of the home. Use the FSA's budget calculator to work out a monthly budget for before and after a move so you can see if you can afford more commitment (www.moneymadeclear.fsa.gov.uk).

Once you know the size of mortgage you can get, plus the size of your deposit, you'll have an idea of the property price range you're working with. Here's where we pause for a reality check! If the total amount isn't enough (that is, your mortgage + the deposit = Barbie's playhouse) then you need to stop and save some more so that you can increase your deposit. All the money-making tips and ideas in Chapters 14 and 15 will help. It's up to you to decide what kind of sacrifices you're willing to make in order to afford the home of your dreams

What 'Borrowing' Really Means

At this point, it's worth reminding you what 'borrowing' really means when it comes to money. As I mentioned in Chapter 4, the term 'borrow' is confusing when it's applied to money, as it implies you get it for free. In fact, if you borrow £100,000 you are in effect paying to borrow. You could say you're 'renting' this money. This rental charge is effectively the fee that lenders take for each day/month/year that you have the money.

Here's the way interest works: you get charged for as long as you borrow the money. So the longer you have the money, the more you pay overall. If you pay a loan off in one year you will pay much less than if you pay it off in 10 years (at the same rate of interest), simply because you get charged for as long as you have the money.

When working out what your 'rent' will cost you on a monthly basis, lenders calculate how much money you've borrowed, how long they're letting you have it and what rate of interest they're going to charge you for it. They'll then say something like: 'Look, if you're going to take 25 years to pay back your £100,000 mortgage, and you'll be paying us 6 per cent interest on that, then ... *[pulling out magical calculator that somehow figures out all complicated mathematical conundrums and voilà]* ... your monthly payment on a repayment mortgage will be £644.30 *[beaming smile]*.'

Ideally, you're not going to take 25 years to pay off your mortgage. That's the usual amount of time that new homeowners are given – but there's no law to say you have to take that amount of time to do it. While you may think that your lender is being generous in giving you so much time to pay off your debt, they're actually thinking about their profit. The longer you take to pay off your mortgage, the more interest you'll end up paying them. Ker-ching for lenders as they cash in and grab all the dosh they can. Don't let them! Pay off your mortgage as quickly as possible.

NEGATIVE EQUITY

You have probably heard the term 'negative equity' bandied around on the news. This is where your mortgage is bigger than the current value of the house. So if your house is valued at £100,000, but your mortgage on the property is £150,000, this means you have £50,000 of negative equity.

If this happens and you find you can't pay your mortgage, you won't be able to completely clear your debt even if you manage to sell the place. And if the lender repossesses your property and sells it on, it's possible that they won't recover all the money they lent to you. This is why mortgage providers get nervous about lending a high proportion of the price of the place you're buying. It's also why they will charge you more for that kind of mortgage – they're pricing in the risk they're taking.

If you are in a negative equity situation but you can pay the mortgage each month and you don't have to sell then you don't need to worry. It's not a happy position to be in but it doesn't matter right now. In time the value of your home will go up so things will improve.

MORTGAGE BROKERS

Whatever your situation, it's a good idea to get advice from a mortgage broker about your situation and see what they suggest. A broker will have specialist knowledge of the mortgage industry and will know the best deals available for particular customers, including the self-employed.

On the plus side, all the research and form filling can be taken care of by a broker. In addition, some mortgage deals are *only* available through them. However, all brokers receive a fee from the lender as thanks for delivering them a new client. This is typically 0.35–0.5 per cent of what your total mortgage will be. So, if you're taking out a £100,000 mortgage, the lender will pay your broker a 'procuration fee' (commission) of £350–£500.

There are two types of broker: fee-based brokers or no-fee (also known as commission-only) brokers. The difference between the two types is that one charges *you* a fee as well as getting cash from the lender, and the other doesn't. A fee-based broker takes his cut – typically around 1 per cent of the total mortgage amount – once the mortgage is agreed. So, for a £100,000 mortgage, you'd usually pay them around £1,000.

No-fee (commission-only) brokers, on the other hand, make their money solely from the commission they get from the mortgage company. Essentially, they don't double dip. They've made their money from the lender, but they won't ask for any from you. Just be aware that some no-fee brokers may not have your best interests at heart and should therefore be avoided. Some make particularly juicy commission on certain mortgage products that aren't necessarily the best for you, but they will try to sell them to you because they're getting so much cash from them.

Be careful and do your homework first. There are lots of mortgage comparison sites available. On Moneymagpie.com we feature an award-winning mortgage brokering service, which covers the whole of the mortgage market. It offers an online mortgage comparison service as well as brokering advice that is trustworthy and free of charge (www.moneymagpie.com/showcomparison/mortgages). You can also look at Charcolonline.co.uk and Moneyextra.com.

Going it Alone

Another option is to approach banks directly, cutting out any broker costs. This requires a bit more effort, time and knowledge, but if you're willing to read up on the latest mortgage deals and what they all mean, you should be in a position to speak to lenders directly if you want to. Keep checking the mortgage section of Moneymagpie.com and magazines such as *Your Mortgage* (www.yourmortgage.co.uk), *What Mortgage* (www.whatmortgage.co.uk) and *Moneyfacts* (www.moneyfacts.co.uk) for new information.

CHOOSING YOUR MORTGAGE

From the outside, mortgages seem more complicated than they really are. There are just a few different things you need to get your head around in order to choose the right mortgage for you.

First, you need to think about the right type of repayment method for you. You have two basic options here: a repayment mortgage or an interest-only mortgage. Then you need to work out what kind of interest rate you prefer. Obviously you'll want the cheapest rate you can get, but unfortunately it's not that straightforward. Some interest rates are fixed for a certain amount of time, while others are more variable – and which type works best for you will depend on your individual situation. On top of this, there are some rather interesting mortgage bundles you could go for. I'll look at all these options in more detail below.

Repayment Mortgages

Good for: *People who want to ensure their mortgage will be paid off in full at the end of the term.*

Bad for: *Borrowers who want to pay off their mortgage quickly or move house in the early years as you'll find the amount you owe won't have gone down that much.*

With a repayment mortgage, your monthly payment covers both the loan and the interest charged for the loan. So when you pay your mortgage each month, you're paying off a portion of your loan plus a lot of interest at the same time.

In fact, when you start to pay off the mortgage, you'll find you are paying mostly interest with just a bit of money going towards the original debt. However, as the years go by, you'll gradually pay more of the debt and less interest every month, as the amount you owe shrinks.

Here's an example: If you have a 6 per cent interest rate on a £100,000 mortgage, you'll pay £6,000 – in your first year – on interest payments alone. If in your second year you manage to pay off £4,000 of the original loan – leaving you with a £96,000 mortgage – you'll only need to pay £5,760 of interest. In other words, you're now paying less interest while continuing to hack away at your mortgage bill.

Every year that goes by, you're handing thousands of extra pounds to your lender. However, by increasing your monthly payments, you can pay off your mortgage faster, thereby paying less interest and saving money. So as soon as you can, reduce the length of your loan term and bring yourself closer to freedom!

If you can afford one, a repayment mortgage is a good option because eventually that happy day actually arrives … you'll become the proud owners of the home you've been living in for the past 20 years!

Interest-only Mortgages

Good for: *Borrowers who want lower monthly payments. Buy-to-let landlords who want to maximise their tax-saving.*

Bad for: *People who are risk averse. You have to be confident enough to hope that other investments you have will grow enough to pay off the mortgage capital, or that the value of the property will grow enough to allow you to sell the property, clear the mortgage and make a profit.*

Interest-only mortgages are just that: your entire monthly payment goes towards paying off the interest, so your original mortgage loan doesn't get any smaller. This means that your monthly payments tend to be a bit cheaper but you're not paying off the actual debt.

Interest-only mortgages can be stretched out over a 25-year period but, at the end of this term, the only thing you will have paid off is the interest. So if you borrowed £100,000, at the end of your term your lender will still be the proud owner of at least part of your house – while you still owe them £100,000. This loan is much like the Mafia's godfather policy where you pay and pay but are never actually freed from the debt.

You're probably asking yourself why anyone would ever get one of these. Well, they are useful in a few situations.

For example, if you need relatively low monthly payments because you can't afford a repayment mortgage (which usually has a more expensive monthly payment) in the short-term. They are also useful for people who are investing in buy-to-let properties, since owners are only able to write off the interest payments on mortgages for tax purposes, not the whole mortgage.

Some people opt for interest-only mortgages because they bank on their property value increasing enough over time. The idea is that when they do sell, they can just pay off the loan in full and take the remaining money as profit. That is fine so long as you are willing and able to keep the property for at least five years. Property prices can go down for a while so you need to be able to sit tight through down times in order to make the money later.

Other people like to play their investments off against an interest-only mortgage. They find the cheapest interest-only mortgage they can get and then, while they pay that each month, they also put money into stock market investments (possibly wrapped in an ISA) and try to make money that way (see Chapter 9: Saving, for more information on ISAs). They work out that if their mortgage interest rate is, say, 6 per cent, but they're able to make 9–10 per cent annually on the stock market, then over time they will make enough money to pay off the mortgage early.

This is a gamble that works well in theory but not always in practice. In order for it to succeed you need to invest long term, and weigh up the pros and cons – particularly on any stock market investments. Also, unless you've secured your mortgage rate for a good 10 years, you're gambling on the fact that interest rates won't sky-rocket past what you are earning on your investments. You could find your mortgage interest rate increases by 1 per cent (which may not sound like much but can equate to hundreds of pounds a month) while the interest earned on your investments is dropping. The result? You're paying out more than you're earning, which is not a good situation to be in for long.

Some people rely on endowment policies to pay off the basic loan. An endowment policy is essentially a life insurance contract designed to pay a lump sum after a set term ('on maturity') or earlier if the holder dies before it matures.

Endowment policies were very popular in the 80s, the idea being that the investment would generate enough income to pay off your mortgage in one lump sum with the added bonus of life insurance that would cover your debts should you die before the end of the term. However, this type of policy usually comes with a lot of extra charges and most of them have performed very badly, leaving investors with a big hole in their finances where there should have been enough to pay the mortgage and more.

TYPES OF INTEREST RATE

Once you've decided on the sort of mortgage you'd like (repayment or interest-only), it's time to choose which interest rate plan is best suited to you. Most people want the cheapest interest rate plan available. However, everyone is different and there's no one-size-fits-all mortgage. Depending on your situation, you may actually be better off going for a slightly higher interest rate that gives you more flexibility.

Also, many mortgages that look like they're the cheapest can actually end up being very expensive. This is usually because they either charge you extortionate arrangement fees, or because they lock you into an extra, more expensive payment period after the introductory cheap rate finishes. So, to avoid being had, make sure you're aware of all the finer points on your payment plan.

Fixed Rate

Good for: *People who want to be able to budget for a defined period of time.*

Bad for: *Borrowers who think that interest rates will fall or those who like to make overpayments and pay off their loan early without penalties.*

Surprise, surprise – this one means that you have a fixed interest rate over a fixed amount of time. Your lender is saying that for a particular period of time (for example two, five or even twenty years) your interest rate will remain the same. In other words, if you lock into a 10-year term at 6 per cent you'll be paying that 6 per cent for the entire 10 years.

On the plus side, because the rate is fixed you won't be affected if the Bank of England base rate goes up. Also, for first-time buyers, fixed rates (at least for one or two years) are regularly the cheapest option. They keep your mortgage down for a couple of years while you spend money on furniture and repairs. The flip side of a fixed rate is that you *won't* benefit if interest rates fall. However, this option makes budgeting easier because you know that you'll have the exact same amount to pay every month.

As its name suggests, there's very little flexibility with this sort of plan. So this is usually only a good option if you're staying put for the entire duration of the period agreed. If you want to get out of the plan before the end of the term, you could be hit with big penalty fees. For example, if you suddenly find you can pay off the whole mortgage in one go – or if you want to switch to another deal – you may have to pay a steep penalty (possibly a few thousand pounds) for doing so. On the other hand, if you decide to move house, you may be able to take your mortgage with you; some fixed rate deals are portable, but not all of them. So if you think you might move during the mortgage term, make sure you pick a deal that can be taken with you.

Finally, make double sure you haven't been tied into a fixed mortgage where the rate is set for the first part of that time but then you have to take whatever rate they want for the rest of the time you're locked into the mortgage. Read the fine print and be very careful. If you're duped by an initial cheap deal, you'll be forced to pay a penalty if you try to get out of the mortgage once they hike up the rates.

Capped Rate

Good for: *Borrowers who want the security of knowing that their payments can't rise above the set level, but will still benefit if rates fall.*

Bad for: *People wanting low costs associated with the mortgage itself and the flexibility to pay off the mortgage early.*

A capped rate mortgage is a variable rate deal where there is an upper limit on the interest rate, but no lower limit. In other words, the lender says, 'All right – we won't charge you more than, let's say, 6 per cent. And if the Bank of England brings down the base rate, we might bring down our mortgage rates too.'

With a capped rate mortgage, the good news is that if the Bank of England base rate goes up, yours won't go higher than that 6 per cent because it's 'capped' at that amount. Also, if your lender's standard variable rate (see below) falls below the capped rate, your rate will fall in line with it.

This is a good option for those of us who love safety and security. You're protected from enormous interest rate increases, but there's still the potential for you to benefit from falling interest rates. On the down side, since a capped rate deal offers both these benefits, a lender will usually set a higher rate for a capped mortgage over, say, four years than it will charge on a fixed rate deal for the same period. Just remember that – as with a fixed rate deal – you'll be committed to this option and will be forced to fork out large sums of money if you want out.

Standard Variable Rate (SVR)

Good for: *People who want flexibility. You will get the benefit of reductions in interest rates. You can come out of it quickly without paying any penalties.*

Bad for: *People wanting protection from increases in interest rates. This is an expensive method of borrowing to buy a home.*

This is the one that the mortgage companies really enjoy offering because – on a whim – they can dictate what the rate will be. It's called 'standard' because it's the rate paid by borrowers who aren't on any sort of special deal. Broadly speaking, the lender has the freedom to decide how much money they feel like making, and therefore what rate they will offer you. Mortgage providers love customers who stay on the SVR rather than making the effort to hunt down a better deal – because this rate makes them a lot of money.

The SVR generally goes up and down vaguely in line with the Bank of England base rate (typically hovering around 2 per cent above it). However, it could go much further up than the base rate and not come down anything like as much. It's an expensive option so you should avoid paying the SVR unless there's absolutely no better deal available to you or you really need the flexibility. On the plus side, because it's flexible, you can come out of it very quickly without paying any stiff penalties.

Discounted Variable Rate

Good for: *First-time buyers who want to keep payments low in the first couple of years to free money up for buying furniture and decorating.*

Bad for: *People who like to have control over how high their mortgage repayments go.*

Discounted variable rate mortgages offer a discount on the lender's standard variable rate (SVR) for a fixed period of time. This period can be as little as three months, as long as five years or even more. If the lender's SVR drops, your discounted variable rate mortgage will too. This sort of deal gives you a bit of a break – but bear in mind that you're still vulnerable to rates going up and down very quickly, depending on what the base rate is doing.

The biggest discounts usually come with the harshest penalties if you decide to pull out of the deal early. Also, remember that you'll end up on the SVR – which will be a more expensive option – as soon as the discounted period ends.

Tracker Rate

Good for: *People who need some leeway in the monthly amount they can afford to repay. Fees are usually lower than for fixed, capped or discounted rates.*

Bad for: *Those who like to know what their monthly mortgage repayments will be because if the base rate rises, so will the repayments.*

This one tracks just above the Bank of England's base rate – so as the base rate goes up and down, so does your mortgage. Let's say your mortgage is set to track 1 per cent above the base rate. If the base rate is 5 per cent, then you'll pay 6 per cent. If the base rate drops to 4 per cent, then your mortgage will also drop – to 5 per cent. The change is immediate, so if the base rate goes up or down your mortgage price will change pretty much the next day.

This option is great when the base rate is going down. However, when it rises, you'll feel the pinch quickly. Tracker rate mortgages are good if you're willing to take a gamble on the Bank of England base rate, and if your finances are secure enough to deal with the possibility of big increases in your repayments.

Really Flexible Mortgages

Good for: *Those who want to be in charge of their finances. Also for borrowers who plan to reduce their home loan by making overpayments, either regularly or by lump sums. Ideal for anyone with a fluctuating income, such as the self-employed or people who work on commission.*

Bad for: *Those who like a straightforward, easy-to-understand mortgage. No point in having one of these if you're not going to use the flexible features.*

If you're disciplined and you want the flexibility to pay off your mortgage fast – or possibly borrow some of the money back later – there are two other types of mortgages you should think about:

- *Offset*
- *Current account*

These are fairly recent entries to the mortgage market, and they're not right for everyone. But if you're self-employed, you have decent savings or you just want to have something that is *very* flexible, check these out:

Offset Mortgages

Good for: *Those with a decent amount of savings. Good for the self-employed who can use the offset to put money aside for tax bills. Also attractive to those wanting to save for home improvements, or children's school or university fees. Those who receive bonuses or an inheritance may find offsetting attractive as you can pay your mortgage without tying up your cash as you would if you overpaid on a standard mortgage.*

Bad for: *People who have little spare cash because if you don't use the flexible features there is a risk you could lose out in the long-run.*

Offset mortgages work by putting your mortgage, current account and savings all together in one big account, but separated out into 'pots' of your money.

It's a mortgage that rewards you for having savings. When it comes to working out how much actual interest you should be paying on your mortgage, they take into account the amount of money you have in your savings and then offset that against your loan. So if you've borrowed £100,000 and have £25,000 saved, they'll charge you interest on £75,000 rather than on the full £100,000.

You still pay the same amount each month, but more of that money goes into paying off the capital of your loan (the actual money you have borrowed), rather than throwing it away on interest, meaning that you should be able to pay off your mortgage more quickly.

If you're disciplined, this kind of loan is a great way to pay off your mortgage quickly and cheaply. It's also a very flexible borrowing option as, once you've paid off some of the mortgage, you can then borrow it back whenever you want and use it as a cheap and growing overdraft facility. However, beware – if you're not disciplined and you have a tendency to go on spending sprees when you shouldn't, keep away from this mortgage. It's so flexible, you might never pay it off!

Current Account Mortgages

Good for: *People who have substantial savings that they can use to offset the mortgage and like the idea of making overpayments and underpayments. Also ideal for those who want to run all of their finances from a single account.*

Bad for: *Borrowers with little savings and those who won't use the flexible features.*

Current account mortgages work in broadly the same way as offset mortgages. However, instead of counting your savings and mortgage as separate entities, they bundle your current account, savings and mortgage into one large account which is constantly, massively overdrawn! You have to keep paying in to it so that you cover the mortgage payments. However, you can overpay when you have money and, again, you can borrow back the money you've paid in.

Like offset mortgages, current account mortgages are really flexible and they're great if you're able to keep saving and making payments. As your savings grow, you're saving on interest payments. Another benefit with very flexible mortgage loans like these is that you can put in large sums of money when you have them. By putting in lumps of money you are paying off the debt quicker and paying less in interest overall.

> Do be aware that flexible mortgages, such as the current account and offset deals, can have higher interest rates to compensate for the flexibility. Sometimes you are better off – at least at the start – going for a basic fixed deal which will allow you to pay off 10 per cent of the total loan each year. That may be cheaper for you in the long run, particularly if you don't have much in the way of savings to offset the loan.

WHAT IS A DEPOSIT?

A deposit is the actual cash that you provide up front as part of the payment for your home. This is your own money, not money you have borrowed. The deposit is now more important than it has been for several years. Most providers won't lend you any money until you've put some cash on the table.

You'll normally need to put down a deposit of, at the very least, 5 per cent of the value of the property in order to get a mortgage. Even then, deals with this 95 per cent loan to value (LTV) ratio are rare, and the interest rates are usually high.

Ideally, you should put down the biggest deposit you can to get a mortgage with a good, low interest rate. To get the very best rates on offer, you should really have a 25 per cent deposit, or as near as you can get to that. Some mortgage lenders now are looking for as much as 40 per cent as a deposit.

THE LOAN TO VALUE RATIO

LTV or 'loan to value' refers to how much the mortgage is as a percentage of the property price. So, for example, if you wanted to buy a property worth £200,000 and you had a mortgage of £160,000 that would be an 80 per cent loan to value (LTV) ratio, because 160,000 is 80 per cent of 200,000.

The loan to value ratio is one of the major factors your lender will think about before lending you money. The less money the provider has to lend you, as a percentage of the property value, the happier they are about giving you that cash and the less they will charge you for it.

This is because the more equity you own in the property (in other words, the more of the property you actually own), the better able you will be to withstand financial problems. That way, they reason, you are more likely to be able to pay your mortgage each month and are less of a risk.

The interest rate charged on any loan is a measure of the risk the lender feels they are taking. The more risky they think you are, the more interest they charge. That's also why riskier investments pay more interest. This is important to remember when you're investing (that is, effectively lending your money to the bank) as well as when you are borrowing. Your credit score or rating will affect a lender's perception of the risk of lending to you. (See box, 'Tame Your Credit Rating', page 53.) Generally, the better your credit rating is, the higher the chances of you getting a cheaper (lower interest rate) mortgage deal.

How to Save for a Deposit

If you haven't got enough money for a deposit, you need to start saving.

> Don't even think about saving for a deposit until you have eradicated your debts.

Saving for a deposit is a useful exercise because it forces you to set a specific financial goal and work towards it. Let's say your goal is to save £20,000 for a deposit. Go through your incomings and outgoings (as shown in Chapter 3) and work out how much you think you could put aside each month. You may need to make some lifestyle changes and sacrifices to do this, so it's only worth it if you *really* want to buy your own place. If you are serious about saving enough for a deposit you will need to *really* cut down on your spending each month. Look at Chapters 5 and 6 for ways to save money day to day and be smart with your spending.

Also, look at ways to increase your income. Could you negotiate a pay rise at your current place of work? Have a look at the Making Money section of Moneymagpie.com for even more ideas. Any extra cash you make through these methods should be earmarked specifically for your 'deposit savings account'.

Keep putting that money away until you have enough for a decent deposit. It may take you a couple of years or more but it will be worth it in the end.

So, with mortgages, as with any financial product, do your homework and shop around and you will be much more likely to get a good deal. Remember that people who manage to save a deposit of *at least* 25 per cent get the best deals – so start saving your pennies.

Once you know what size of mortgage you can get and how much you have saved for a deposit, the next stage is to go looking for a fab place to live.

The Property Hunt Begins

So now you've got enough money to make an offer, it's time to look for properties. This is where the fun starts.

One of the many downsides of looking for a property used to be having to deal with estate agents. Even now, the majority of home purchases are done through agents but there are also some serious alternatives. There is nothing to stop you looking around yourself. Look at adverts in national and local newspapers and on sales websites like Gumtree.com, Loot.co.uk and even eBay. Look at the various property websites that have been set up in the last few years such as First4sale.com, Housenetwork.co.uk, Houseladder.co.uk, Homesonsale.co.uk and Homepages.co.uk. Many other property websites are directly linked to estate agents so they don't give you much of an advantage except that you can do some searching from the comfort of your own computer. Sites such as these include FindaProperty.com, Hotproperty.co.uk and Propertytoday.co.uk.

Another way to find the property you want is to ask locally. Simply talking to people in the area can often uncover news of someone locally who is selling their property. You could also try a property auction but be on your guard as the property might be in poor condition and need redeveloping. Find out more at www.propertyauctionzone.com.

Plenty of people buy direct from a builder or developer. The developer may take your home in part exchange and offer incentives such as paying for legal fees or giving you carpets and curtains or white goods.

DO YOUR RESEARCH

Thanks to the internet, there are now lots of ways you can find out about an area and get a clear idea of house prices without having to take an estate agent's word for it. Even if you do end up using an agent, it's definitely worth mugging up on local facts first. Check out Hometrack.co.uk for the most up-to-date independent survey of UK house prices and market trends. Find out about local property prices at www.

ourproperty.co.uk and check out what homes have sold for in your chosen road at www.thinkproperty.com/soldhouse-prices.htm.

Also look at sites like Upmystreet.com, Homecheck.co.uk and the government website Neighbourhood.statistics.gov.uk for information on local schools, crime levels, ecological data and so on.

ESTATE AGENTS

Incredibly, estate agents are not licensed in the UK, unlike the rest of Europe, the USA and Canada. This is probably one of the reasons why they have such a bad reputation here. The Ombudsman for Estate Agents (OEA) keeps calling for agents to be licensed but so far all that has happened is that more agents have joined its voluntary scheme. This is not as good as a licence, but it does at least mean that if you use a member estate agent and you have a complaint against them you can take it to the Ombudsman and possibly get compensation of up to £25,000.

Have a look, too, at tips and advice given by the Office of Fair Trading (www.oft.gov.uk) and the National Association of Estate Agents (www.naea.co.uk). Both have downloadable sheets of advice on various aspects of buying and selling through an estate agent.

It is a good idea to visit all the estate agents in the area where you are looking to buy a property. Sign up with all of the ones that you know are members of the NAEA or the Royal Institution of Chartered Surveyors (RICS). You will find out very quickly which are the efficient and keen ones as they will be the ones that contact you with details of potential properties.

If you do intend to contact estate agents then make sure you read *Freakonomics* beforehand (for details, see Resources). This book beautifully exposes some of the shadier behaviour of estate agents that most people fall for.

LOCATION, LOCATION, LOCATION

Think hard about the kind of place you want to buy and don't rush into any purchase. This is probably the biggest thing you will spend on in your life – you need to do it right! Your lifestyle and personal preference will decide the type of property that is best for you but keep these points in mind:

- *As they say, location is of prime importance if you are thinking of selling the property a few years down the line. It's also important for you. Think about how convenient the location is for your needs, what the transport links are like and how close the good local schools are if you have children. The Department for Education and Skills (www.dfes.gov.uk) will have details of schools, while Ofsted (www.ofsted.gov.uk) inspection reports show a school's performance.*
- *What amenities are on offer? Desirable properties will be near to shops, restaurants, public parks, sports and leisure facilities.*
- *How much outside space do you want? Are you happy with a balcony or would you prefer a roof terrace or garden?*
- *Size is a factor, even if you are buying on your own. If you can afford it, consider having an extra room that you could let for a while to help with mortgage payments.*

- *Only buy a place 'in need of modernisation' (in other words a dump) if you know you have the money to do it up and either the ability to do it yourself or access to good builders you trust and can afford.*
- *Think about how much it will cost you to keep the property going each year. For example, if you buy a flat you will probably have an annual service charge to pay. Will you be able to cover that? Also, the bigger and the older the property, the more likely you are to have to pay for maintenance and repairs. Keep that in mind if you hanker after a stately home!*

So, you have found a place you really want. Now it's time to look at the figures again!

Don't Forget the Extra Costs

Once you have enough of a deposit to get a half-decent interest rate on your mortgage, sadly there are other costs you will have to cover. You'll need to have extra cash put aside to cover stamp duty, surveying fees and legal fees. If you opt for a mortgage broker who charges, you'll also have to fork out for broker's fees.

STAMP DUTY

Stamp Duty is a tax that the government collects on property that is purchased. It's the buyer who pays this tax, not the seller, providing it's their primary home (not a second or holiday home). Why do they do it? Because they can. That's all you need to know. It's a tax for nothing and a very lucrative one for the government. Great, huh?

What you do need to know is that stamp duty is calculated as a percentage of the purchase price. So the more expensive the property you're buying, the higher percentage of stamp duty you'll have to pay.

HOW MUCH STAMP DUTY YOU'LL PAY

Up to £125,000 (until 1 September 2009 this is temporarily raised to £175,000): Nil
Over £125,000 (£175,000) to £250,000: 1 per cent
Over £250,000 to £500,000: 3 per cent
Over £500,000: 4 per cent
The percentage is paid on the full amount, by the way, so if you buy a property for £600,000 you will pay 4 per cent duty on the *whole* amount.

LEGAL FEES

The legal fees that you pay will depend on your individual circumstances. You can generally expect to pay anywhere between £150 and £1,000 for the basic conveyancing costs (conveyancing being the legal process of transferring ownership from the seller to the buyer).

Other legal costs include search and Land Registry fees. These cover the cost of a variety of checks on the property. For example, your solicitor will check with the Land Registry that the seller of the property actually has the right to sell it. Land Registry fees are between £40 and £700, depending on the value of the property you would like to buy. For example, there is a £200 charge for houses valued between £100,000 and £200,000. Then there are local authority searches (around £180), drainage searches (around £50) and environmental searches (around £40).

FINDING A SOLICITOR

You don't have to use a local solicitor; there's nothing to stop you using a cheaper solicitor elsewhere. Online services offering conveyancing are, not surprisingly, the cheapest, but you have to allow for the lower level of service with these organisations. If you have a slightly complicated situation then you might want to consider a real-life conveyancing solicitor or agent who can answer your questions when you telephone or email. As always, it's best to go for professionals recommended by friends if possible as competence seems to vary wildly!

You could also use a licensed conveyancer. These are a relatively new idea in Britain. They are qualified, specialist lawyers who concentrate on conveyancing and tend to be cheaper than solicitors. Ask family or friends if they can recommend anyone. Otherwise you can find a local one through the Council for Licensed Conveyancers (www.conveyancer.org.uk). Their website has a directory of licensed conveyancers and you can search for one in your area just by clicking on the map of Britain on their 'directory' page. You can also get details of conveyancers from the Law Society (www.lawsociety.org.uk/choosingandusing/findasolicitor.law). In Scotland use www.lawscot.org.uk/find. As with standard solicitors, your licensed conveyancer doesn't have to be local. You may find a cheaper one based much further away.

If you feel confident enough, you can even do your own conveyancing but you should be fully conversant with the legal processes. Bear in mind that if something goes wrong you'll only have yourself to blame, whereas if you use a solicitor or licensed conveyancer, you'll be able to claim compensation. If you are interested in the DIY conveyancing route, check out: www.mortgagesorter.co.uk/buying_home_conveyancing.html and www.theadvisory.co.uk/diy-conveyancing.php.

SURVEYING FEES

All mortgage companies will want to get the property you're interested in surveyed before they offer you a loan. And guess what? They'll charge you for this. There are different levels of survey from which to choose:

Valuation Survey

This is the simplest form of survey. Its cost will depend on the property value but will typically be between £150 and £300. It is solely for the benefit of the lender and is simply to assure them that they are not investing in a property made of cardboard held together with glue. A valuation survey is not meant to flag up all the details that you should know about before purchase. As you're going to be spending a good chunk of your life paying off this property, it's a good idea to have it thoroughly inspected first.

Homebuyer's Survey

A homebuyer's survey is considered to be a mid-level inspection and will cost you twice as much as a basic valuation. It will cover the structure in much more detail and should highlight any problematic areas that need to be dealt with – or at least require further investigation – before purchase. It will also come up with a list of repairs that need tackling.

Full Structural Survey

This valuation will examine everything from wiring and plumbing to beams and structural engineering. It will outline any issues that currently exist, flag up problems that are likely to arise in years to come, and suggest measures that could be taken to prevent them. You will be more likely to discover the hidden horrors of a house, such as subsidence, damp and structural problems. These could cost thousands to put right; indeed, they could even make the property unsaleable. So even though a structural survey will cost upwards of £800 it's well worthwhile paying for one. It will also put you in a better position to negotiate money off the price for problems and so make the cost back several times over. It may even throw up problems that scare you away from the purchase – saving you huge amounts of money and tears. In which case it will be money very well spent indeed.

Check out the Royal Institute of Chartered Surveyors' (RICS) guide to understanding surveys so you know what to expect at www.rics.org/Services/Usefulguides/Consumerguides/understanding_surveys.htm.

ARRANGEMENT FEES

Thought you'd paid enough already? Nope. Lenders also want to charge you for the blood, sweat and toil they go through in the five minutes it takes them to set up the mortgage. They quaintly refer to this as the 'arrangement fee'. Arrangement fees can be £1,000 or even more – and over the past few years they've been going up.

There are some 'no arrangement fee' deals around. However, be wary of these and do your sums carefully. When you work out the *total* amount you'll pay for the whole mortgage, you may find that with 'no arrangement fee' offers, you end up paying more in the long run.

Conversely, when you're choosing a mortgage, make sure you add on your arrangement fees as well as your monthly payments to find out what you will be paying in total for your mortgage. Low-interest deals that *seem* to offer great value very often have a nasty sting in the tail in the form of enormous arrangement fees.

Here are three real examples of different two-year fixed rate mortgages from the same lender, one with no fee:

Rate	**Fee**	**Interest over 2 years**	**Fee**	**Total cost over 2 years**
6.03%	£999	£6,030	£999	£7,029
6.18%	£599	£6,180	£599	£6,779
6.58%	Nil	£6,580	Nil	£6,580

Your Financial Checklist

To recap, let's run through all the different pots of cash you'll need to start off with:

Deposit: at least 5 per cent but ideally 25 per cent or even 40 per cent
Stamp duty: if buying a property for over £125,000 (£175,000) it's 1 per cent, 3 per cent or 4 per cent of the total value, depending on the price
Survey: £250–£900, depending on the sort you choose
Legal fees: £400–£1,000
Arrangement fees: around £1,000
Broker fees: typically up to 1 per cent of the cost of the mortgage unless you go for a free one

Here's an example of what the total cost might be if you're a first-time buyer going for a £150,000 property:

A 5 per cent deposit for this £150,000 home will set you back £7,500. If you want a 10 per cent deposit, you'll need £15,000. For a recommended 25 per cent deposit you'll have to save £37,500.

You will then need around £4,850 to cover your other costs.

- Work at getting together a healthy deposit by using the tips in this book for spending less and making more.
- Never get more of a mortgage than you can comfortably pay back. Do your best to pay it off as fast as possible once you get one.
- Go to Moneymagpie.com's online mortgage guide for details of a recommended free brokerage service, and more information on getting a mortgage or remortgage (www.moneymagpie.com/downloadPDF/The_Friendly_Mortgage_Guide_from_Moneymagpie).

part three

SECURING YOUR FUTURE

chapter nine

Saving

Saving is all about 'paying yourself first'. It's a very satisfying thing to do and is the basis of future wealth. In this chapter you will find out:

- *How to save step by step (see opposite).*
- *What types of savings accounts exist (page 184).*
- *How to save when you don't have any money (page 195).*
- *How to get your hands on free money (page 196).*
- *Sneaky ways to save (page 199).*

Saving is a fundamental part of getting on top of your money. When you see money going out of your bank account and into your savings account(s), remind yourself that this is you paying *you*. Believe me – it's a nice feeling. In this chapter I am talking about saving for short-term goals, not about long-term investing (putting your money away for more than five years). I'll give you simple and straightforward ways of investing for your future in Chapters 10–13. But before you think about putting money away for the long term, you need to get the short term secure first.

How to Save

There's really no secret to it – saving is all about living below your means (that is, spending *less* than you earn) and putting whatever is left over into at least one savings account. Once you have paid off your debts, if you find yourself with money left over each month, you're in an ideal position to start saving a regular sum towards your future financial targets. Your targets might include next year's holiday, a deposit for a house, your child's university education or, most importantly, a nice, fat emergency fund to cover you if you suddenly can't earn for a few months. In fact, canny savers often have several savings accounts and they give each one a specific goal, such as the dream holiday, a new car or a Christmas account.

Even if you can't think of an immediate reason, target or priority for *why* you should save, the discipline of regular saving is worth it. At some point in the future, as you contribute more to the account and the interest snowballs, you could surprise yourself by how quickly the money grows. So follow this step-by-step plan and you'll find yourself saving quite surprising amounts over even a short period of time. It can be really exciting!

STEP 1: PAY OFF YOUR DEBTS *BEFORE* YOU START SAVING

We have already looked at how to rid yourself of the debt demon (see Chapter 4). Just to recap: you must pay off debts before you start saving, unless your debts are on 0 per cent credit cards, in cheap student loans or loans that you cannot pay off early without a penalty charge. This is because the amount you get charged in interest on debts is nearly always more than the interest you would make on your savings. So, by saving on the one hand and paying off debts on the other, you will actually lose money over time.

Say you have £1,000 deposited in Acme Bank and it's giving you interest of 5 per cent a year. That means that over a year you'll get £50 of interest. Annoyingly, you have to pay 20 per cent tax to the government on that (£10), leaving you with £40. However, if you also have £1,000 of debt on an Acme Bank credit card that charges 15 per cent a year and you don't pay off any of the interest every month, that debt will cost you £150 a year in interest added to the £1,000. So you will end up *paying* £110 as your savings will have been swallowed up.

In this example, your debts cost you three times more than the interest earned on your savings. It would be better to put that £1,000 of savings into paying off your credit card and then start again. It would be saving you £9.17 per month that you would otherwise just be handing over to Acme Bank.

STEP 2: CUT THE COST OF LIVING

In order to save, you need to free up as much money as you can day to day. There are two ways of doing this:

1. Cut down your essential bills each month. If you haven't already done so, switch to much cheaper suppliers so that you can save money every month (see Chapter 5).
2. Cut down on your general, day-to-day spending. Keep a

spending diary for a few weeks and you'll soon find out where the money is going (see Chapter 3)!

STEP 3: SET UP A SAVINGS SAFETY NET

This is money you save to cover you and your family if you lose your job and can't work for a few months so there's no money coming in. Work out how much you need to keep the roof over your head and body and soul together each month (you can get this from the budget you've already done in Chapter 3). Add up all your essential outgoings. This will give you the amount you *have* to have each month to keep everything going.

Once you have that figure, multiply it by three to six times as this is the amount of money you plan to set aside. So, for example, if you work out that you spend £1,000 a month on your mortgage, bills, food, travel and so on, you should aim to have between £3,000 to £6,000 in your safety net savings account. This should be an easy-access account (one you don't have to pay a penalty on if you withdraw money) and it's a good idea to get one with a decent interest rate.

Once you've saved this amount in a savings account, don't touch it unless you really are in an emergency. Forget about this money because it's your own personal insurance and you should just keep it there to fall back on. The great thing about this account is that it is your self-insurance policy. Unlike income protection policies, if you don't use the money, it still stays there, growing quietly for you to use later.

STEP 4: SET UP OTHER SAVINGS POTS

Set up different savings 'pots' for different things. We're talking here about saving for a rainy day – or several rainy months in a row – as well as for holidays, Christmas, a new kitchen or a car. Set up at least one other high interest account where you'll put a bit of money in each week or month to save up for big things like a new kitchen, a car, a good holiday and Christmas. In fact, you could set up a lot of different accounts for your different goals if you like. There's nothing to stop you having a 'Christmas savings account', a 'holiday savings account' and a 'new kitchen savings account' and so on.

Having decided to set up these accounts, you now need to sort out the best account for your circumstances (see pages 184–188).

STEP 5: KEEP AN EYE ON YOUR ACCOUNTS

Financial companies often drop their rates without warning. If this happens to you, move to a better account. The bank could get you in with a headline-grabbing account that tops the best-buy tables only to quietly drop the rate later on, so be vigilant. If your bank or building society sends you statements of how much your account is worth, always check the rate of interest on that statement against the rate on the previous statement. If it has dropped, make your displeasure known. Your bank may move you to a better rate. If not, find an account paying the rate you want and move your money.

Remember to take tax into account when calculating how much you will make on your savings. Any interest will be taxed by the government so the rate you see is usually not quite the amount of money you will make in the long run, unless you have wrapped your savings in an ISA (see page 187). To figure out what you'll get if your savings are not in an ISA, take 20 per cent off the quoted rate, that's how much you will get. So for example, if you're being quoted an interest rate of 5 per cent, once the tax has been taken out you will really get 4 per cent.

Also remember to keep your money safe and don't put more than £50,000 in any one banking institution.

WHAT IS AN AER?

You'll see the term AER quoted in savings accounts. It stands for 'annual equivalent rate'. This is the annual rate of interest, taking into account how often the interest is added to your account. The higher the AER, the better the return. This is not to be confused with APR or 'annual percentage rate', which is the real amount of interest you'll be charged on a loan, credit card or mortgage on a yearly basis. Basically, APR applies to money you *borrow* and AER applies to money you *save*.

The AER allows you to compare how much you'd earn on an account where interest is paid monthly with one where interest is paid annually. If you look at the savings rates advertised by banks, you'll see two rates quoted – the rate in huge numbers and, in the smaller print, the AER. The AER is the 'true' return as it factors in charges made by the bank for running the account. Also, if there's a charge for withdrawing your money, the AER will take this into account. So, for example, if you're charged

30 days' interest for a withdrawal, this will be reflected in the AER. Also, if an account gives you one rate for the first six months and then another for the next six months, the AER adds these up and comes up with the overall average interest you'll make for that whole year.

Different Types of Savings Accounts

Your money will earn more interest in a proper savings account than it will in your current account at the bank. Most current accounts don't pay much interest on your money. You need to look for a nice, high interest savings account or two to put your money in so that it will grow more each year.

There are lots of different types of savings accounts on the market – and this can make it difficult to work out which one is the best for you. To add to the confusion, some accounts fall under a couple of different categories. So you could have an 'easy access''online' account, or a 'no notice''monthly interest' account and so on. However, it's not too hard to grasp what the different types of accounts really are. Most do what they say on the tin. Here's a basic guide to the main ones.

EASY ACCESS ACCOUNTS

You can put money into and take money out of these accounts whenever you like. They might be online accounts that you have to set up over the internet or ones where you have to go into a branch. Quite often (though not always), the rates are a little bit lower than other accounts, which is the price you pay for this flexibility. If you think you may need to withdraw some of the money you deposit at short notice, then these are the accounts to consider as they won't sting you with financial penalties for doing so.

PENALTY ACCOUNTS

They're not really called this (would you take one out if they were?) and usually come in the guise of online, easy access savings accounts. They tend to give a good rate of interest, but the downside is that you'll probably suffer 30 days' loss of interest on any money you withdraw. You have to look at the small print to find this – or check on a comparison website for the details. It's sneaky but, if you can't resist the temptation to dip regularly into your savings, this kind of account can be a useful deterrent!

NOTICE SAVINGS ACCOUNTS

A notice savings account, obviously enough, means you have to give notice to the bank or building society before you take out your money. If you don't, you could be penalised and lose interest on your savings. It used to be that these accounts gave the best rates but that's not always the case now. If you find one that is paying a keen rate of interest, it may suit you if you can deposit the money safe in the knowledge you won't need to draw on it for the foreseeable future and, if you do, you can give the notice period – usually 30 days – and avoid any penalties.

FIXED RATE SAVINGS BONDS

You put a lump sum into these accounts for a specific amount of time (say six months or three years). In return you get a fixed rate of interest for the whole time but you can't take any of your money out until the end of the fixed period. Rates for savings bonds can often be quite good, although it's a bit of a gamble. If the Bank of England lowers interest rates while you have your bond then you're laughing as the bond has to pay the agreed rate of interest on your savings. If interest rates go up in that time, though, you could feel fed up that you're stuck with a bond with a suddenly uncompetitive interest rate. Like notice savings accounts, these bonds are good for people who can commit the money for a fixed period of time and won't need to take the cash out in that time.

MONTHLY INCOME SAVINGS

These are similar to the savings bonds. The main difference though is that these accounts pay you interest every month, rather than annually or on account maturity. These can be useful if you're looking for an income from your savings. Retired people often go for these accounts as they can ask for the interest to be paid out as income every month rather than be reinvested in the account – a useful feature if you're living on a fixed pension but have cash in the bank and need the interest it generates to supplement your income.

CASH ISAS

These are savings accounts where you don't have to pay tax on the interest you make. You have to be a UK resident for tax purposes and aged 16 or over to have one. You can only put up to £3,600 per tax year (at time of publishing but check Moneymagpie.com for updates) into an ISA. Cash ISAs can be instant access accounts or notice accounts.

If you're retired and you can claim back the tax deducted from your interest, you may not want to bother with a cash ISA as its chief advantage is you don't pay tax on any interest. If, however, you are a taxpayer, you're effectively getting an extra 20 per cent on your investment simply because that's the rate of tax not being deducted from your interest.

The catch with cash ISAs is that the highest rate will only be applicable to savers who deposit the whole £3,600 allowance as a lump sum. Also, a high number of cash ISA rates include a 'loyalty' bonus – usually 0.5 per cent – that is paid only if no withdrawals are made during the first 12 months. If you have to take money out, the rate drops.

You could say that, if you're a taxpayer, a cash ISA should be your first consideration for saving cash, simply because it's tax-free. For example, if you paid £3,000 into an ISA paying 6 per cent, you would earn £180 in interest. Whereas if you saved the amount into a normal savings account paying the same rate, basic rate taxpayers would lose £36 to the tax man and higher-rate taxpayers would be taxed £72.

However, as you will see in Chapter 12, you could put a whole £7,200 into a *shares* ISA (a stock market investment like a fund or individual shares that are wrapped in an ISA), which would make you even more money in the long term. If you did that then you wouldn't be allowed to put money in a cash ISA too. Personally I always put all of my ISA allowance into a shares ISA as I look to invest for the long term. So read that chapter before you make any big decisions this tax year.

ONLINE SAVINGS ACCOUNTS

Most online savings accounts allow you to check your balances, review transactions, transfer money and set up standing orders online. If you have internet access, can't be bothered queuing up in a bank or building society and have no qualms about transferring your money from your home computer, online savings accounts are worth considering, especially as the rates offered tend to be slightly higher than branch-held accounts.

> If you're retired or a non-taxpayer, ask for a R85 form when you open a savings account. Fill it in, send it off and the interest on your savings will be paid to you in full with no tax deducted.
>
> This means, for example, you could plump for an account which may not necessarily have the best interest rate but offers you more flexible terms and conditions.

Alternative Savings Accounts

PREMIUM BONDS

If you want to save with the chance (albeit slim) of big winnings, consider Premium Bonds from National Savings and Investments. Premium Bonds are an investment where, instead of interest payments, savers have the chance to win cash prizes. The minimum purchase is £100 (or £50 if you pay by monthly standing order) and you can hold up to £30,000 in bonds. The average return is around the same as (or a little less than) what you would get from an average building society, but returns are tax-free, and you don't lose your money as you do with ordinary gambling. Of course, there's always the possibility that you could win a big prize of up to £1 million, and also the chance that you might win absolutely nothing. Which.co.uk estimates the odds of winning at 24,000 to one which is not great.

Premium Bonds are also popular because they are backed by the government. This means that although they are a form of gambling, they are in some ways safer than ordinary bank and building society savings accounts. Daft huh!

Personally, I'm not keen on premium bonds and I've never invested in them. I never gamble and I'm not impressed by the average returns on these as an investment. Many people love them though because they're excited by the possibility of winning 'the big one'. If you're like this then by all means put some cash in, but not too much. Really, on average you would be better off putting more money in a high interest savings account instead.

ZOPA.COM

Crazy name, crazy concept – but it can work. Zopa stands for Zone of Possible Agreement, which is the area between the lowest amount one person is prepared to get for something and the most someone else is prepared to give for it. It's basically how people negotiate a price between themselves.

Zopa.com is the first online financial 'exchange' – a type of web marketplace for loans to and from ordinary people. It works by putting together people who want to borrow from, and lend to, each other. By joining you can become a borrower if you need money, so that you apply to borrow money from several lenders (you never borrow from just one person). Or, if you have money to invest you can become a lender, which is like being a saver in a bank except you're lending your money to real people instead of an actual bank. Zopa makes money by charging lenders and borrowers a fee – borrowers pay a set fee of £94.25 and lenders are charged an annual service fee of 1 per cent of their gross lending.

The interesting thing as a lender is that you get to choose what interest rate you want to lend at. Obviously, you would want to choose a high interest rate but that may mean that your money doesn't get lent out very quickly so it sits in your account making minimal interest for a while. Lending at a low rate means it's annoying when you see interest rates in the country going up and you realise what return you're missing. However, if interest rates go down you will be pleased that you have a fixed amount coming into your account.

You also need to decide how long you want to lend for (how many months your money will be tied up) and what kind of borrower you want to lend to. You have a choice between A*, A, B, C or Young (for borrowers aged 20–25). A* borrowers have high credit scores so present less of a risk whereas C-rated borrowers are more creditworthy than most of the population, but have lower credit scores than A*, A and B-rated borrowers. It certainly helps you realise what banks go through when they work out interest rates for their savers and borrowers!

There is a limit of £25,000 that you can put into Zopa. Also, it is a properly regulated financial institution (backed by US venture capitalists) so everyone who wants to borrow has to have their credit rating checked, and they must have been on the electoral roll for at least six years. Although Zopa has a strict credit-checking system it has a rather more creative approach than some banks. For example, it might even take someone's eBay rating into account if they don't have many other things to show for themselves.

Although this is an alternative to investing with the banks, it's not necessarily a safe haven. One or more of the people who borrow some of your money (the loan is spread around various savers) could default, although few have so far. Also, you have to tie up your money for some time, and that could be a problem if you need to access your money quickly.

CREDIT UNIONS (CUS)

Credit unions are particularly good for people on low incomes who want to save or borrow small amounts. Many, however, are getting bigger and now offer a range of services including current accounts, mortgages, savings accounts, Christmas savings, children's accounts, mini cash ISAs and fixed term savings. If you're a saver, rates of return can be higher than those offered by the main banks.

The way they work is that they are set up and run by a group of individuals who have something in common – for example, they live on the same estate or they do the same job (like a nurses' credit union, cab drivers' credit union). They're basically financial co-operatives and they offer a low-interest and easy-to-use saving and borrowing method for their members.

Credit unions aim to pay a dividend on savings once a year to all their members. This can be as much as 8 per cent of the amount people have saved, but is typically 2 or 3 per cent. Another bonus offered by credit union savings accounts is that life insurance is included at no cost to the member, making it easy to build up a useful nest egg for you and your family. On a member's death, the amount of savings can be as much as doubled by the insurance and paid to whomever the member chooses.

It's also pleasant to know that City fat cats aren't pocketing profits on your transactions. Credit unions have a lot of volunteers running them. If you volunteer then you get some useful training in money management and working in finance while being involved with like-minded people.

There aren't many credit unions in Britain, mainly because of restrictive financial rules in the past, and they're not very well known generally. However, they are big in America, Ireland and several other countries. As the rules for credit unions in the UK have improved they have been able to increase the services they offer. To find out if there's a credit union near you, or one that you could join, go to the website for the Association for British Credit Unions (ABCUL) at Abcul.org.

- Once you are out of debt, set up a standing order from your bank account into a high interest savings account. This is your savings safety net. Keep putting the money in until you have enough to cover you for at least three months.
- Once you have the safety net, set up another account (or more than one), which will be for other savings.

SIX SAVINGS BASICS

1. On the whole, it's best to go for the highest rate of interest you can find. The more interest your account gives you, the more money you will make each year.
2. Safety first. Make sure you don't have more than £50,000 in any one banking institution as only that amount is covered by the Financial Services Compensation Scheme. Be careful, too, as some banks and building societies are owned by the same institution.
3. If you want a totally safe bet then organisations backed by the government, such as National Savings and Investments and Northern Rock, are best. However, for this extra safety you will have to sacrifice good interest rates so your money won't grow as well.
4. There are different types of savings schemes and some will be more useful to you than others. If you don't need your money

for a year or so and would like high interest rates on it then put it in a savings bond (see page 186). If you want to be able to put money in and take it out at any time then go for an easy-access account (see page 184). If you're undisciplined and you tend to take your money out when you shouldn't then go for an account with penalties to deter yourself (see page 185). Look at Money Facts (Moneyfacts.co.uk) for lists of the different kinds of accounts and pick the ones that meet your needs the best.

5. It's a good idea to check the interest rate on your savings accounts about once every six months (make a note in your diary to remind yourself). Banks and building societies will regularly introduce a new savings account with a really high interest rate to lure you in and then, some time down the line, they may reduce the rates, hoping you won't notice! Compare the rate you are getting with the other best rates (look at the comparisons section on Moneymagpie.com to see what's top of the tree at any time). If yours is nowhere near the top then switch!

6. Setting up a savings account, or switching, is easy. You can go into a branch of the bank or building society you want to join and fill in forms there and then. Just take along proof of your identity in the form of a passport or driver's licence and a bill with your name and address on it to prove where you live. Give them some cash or a cheque and you're all ready to go. Or set up an account online. With this you will need to fill in the form online and they will send you printed forms to fill in and send back with proof of your identity. Once it is set up you can start to move money, via the internet, from your nominated bank account into the online account. Simple!

How to Save when You Don't Have Any Money

This is all very well and good, of course, if you have money to save, but if you're only just about managing day to day, saving could seem like a far-off dream. However, if you have a little spare time and a bit of energy, there are ways to do it. Whatever it is you feel you can do to make some money, ensure the money is earmarked for savings only. If you make the money over the internet then move it straight into an internet-based savings account. If it's cash, then put it in an envelope and deposit it in your special savings account immediately to stop yourself spending it on treats.

Here are my tips for saving when you think you don't have any money:

- **Set aside an evening a week to make money:** *It could be one night babysitting or tutoring. If that sounds too much like hard work, how about one night in which you spend a few hours in front of the computer getting paid to surf by doing online surveys, trying to recruit friends to new jobs on commission-based site Zubka, or even doing your own blog and putting Google-Ads on it. (See Chapters 14 and 15 for more ways to make money in your spare time. Also, take a look at the Making Money section on Moneymagpie.com, which is updated weekly.)*
- **Make one weekend a month your money-making time:** *If you have loads of energy you could spend every weekend, or perhaps just every Saturday, making money. Perhaps you could work in a local shop at the weekend, or*

make things to sell at a local market or car boot sale once a month.

- **Set up a savings account with penalties:** *If you're naughty and keep dipping into your savings for bits and pieces then put your money into an account with penalties. These accounts can be a useful way to force yourself to save regularly and not take the cash out (see page 185).*

Free Money

Ferret out all that money you've forgotten about. It's estimated that Britons have over £4 billion worth of unredeemed loyalty card points, gift vouchers, credit notes, coupons and air miles – just lying around the house! So hunt down all that 'free money', and the next time you book a flight, do a food shop or splash out on some new clothes, try to avoid spending any more than you have to. And the money you've saved? Straight into the savings account, of course!

DORMANT SAVINGS AND INVESTMENTS

The Unclaimed Assets Register (UAR) says some £15.3bn of forgotten money is kicking around in bank accounts, life insurance and investments in the UK. This is usually because people lose track of their savings accounts when they move house and forget to pass on their address, or when people die and their executors hadn't realised they had an account. So to track down what's rightfully yours, here are some useful starting points:

- *Go to Mylostaccount.org.uk to see if you have any old savings accounts lying dormant that you could raid to add to your stash. The British Bankers' Association (www.bba.org.uk) and Building Societies' Association (www.bsa.org.uk) also offer services to help you trace forgotten savings.*
- *For insurance plans, old pensions or lost shares, try the Unclaimed Assets Registry (www.uar.co.uk or phone 0870 241 1713) but it does charge a fee of £18 for each search.*
- *The Investment Management Association (www.investment uk.org) can help in tracing lost unit trusts.*
- *The Association of Investment Trust Companies (www.aic. co.uk) also has a search facility.*
- *The Government's Pension Service (www.thepensionservice. gov.uk) runs a tracing service to help track down occupational pensions and those of close relatives who have died, as you may be entitled to that pension fund.*
- *National Lottery prizes have to be claimed within 180 days. Check your numbers by visiting www.national-lottery.co.uk.*
- *To track down Premium Bonds prizes visit the National Savings and Investments website (www.nsandi.com). Type in your bondholder's number and a free search will be done for you.*

DON'T PAY TOO MUCH TAX

The tax man may be scary, but it could be worth your while getting in touch. According to Unbiased.co.uk, the organisation for independent financial advisers, failure to claim back tax overpayments left us £322 million out of pocket in 2007–08. Here's how to reduce your tax and keep more of your cash:

Claim Your Tax Credits

Contact HMRC (www.hmrc.gov.uk) and the DWP (Department of Work & Pensions, www.dwp.gov.uk) to ensure you are receiving your full entitlement to Pension Credits, Child Tax Credits and Working Family Tax Credits.

Check Your Tax Code

You could be paying too much income tax. Your tax code is three numbers followed by a letter and is calculated by adding up all your allowances and then taking away the deductions from this total, such as tax on perks like company cars. Most people in the UK who are below the age of 65 and in full-time paid employment have the tax code 522L. If you add a zero to the end of the three numbers you get the amount you're allowed to earn in a tax year before you pay tax. (In 2008–2009 this is £5,220.) If your tax code is higher, it could be because you're in receipt of various forms of tax credits or other allowances. If your tax code is lower than 522, it could be the taxman believes you're getting a perk via your employer, such as private health insurance, and so your personal allowance is lowered to offset the cash benefit you're deemed to receive. If you've changed jobs and have no perks in your new job, the taxman doesn't know this and needs to be told, as you're effectively being hit by a double-whammy of no perks and higher taxes!

If you think your tax code is wrong, contact your local tax office. This is not as logical as you may think, as you could live and work in Leeds and your tax office could be in Cardiff! So your first enquiry should be directed to your employer's payroll office, or the person who looks after the payroll for your employer. They should be able to give you the name and reference of the employer's tax office, the address and telephone number. Once you talk to someone at the tax office and tell them you believe you've been allocated the wrong tax code, they should be able to tell you how to proceed.

Check Your Council Tax Banding

If you live alone you are entitled to a 25 per cent reduction. You may also qualify for the Second Adult Rebate if you share your home with another adult who isn't your spouse or civil partner and is unable to pay council tax. Out-of-date valuations mean thousands of homes are in the wrong band. If you can prove your property is in a higher band than it should be, you can reclaim overpayments. Speak to your local council about getting a revaluation.

SNEAKY WAYS TO SAVE

This is where you have to use low cunning to come up with ways of kidding yourself into saving without you even realising it. Try some of these yourself:

- **Pay yourself first.** *Think of your savings account as your own personal account, while your current account is just business. Whenever you get paid, whether it's a monthly salary or bits and pieces of freelance payments, put a percentage (1 per cent, 5 per cent, 10 per cent – whatever you can afford) into your savings account before you do anything else. Set up a standing order to whip it straight out of your current account and into your savings account to avoid any temptation!*

- **Get cashback.** *When you get any money back from cashback credit cards or cashback sites (see page 109), stick it straight into your savings account. Remember: a credit card that refunds a percentage of your spending to you as cash only makes sense if you clear your outstanding balance every month. Any interest you have to pay on a balance left over from one month to the next will eclipse the cashback reward.*
- **Spend one pay rise behind.** *If you get a pay rise, you might be tempted to increase your spending – but don't! Instead, try to stick to the smaller budget you're used to, and put the extra pay into your savings account. In fact, change your monthly standing order so that all of the money diverts into your savings before you even think about the raise.*
- **Exercise and save.** *If you walk, cycle or get a free lift for a journey that you would usually pay for, put the fare into your savings. So if you would have paid £2 for the bus ticket, put that money in your piggy bank. Cycle to work for a month and you could save £60 or even more.*
- **Set up a bad habits box.** *It could be just a swear box or it could be a chocolate, fast food or crisps box. Whatever your secret – or not so secret – naughtiness is, impose a fine on yourself when you indulge. Come up with an amount that suits you – 10p or £1 – and stick it in the bad habits box. If your particular vice is a McDonald's or a quick curry on the quiet, then putting money in the box each time you succumb will help you kick the habit.*
- **Be the agent for your friends.** *Be the one to book group holidays – you could get a discount or even a whole holiday for free for yourself. Put the amount you've saved into your account. If you have a car, join up to car-sharing websites like*

Liftshare.co.uk or NationalCarshare.co.uk or just arrange to give friends lifts. Any money they give you for petrol should go straight into your savings pot.

- Keep open to opportunities for free money. Use extra money that comes in to top up your savings and, later, to put into investments for your future.
- Set up a standing order to move money from your everyday account into your savings account.

chapter ten

Making Money Work for You – the Essential First Steps of Investing

This is the first of four chapters which will take you through the steps you need to take to create a nice, fat retirement fund for your future. In this chapter, I'll be looking at:

- *The Seven Golden Rules of investing (see opposite).*
- *Laying the foundations for investing (page 206).*
- *Paying off your mortgage (page 207).*
- *Cutting down on tax (page 210).*
- *The joy of compound interest (page 212).*
- *How much you should aim to have in your fund (page 214).*

Investing for your future (and for your family's future) seems such a mysterious and scary art that most people don't know where to start. Most just contribute to their occupational pension and maybe put money into an ISA or two. If they venture into serious stuff, they tend to get someone else to do it for them, such as an independent financial adviser (IFA).

Now, many IFAs are very good and worth the money (I will explain later in this chapter how to find a good one). However, many are not really capable of doing as good a job as you are. Seriously. This is because no one, not even your mum, has your financial future as much at heart as you do. Who else is going to know as well as you do what your attitude to risk really is? Who else knows what big things you're really planning in the future? Given a bit of effort and a little time on your part, you can learn enough about investing to do as good a job – in fact, better – than the City boys. Read the next four chapters and you'll see what I mean.

The Seven Golden Rules of Investing

GOLDEN RULE 1: THINK FOR YOURSELF

A sure way of losing money is to copy what other people are doing without really knowing what you are doing or why you are doing it. This happens regularly with stock market investments and, recently, with property. It's no good just going along with the crowd – if you do, you will buy when everything's expensive and you will probably panic and sell when the market has dropped down to the bottom. Think for yourself. Make up your own mind and don't be tempted to panic when others are panicking or be greedy when others are throwing caution to the wind and piling into something you don't completely understand.

GOLDEN RULE 2: DO YOUR OWN RESEARCH

You will be told all sorts of things by friends, strangers, newspapers, television programmes, websites and even the government about what is a good investment. Don't just follow what they say. Do your own reading. Work out the sums for yourself. If you find yourself getting excited and thinking you should put money in *right now*, sit back, take a big deep breath and, before you plunge in with your hard-earned cash, make sure that the figures add up and it really is common sense.

GOLDEN RULE 3: SPREAD YOUR INVESTMENTS

Don't ever put all your eggs into one basket. If you spread your money into different 'asset classes' (such as shares, property, commodities, cash) then, if one crashes, you will have the others to fall back on. I get very fed up when I hear people say, 'Oh, I'm not going to bother with pensions, I'm putting all my money into property,' because even houses are not as safe as houses.

GOLDEN RULE 4: NEVER INVEST IN ANYTHING YOU DON'T UNDERSTAND

Many of the mis-selling scandals in the past happened because people put money into products they didn't understand. A financial salesperson told them that a particular product was good, and they were too embarrassed to admit that they didn't understand how it worked. Never be shy about asking and asking and asking until you understand.

If someone has kept explaining how something makes money and it *still* doesn't make sense to you, then it's probably because that product is actually rather bad and *doesn't* make money. Trust your gut instincts.

GOLDEN RULE 5: START INVESTING AS EARLY AS POSSIBLE

The longer you have your money in a good investment product, the more money it will make, thanks to compound interest (see page 212). It looks like magic when you first see the figures. Basically, the idea is that every year your investment grows by a greater percentage than the one before. After a while, time itself makes money for you. In fact, if you put a big lump of money into an investment and then just leave it for 40 years, it's likely to be bigger when you take it out after that time than it would be if you had done nothing for 20 years and then started investing every year.

GOLDEN RULE 6: INVEST REGULARLY

By investing regularly (every week or every month) your money will grow steadily. Also, by setting up standing orders or direct debits for this money to go into your investments, you will be 'paying yourself first' and there will be much less temptation to spend that money on things you want *now* rather than investing for a much greater reward later in your life.

GOLDEN RULE 7: BE PATIENT

Making money safely and without hassle and worry is a long-term thing. Compound interest works in your favour over time. Think hard about what to put your money in for the long term and then leave it there ... and leave it ... and leave it.

Laying the Foundations

It's no good rushing into any type of investment and it's certainly no good putting money into anything until you have laid the right financial foundations. Here's what you should do first:

STEP 1: MAKE SURE YOU'RE OUT OF DEBT

There is no point in saving (or investing) at all while you are still paying off loans, credit cards or overdrafts. You will simply be losing money (see Chapter 9). So if you have debts on any of these, go back to Chapter 4 and follow those steps until you have eradicated all non-mortgage debt.

STEP 2: SORT OUT YOUR SAVINGS SAFETY NET

If you are out of debt, the next step you need to take before you even think about starting to invest is to set up a nice plump savings cushion for yourself (see Chapter 9). Essentially, this is a savings account that has enough money in it to cover you for *at least* three months of expenses in case you suddenly lose your income. Ideally, it should have enough to cover you for six months. If you don't have this 'safety net', then you might have to dip into your investments to pay for essentials in an emergency. This could be very difficult as you might not be able to get your hands on the money quickly, particularly if you have invested in, say, property which can take months to sell; or your investment might be in a down-cycle in the stock market so you would lose money by taking it out just then.

DON'T TRUST IN CASH FOR LONG-TERM INVESTING

When it comes to investing for the long term, keeping your money in savings accounts can actually make you lose out in real terms. It's all because of inflation. Remember inflation? Yuk! Nasty concept. It's basically about how the prices of things go up over time. For example, £1 today buys a lot less than £1 did ten years ago, and £1 ten years from now will buy even less.

The government wants inflation to be around the 2 per cent mark, but in recent times it's reached peaks close to 5 per cent. If you just keep your money in a savings account it may grow (earn interest) by, say, 5 per cent. You have to hope that inflation is less than 5 per cent otherwise your money will actually be worth *less* than when you put it into the savings account. Therefore, in order to counteract the effects of inflation over the long-term, you need to choose an investment that will give you the best return while not being too risky.

STEP 3: CONSIDER PAYING OFF YOUR MORTGAGE FIRST

People don't usually start sections about investing with this tip but I truly feel that the best and safest investment you can make right now, if you have a mortgage, is to pay it off – and to do that before you do any other investing.

There are various reasons for this:

- **It is relatively secure.** *All investments, including cash (savings accounts), government bonds (gilts), the stock market, pensions and so on have an element of risk in them. Some more than others, certainly, but there is still an element of risk. When you pay off your mortgage, however, you pay it off. That's it. It's gone and you own your home outright.*
- **It is tax-free.** *If you have a spare £5,000 and you put it into a savings account at 6 per cent, you will make interest on it but you will also have to pay tax on that interest, so you will actually make just under 5 per cent. However, if you put that £5,000 into your mortgage which is charging 6 per cent, you will save the full 6 per cent interest as the tax office doesn't count it as an investment. As far as HMRC is concerned, you have paid off a debt (which is true) so you don't get taxed on it.*
- **It gives a good return.** *Admittedly, mortgages are among the cheapest ways to borrow, but average rates of return on property are still lower than the stock market. Over the last 25 years, the average mortgage rate has been roughly 10 per cent. The average savings rate has been around 5 per cent and the average stock market return over the last 35 years has been over 10 per cent. Now you could say that it would be better to put extra money into the stock market and then pay off the mortgage in a lump. That's certainly how endowment mortgages are calculated (see page 154). However, nothing is certain with investments and you would be more secure if you paid off the mortgage, rather than hoped for the market*

to rise as you pay it off; particularly if, like me, you want to pay your mortgage back in under 10 years (which, incidentally, I did – so you can too!)

- **You save so much in interest.** *Imagine the usual 25-year mortgage. Say you borrow £200,000 over 25 years and over that time the average rate you pay is 10 per cent. On a normal repayment mortgage you will pay £350,840 in interest alone over that time. If you overpay your mortgage each year so that you pay it off in just 15 years, the actual amount of interest you will pay will be £194,421, a saving of £156,419.*
- **It gives you such freedom!** *When I paid off my mortgage, for the first few months I would wake up in the morning thinking, 'Shall I bother to work today?' Being self-employed, sometimes the answer was 'Nah!' If you harbour desires to go round the world, set up your own business, start a family or just have a break for a while, paying off your mortgage can enable you to do any of these things . . . or nothing at all. Talk about quality of life.*
- **It really annoys the mortgage lenders!** *Mortgage lenders collect about £70 billion in interest from us each year. Of course, much of that goes out in the interest they have to pay on the money they have borrowed (either from us in the form of savings or from the Bank of England or, more controversially, from the global money markets). However, much of it goes into their pockets. So, who would you rather give money to: mortgage lenders over years and years, or your own investments? Tricky . . . keep thinking . . .*

How Do You Do it?

- *It depends what kind of mortgage you have. If you have a fixed rate mortgage, you will probably only be allowed to pay off an extra 10 per cent of the full loan each year without incurring penalties. If you are able to do that, then by all means use that facility. If you are able to pay off more than the penalty limits allow, then it would be worth putting anything over 10 per cent of the loan into a savings account until the end of the fixed rate period. At that point, put the lump of money into your mortgage and then decide if you want another fixed rate or to move to a more flexible deal.*

- *Many, but not all, variable rate mortgages will let you overpay when you want to. Speak to your lender to see what they allow.*
- *There are also all kinds of flexible deals that people have taken out (fewer now than there were before, but they still exist). Most of these will allow you to overpay when you want to but, again, check with your lender to see what their rules are.*
- *The best for overpaying are offset or current account mortgages. With these you can overpay as much as you want, when you want. You can also take the money out again if you need it. For this extra flexibility you often pay a slightly higher interest rate than many other deals, but if you have enough in savings it may still be worth it.*
- *For more information on mortgages and the various types of mortgage deals around, see Chapter 8. For information on pensions, see Chapter 11.*

STEP 4: CUT DOWN ON TAX

You can save a lot of money over time by using ISAs to protect your money from tax (see Chapter 9). ISAs are not products in themselves; they're like wrappers into which you put an investment, and that wrapper stops you having to pay tax on anything you make.

With a cash ISA, effectively you set up a savings account (with a building society or bank) but when you get your interest (usually monthly or yearly) the government won't take tax out of it. With shares ISAs, if your investment grows, you won't be taxed on that growth. We all have an ISA allowance each tax year (6 April one year to 5 April the next), which is essentially a limit on how much money you can contribute to your ISA.

ISAs were set up to encourage people to invest for the long term. This is why the government allows us to put the full allowance (currently £7,200) into a shares ISA, but only £3,600 into a cash ISA (plus another £3,600 into a shares ISA, if you want). The government knows that in the long term, shares offer us a much better chance of making money for our retirement than cash does.

It's up to you how you put money into your shares ISA. You can put in a lump sum or a few lump sums, or you can make monthly investments. If you have a lump of money to invest now, then go ahead and put it in. If you don't, and you think you can afford a certain amount each month, then set that up as a direct debit from your bank account.

You also save tax when you contribute to a pension (see Chapter 11). Any money you put into a pension has the tax you would have paid on that money added back by the government. So if you're on the standard tax rate of 20 per cent, for every £80 you put in, the government adds another £20 (the assumption being that you have really put £100 in from your *gross* earnings).

STEP 5: BE BOLD

Aim to invest your money in products that will go up in value much more than inflation. Investing is a long-term thing, though, so you need to look at the *average* growth of different products over time to decide what you should invest in. For example, it may be that cash is currently giving 6 per cent, shares are giving 2 per cent and property is losing a worrying 5 per cent. However, if you look at the figures over two or three decades, you will find that, on average, cash gives 4 per cent, shares give 10 per cent and property gives 9 per cent. So, ideally, to make really good money in the long term, you should be investing in a few products that give you the highest average amount year on year.

One really good piece of news – probably the best piece of news you could have about investing – is that the longer you have your money in one of these good investments, the greater your money will grow year on year. This is because of the joy and wonder of compound interest.

What is Compound Interest?

It works like this: when you invest money you earn interest on it (or you should do anyway!) The following year you earn interest on the combined total of the money you originally put in *plus* the interest you made during that year. The next year the same happens and so on and so on.

So, for example, if you put £100 into something that gives you 10 per cent return in that year, at the end of the year you will have made £10. If you keep that money in there then you will make 10 per cent on £110, which is £11 – this is added to your total, meaning that you now have £121 earning interest. Then in the next year you will earn 10 per cent on £121, which is £12.10. So you can see that each year it goes up just that bit more.

Two things you need to know about compound interest:

1. Small differences in interest rates make a *big* difference in the long term (see box, below).
2. Saving regularly over long periods of time can build up a big sum of money. Look at that compounding box, below. Imagine putting £100 a month into something giving you 10 per cent a year for 40 years. Think about how much you could invest on a monthly basis and then put it into the online compound interest calculator on Moneymagpie.com/bookgift to see how your investments could grow over time. It's pretty impressive!

COMPOUNDING OVER 40 YEARS

This is an illustration of how much compound interest can be earned over 40 years:

£100 a month in a savings account giving an average of 4 per cent = £116,486

£100 a month in a fund giving an average of 7 per cent = £248,552

£100 a month in a stock market fund giving an average of 10 per cent = £559,461

The Rule of 72

One way to work out how long it would take for your investment to double is using what is called the 'Rule of 72'. This is where you divide 72 by the percentage rate of growth of your investment. So if your investment gives you 8 per cent a year on average, it will take 9 years for your money to double (72/8 = 9). It will only take 6 years if you're getting 12 per cent, and so on.

STEP 6: AIM FOR ENOUGH MONEY IN YOUR RETIREMENT FUND

How much should you have as your investment goal? It's a question many people ask and the answer really depends on how much you would like to have to live on when you retire.

However, to give yourself an idea of what you might be able to get, work it out like this:

1. Once you retire, you will use the pot of money you have amassed to create an income for yourself, either by buying an annuity (a regular payment every month that you are promised until you die) or by investing in something that gives you regular interest (such as a monthly interest savings account) or a mixture of those.
2. The amount you get will depend on a) how much is in your pot of money and b) what kind of interest you can get on it.

3. On average, you should expect to make around 5–6 per cent in interest/annuity payments on your money each year. So, for example, if you have £100,000, you would get £5,000–£6,000 a year from it.
4. The current national average wage is about £22,000 for women and £25,000 for men. If you assume that you would get 5–6 per cent for your investment, then just to get roughly the national average wage each year once you retire, you would need (in today's money) around £400,000 in your retirement pot.
5. However, if you're not going to be retiring for 10, 20, 30 or even 40 years, remember that inflation means you will have to have a lot more than that in your pot to keep up with costs. Tell yourself that you will need *at least* £400,000 to have even a shot at the standard of living you're enjoying now.

Now, remember those Seven Golden Rules at the beginning of the chapter? Remind yourself of them now – they're important when you are thinking about what to invest in and how to do it for your future. Move on to the next three chapters to find out about products you should be thinking about investing in for the long term.

HOW TO CHOOSE A GOOD IFA

Independent financial advisers (IFAs) come in all shapes, sizes and abilities, like accountants. It's important to see at least three or four before you plump for one:

- Ask friends, colleagues and family for personal recommendations. Ask them why they like them (not just because they're a nice person!) Have these advisers genuinely saved or made them money?
- Get a free meeting with them. Most IFAs will give an initial consultation for free.
- First check that they are genuinely independent. If the answer is anything other than 'yes' (such as 'sort of' or 'partially') then, no matter how persuasive they sound about how that doesn't affect their ability to recommend great products, just walk out.
- Ask about fees. Do they charge fees on an hourly basis, do they earn their money from commission or do they offer a mixture of the two? IFAs shouldn't charge fees as well as taking commission. If you pay a fee, all the lump sum commission the IFA earns on financial products they sell you should be refunded to you.
- If you decide to go down the commission route, make sure you know how much your IFA will receive.

For more information, including details of the qualifications your IFA must have, see Unbiased.co.uk (the website of IFA Promotion, the association for independent financial advisers). You can also find out more information on the Financial Services Authority (FSA) website at Moneymadeclear.fsa.gov.uk.

- Read through this chapter again to make sure you have understood the various points.
- Read the next three chapters before making any decisions about what you will invest in.

Now that we've covered the foundations for investing, I'm going to move on to the various different products into which you could put your money. I'm going to start with a relatively easy, very tax-efficient one – pensions …

chapter eleven

Pensions

Yes, this is a chapter on pensions, but don't skip it! In this chapter I'll be looking at:

- *Whether you should invest in a pension now or pay off your mortgage first (see opposite).*
- *The state pension – what you can expect to get (not much!) (page 223).*
- *Company pensions – why you should grab one if it's offered (page 227).*
- *Personal pensions – the good, the better and the really rather interesting (page 232).*

The best way to think of a pension is as a kind of unpaid bank manager who keeps handing you cash once you stop working. The idea is to squirrel away as much money as you can over your working life so that when you retire you are able to access that money and live your life comfortably. However, you don't have to put money into a pension alone for your retirement. In fact, you don't have to invest in a pension at all if you don't want to. There are lots of other things in which you can build up money (see Chapters 12 and 13 for ideas) but pensions are a very good place to start.

A pension is simply a type of investment that has different rules attached to it, particularly the rule that any money you put in has added to it the tax you would have paid. Also, you're not allowed to touch the money in your pension pot until you retire.

Mortgage versus Pension

In Chapter 10 I said that, in my view, it's a good idea to pay off your mortgage before you do anything else. When it comes to pensions, however, this may not work completely for you. You may, for example, already have an occupational pension with your company before you get a mortgage. If so, you should continue contributing to your pension scheme while paying your mortgage. You may decide to keep your pension contributions low while paying extra into your mortgage; or, you may prefer to increase your pension payments gradually, keeping the same mortgage repayment each month. I went for the first option – I kept my pension and other investments low while putting all extra money into my mortgage. Once I had paid off my mortgage, I made sure I increased my payments into pension and stock market investments. I could do that easily because I didn't have a mortgage any more.

When you pay off your mortgage, although the saving you make on the interest is tax-free (see page 208), you don't get the advantage of having the tax you would have paid on it added to your investment, as you do with a pension. However, when you pay off your mortgage, you do have the freedom to do what you like with that asset – you can sell it or make money by renting it if you want. With a pension, although you can take a tax-free lump sum of up to a quarter of your pension pot out when you retire, with the rest of it you *have* to buy an annuity (see opposite) by the age of 75. This is not necessarily a bad thing (at least it guarantees you a specific income for the rest of your life) but if, like me, you prefer to make up your own mind about where you put your money, this can be quite annoying!

The other argument for paying into both a pension *and* your mortgage is that you then automatically spread your bets between a pension and property. That's a good start towards diversifying your investment 'portfolio'.

What is a Pension and Why Should I Bother?

Pensions are really just a special type of investment. The difference between pensions and all other investments is that pensions have separate rules governing them, particularly when it comes to tax. If you're wondering whether it's worth your while contributing to a pension, consider these points:

- *The government adds in the tax you would have paid on any money you put into a pension fund. So if you're paying higher-rate tax (40 per cent), then that's a really big incentive to put money in.*
- *Pension rules say that you can't take money out of your personal pension pot until you're at least 55 (from 2010) so it can be a very good way to invest if you're the sort of person who's likely to try to dip into your investment.*
- *The fact that you have to buy an annuity (see opposite) with at least part of your pension pot by the age of 75 means that*

you know you're going to get a secure, regular income every year for the rest of your life.

So, even though pensions have become pretty unpopular over recent years, it's worth considering having one or more yourself at least as *part* of your retirement fund.

WHAT'S AN ANNUITY?

Annuities are basically a kind of insurance payment that we get every month for the rest of our lives. The company that pays out this annuity promises to pay a certain amount every month for as long as we live – whether that be another two, twelve, twenty or two hundred years (unlikely, but you never know!) Naturally, these annuity companies don't want to lose money, so the longer they *think* you will live, the less they want to pay you each month. This is why women tend to get worse annuity rates (lower payouts) than men. It's also why, the older you are when you retire, the better your annuity rate will be. If you have certain illnesses, high blood pressure, high cholesterol, are obese or you smoke, you could get a higher income with an enhanced or impaired life annuity, as you are statistically likely to live for a shorter period. Also, some annuity providers offer better rates to those approaching retirement in certain poorer postcode areas because again, statistically, you're likely to live a shorter life if you are from these areas.

As with everything, it's really important to shop around for the best annuity rate you can get. Most people just take the annuity that is offered by their pension fund (bad idea) so they miss out on loads of extra money they could have got if they had gone to other pensions and insurance companies to see if they could find a better offer (you usually can). This is known as your 'open market option' and you should always use it to shop around for a better annuity income. You can shop around for the best annuity rate through various brokers such as AWD Chase de Vere (www.awdplc.com), Hargreaves Lansdown (www.h-l.co.uk) or The Annuity Bureau (www.annuity-bureau.co.uk).

The Pensions Advisory Service website (www.pensionsadvisoryservice.org.uk) features an annuity planner which guides you through the steps you need to take to convert your pension fund into an annuity.

HOW TO USE THIS CHAPTER

- **If you hate the idea of pensions** – *at least look at the information on state pensions (see opposite) and also the sections on stakeholders (page 233) and SIPPs (page 236). You may be pleasantly surprised!*
- **If you are employed** – *you should certainly read the section on occupational pensions (page 227) and the state pension (opposite). The stakeholder section (page 233) could be useful if you're with a small company that only offers access to one of these and doesn't have a contributory occupational pension. If you would like to set up your own pension separately to add to your work one, have a look at the personal pensions section (page 232).*
- **If you are self-employed** – *read the personal pensions section, including stakeholders (page 233) and SIPPs (page*

236). Also check the state pension information (below) to make sure that your National Insurance contributions are up to date – something a lot of self-employed people forget.

- **If you are not employed and not earning** – *look at the information on stakeholder pensions particularly (page 233), and also see the note in the state pension information (below) about how you could get National Insurance credits.*
- **If you want security above all else** – *read the whole lot. You might feel you want to invest in all sorts of pensions.*

The State Pension – What You Can Expect from the Government

This is the pension that most of us get whatever our work status has been.

Your retirement income starts with the basic retirement ('state') pension. Find out when you'll reach state pension age at www.thepensionservice.gov.uk/state-pension/age-calculator.asp.

You will get a state pension only if you've paid enough National Insurance contributions (NICs) over your working life. That means that if you're retiring before April 2010, you'll need to have paid a total of 44 years of NI contributions if you're a man and 39 if you're a woman. For everyone else, though, it's going down to just 30 years if you retire on or after April 2010.

If you've taken time off to care for someone or to have a baby, and have therefore not paid enough into your National Insurance pot, you can get National Insurance credits to top it up. Go to Thepensionservice.gov.uk to find out how you qualify for these and how to apply for them. Otherwise, if you haven't contributed National Insurance payments for long enough, you'll receive a reduced amount of state pension. If you haven't paid any NICs, you may get nothing at all, which will mean you will need to be supported with state benefits instead.

Believe it or not, the current basic retirement pension for a single person is barely £5,000 a year. Could you live on that? Not many people can, which is why it's so important for you to invest in other products as well so that you can build up a really good pot of money for your retirement.

You can find out how much you're likely to get in your state pension (dependent on the NI contributions you've paid so far) by applying for a pension forecast from the Pension Service (www.thepensionservice.gov.uk). This will give you an idea of how much of the state and state second pension you will be entitled to when you retire. The state second pension, by the way, is an additional state pension for low and moderate earners, and certain carers and people with a long-term illness or disability. It will also let you know if you have any missing years of National Insurance (NI) contributions, whether or not you can make them up, and at what cost. Go to the website www.thepensionservice.gov.uk or ring 0845 601 80 40. The Pension Service can also provide a combined state and occupational forecast if your employer takes part in its combined pension forecast scheme – check with your employer or the Pension Service to see if you can benefit from this.

What you should do about your state pension

- Contact the Pension Service (www.thepensionservice.gov.uk) to see if you are up-to-date with your NI contributions and, if not, whether you can put money in to top them up.
- If you have been unable to pay your NI contributions because you have taken time off to have a baby or care for a relative, make sure that you have National Insurance credits. If you're not sure, contact the National Insurance Office (part of the HMRC) at www.hmrc.gov.uk/nic/offices.htm.

Non-state Pensions

There are various types of pensions that we can contribute to ourselves. The pension scheme you opt for depends on your circumstances. For example, if you're employed, your employer may run a pension scheme that you can pay into (see page 227). If you don't work, you could still pay into a stakeholder pension (see page 233).

The general rules about how much we can put into our pension 'pot' over time have changed recently. Here are some of the big changes that the government has made that, I think, make pensions rather more interesting as an investment:

- *You can now contribute as much as you want into any number of pension schemes (personal and/or occupational) each year.*
- *From 2010, you can put up to £255,000 per year into your pension. That amount will be reviewed (probably raised) every five years after that. It used to be that you could only put a limited amount in each year, according to your age.*
- *Pensions have also become more flexible. Some pension schemes are now allowed a wider choice of investments, giving them the opportunity to make more money for you.*
- *All types of pension schemes are now allowed to pay a tax-free lump sum of up to 25 per cent of the value of your pension pot when you take your pension out.*
- *Also from 2010, you are allowed to have a total pension pot of up to £1.8 million (with this limit to be reviewed every five years after that).*

MAKE SURE YOU'RE REGULAR!

It's important to remember that whatever you put your money into for your retirement, the best way to build up a nice wad of cash over time is to pay in *regularly*. Even if you can't pay much each month, make sure you set up a standing order that will go out every week or every month into your pension or stock market fund and whatever else you want to invest in. If you have that cash going out each month, after a while you will hardly notice it and the money will quietly build itself up without much effort on your part. To find out exactly how much you would have to pay each month to reach your pension target, you can use the online pension calculator at www.pensioncalculator.org.

OCCUPATIONAL PENSIONS

This is something you may get if you're employed or have been employed at some stage.

Occupational – or company – pensions can be a pretty good proposition as you benefit from your employer's contributions (free money!) Every month, both you and your employer make a contribution into the pension fund (Contributory pension). Typically, an employer will pay in 6.8 per cent of your salary and you, the employee, will contribute around 3.6 per cent to a company scheme (source: http://uk.mercer.com/home.htm). Contributory pensions can be a really good perk of your job. Think of your employer's contribution as a kind of pay rise for the future. One downside to company pensions, though, is that you generally have little control over the choice of fund – you're just stuck with it. It's good to have someone else paying into your pension, but that good could be wiped out if the chosen fund performs badly.

Other, probably smaller, businesses may offer a stakeholder pension (see page 233) through the company, although they won't add any money to it. It's just a useful way for you to contribute without effort.

Some really fortunate employees are on what's called a 'final salary' scheme (see page 230), where you are guaranteed a certain pension when you retire. They're dying out pretty quickly as they're really expensive to run and a lot of businesses don't have the cash to keep them going. However, the other type of company pension – defined contribution (see page 231) – can also work in your favour as some companies put a generous amount into these each month to top them up.

When it comes to building up a nice, fat pension pot for your retirement, it really does make a difference if you can put extra in each month. If you can possibly manage it, put as much of your money into the company scheme as you are allowed. It's obvious really, but the more you put in each month, the more you will have when you retire – and it grows exponentially (that is, even more than just the money you put in). You can see how much of a difference it can make over time in the table below or by using the online pension calculator at www.pensioncalculator.org.

HOW PAYING A LITTLE EXTRA CAN SERIOUSLY BOOST YOUR PENSION POT

The table below shows the projected change in pension for a pension scheme member who increases his contribution from £100 to £150 per month and then to £200 per month, assuming that the employer contribution remains stable at £150 per month.

Member contribution	Employer contribution	Projected pension at retirement (£ per annum)	Difference (£ per annum)	% change
100	150	5,300	--	--
150	150	6,400	1,100	20.75
200	150	7,700	2,400	45.00

Source: Friends Provident

You get tax relief on pension contributions, which makes them even more attractive. So a basic-rate taxpayer, paying tax at 20 per cent, who puts in £80 a month, will effectively get the benefit of contributions of £100.

If You Change Jobs ...

If you change jobs, you should be able to take your pension with you if you want to. Under an occupational scheme, if you've worked for an employer for two years, you get to keep the value of any pension benefits that have built up too. If you've been paying into the company scheme for less than two years, you'll get your contributions back, minus tax and National Insurance, as a lump sum.

You can either keep the 'preserved benefits' in the old scheme, or you can get the old scheme to transfer enough money (called the 'transfer value') to the new scheme to give you some of the benefits you had already built up in the old scheme. Mind you, it doesn't always work because different pensions companies have different rules, so if you're thinking of doing this, get advice from an independent adviser before you try to move your money.

It's hard to say whether you're better to keep your preserved benefits or transfer to a new scheme. The trouble with transferring is that it often costs you money to do it. This can make the transfer value less than what you'd have if you left the preserved benefits alone. Talk to your boss or personnel manager (or, better, to a fee-based independent financial adviser) about whether you would make enough money in another pension to make it worth moving.

With people changing jobs more frequently these days, some are ending up with lots of little pension policies scattered around. If you've flitted between a number of jobs and think you may have bits of pensions sitting around unclaimed, you can search them out through a pension-finding service. Try the Unclaimed Assets Register (www.uar.org.uk, 0870 241 1713), the Pension Schemes Registry (0191 225 6393) or the AMP Pension Find Service (0800 068 5456).

Basically, if you put twice as much in you get roughly twice as much out, but if you put it in over a longer period of time then it really makes a difference. In this illustration, just an extra five years adds nearly a third to the final pension received:

Gross contribution	**How many years to retirement** *40 years (someone age 25)*	*35 years (someone age 30)*
£50 pm	pension fund £103,098 = £6,706 pa pension	Pension fund £72,423 = £4,729 pa pension
£100 pm	pension fund £208,435 = £13,558 pa pension	Pension fund £146,625 = £9,574 pa pension

FINAL SALARY AND DEFINED CONTRIBUTION PENSIONS

What's the difference? Quite a lot actually:

- Final salary (or defined benefit) pensions give you a definite amount of money each month when you retire based on the salary you have in your last five years of work. It's worked out on an 'accrual rate' where you get a 60th or 80th of your final salary times the number of years you have worked there. This type of pension is generally considered to be the better option, but there are very few left now, apart from in some civil service organisations. Even if you're currently paying into a company pension scheme which is 'defined benefit', it can be changed into a 'defined contribution' (or 'money purchase') scheme at any time before you retire, and this is happening more and more. This increases your risk but gives you more control over your pension contributions.

- A defined contribution (or money purchase) pension means the amount you pay in is defined (for example, you pay £100 per month), but how much you get when you retire depends heavily on the performance of the fund's investments, the level of charges, the whims of the pension fairies and so on.

Your company pension

- Ask your company to show you how the pension fund has been performing. If necessary, speak to a pensions adviser or independent financial adviser to see if it is performing well compared to other pension funds. If so, try to put more money in each month if you are able.
- Speak to your head of personnel or your line manager to see if you could contribute more to your company pension each month.

NON-COMPANY PENSIONS

If you're self-employed, you're not earning or your company doesn't provide a pension scheme – or you want to have your own pension as well as a company one – there are a few options to choose from.

Personal Pensions

Personal pensions are designed particularly for self-employed people and those who would like to have an extra pension on top of their company pension.

Personal pensions are essentially defined contribution schemes (see page 231) into which you pay a percentage of your income. Like company pensions, your contributions have the tax you would have paid added to them by the Inland Revenue, which means that if you're a higher-rate taxpayer they are worth considering.

It works like this: for every pound a basic-rate taxpayer pays into their pension, the provider will claim back tax from the government at 20 per cent, which means it costs you just £80 to pay £100 into your pension pot. The same goes for higher-rate taxpayers who receive 40 per cent tax relief on contributions, although it works slightly differently. The first 20 per cent is claimed back on your behalf by the pension provider, but you must claim the remaining 20 per cent back yourself when you file your annual self-assessment tax return.

However, personal pensions are not nearly as good as company pensions because it's only you who pays into them. Also, until the introduction of stakeholder pensions (see below) the pension companies tended to charge high management fees, which generally made them perform quite poorly (I speak from experience – I have two small ones and I'm thoroughly underwhelmed by them!) Some personal pensions have done well over time, but most have not. The only types I think are worth considering are a stakeholder or a SIPP (self-invested personal pension, see page 236) to get past the high charges and generally poor performance. SIPP charges can be high too, but you do have more control over the pension pot generally.

Stakeholder Pensions

Simple, cheap and effective. If you want a pension you don't have to think about, these are definitely worth a look.

Back in 2001, in a bid to make personal pensions a little more useful and exciting (as if they could be any more thrilling than they already are), the government changed some of the rules and introduced stakeholder pensions. Stakeholders are pensions that anyone can have – even children and non-workers. They are essentially private pensions but, unlike traditional ones, they are simple, transparent and cheap – altogether a better product than other personal pensions, in fact.

You can get stakeholder pensions from all sorts of financial services companies, such as insurance companies, banks, investment companies and building societies. Stakeholder pension funds are mostly set up as tracker funds, 'tracking' stock market shares for example, which helps them charge such low fees (for more information on trackers see page 251). Some stakeholders charge less than others, so look at the lower-charging ones first. Stakeholder charges are capped at 1.5 per cent a year.

If you're employed by a firm that has five or more employees, then your employer must provide you with access to a stakeholder pension scheme if they don't already offer an occupational pension. This can be useful for employees, but it is nowhere near as good as a traditional company pension because the employer is not likely to put some of their own money into the pot.

Visit www.unbiased.co.uk or call 0800 085 3250 to find local independent financial advisers with specialist pension qualifications. Compare stakeholder pensions from a range of providers using the Financial Services Authority's comparative tables (www.fsa.gov.uk/tables/bespoke/Pensions).

The Rules for Stakeholder Pensions:

- *You no longer have to be earning an income to contribute to a personal pension. This means, basically, that most people are able to contribute up to £2,880 a year (before tax relief) to a personal pension, even if they have no earnings of their own. Actually, this is true for other personal pensions too. When the government brought in stakeholders, it allowed anyone to pay this amount into any personal pension, not just stakeholders.*
- *On top of that, the government adds a contribution which is calculated using the basic rate tax (now 20 per cent), making a total of £3,600 per year. This is particularly useful for people going through career breaks or people on low incomes, as it means they can keep their pension contributions going.*

- *The catch is, of course, that many people without an income can't contribute anything much to a pension of any sort, as they are only just coping day to day. But a generous partner can contribute on your behalf.*
- *Parents and grandparents can also make pension contributions for children and grandchildren. In fact, some start off a stakeholder pension for children when they are just babies.*
- *Stakeholder pensions are great for self-employed people who don't have access to a company pension. As they are a type of personal pension, they can be taken out by anyone. If you are earning then the usual pension rules apply (see page 226). You're not restricted to just £2,880 a year.*
- *Stakeholder pensions are offered by some employers. If you haven't been offered access to a scheme but are interested, ask your employer. Your employer will have already chosen the pension provider and may have arranged for contributions to be paid from your wages or salary. Your employer may even contribute to the scheme although many won't.*
- *If your employer doesn't offer any pension, or you're self-employed or even not working, you can start a stakeholder pension yourself with a minimum contribution of £20. You choose the pension provider yourself and make your own arrangements to pay contributions.*

Your personal pension

- If you have one or more personal pension, then look at your latest statement from the company to see how it is performing or speak to an independent financial adviser about it.
- If the personal pension is doing badly, either move the funds into a new stakeholder pension or SIPP (see below) or just freeze it and set up one of these other pensions.

Self-invested Personal Pensions (SIPPs) – for the Sophisticated Investor

If you like to manage your investments yourself, SIPPs are certainly worth a look. However, they are very much an advanced option – only really a good idea for people who are very experienced and confident in stock market investing – and they can be pricey.

SIPPs are a bit like ISAs in that they're not an investment in themselves, just a sort of pension 'bag' into which you can put various different investments. You can't put in any old investment, though. For example, you still can't put residential property into a SIPP. However, you can include the following:

- *Commercial property*
- *Stocks and shares*
- *Investment trusts*

- *Unit trusts*
- *Open-Ended Investment Companies (OEICs)*
- *Gilts*
- *Collections (art, wine, stamps and so on, although the charges for including these can be too high to be worth it)*

On the plus side for SIPPs, you get to control what you invest in, rather than some faceless, obscure, high-charging bunch of fund managers. Also, by putting a range of different things into a SIPP, you spread the risk. The charges for running a SIPP have dropped with the introduction of online SIPP providers (these charges used to be quite high), so they're more accessible than they used to be.

On the other hand, most of us can't even run our bank accounts properly so, unless we get a whole lot better at managing our money very quickly, we're not going to run our SIPPs at all well. Also, different SIPP providers will accept different products, so you might find that you can't include, say, foreign property when that was the whole reason for setting up the SIPP in the first place. Not only that but the rules governing collections such as wine, antiques and stamps are rather muddy. You'll need good advice on those and should contact a reputable independent financial adviser with specialist pensions knowledge (see page 234).

However, if you are brave, strong and interested in investment and pensions generally, then a SIPP is probably the way to go for you. You can get SIPPs from various fund management companies or create and run your own. If you want an investment company to run yours for you then you need to check the annual fees that they levy. As far as I am concerned, the best providers of managed SIPPs, in terms of their low charges, are:

- *Hargreaves Lansdown (www.h-l.co.uk), which has the lowest annual management fees*
- *Fidelity Funds Network (www.fidelity.co.uk)*
- *James Hay (www.jameshay.co.uk)*
- *Killik (www.killik.com)*

SIPPs

- If you like the sound of SIPPs and want to run your own then read *The Naked Trader* (see Resources for details) for more ideas.
- If you want a company to manage your SIPP for you then get in touch with one of the companies above to find out about what they offer.
- Make sure that the managed SIPP will include the kinds of sectors you want to invest in, such as foreign property and specific collections.

How to Tell if Your Pension is Doing Well

When you get the annual review of your pension, scour the pages to find out how much you are being charged each year for the management of your fund (the annual charges). It's not easy as pension companies like to write in very confusing terms. So if you can't see it in the literature, phone the company up and nag them until they tell you. If the charges are higher than 1.5 per cent a year, then the fund has to have performed particularly well to make it a worthwhile investment. If it hasn't (and you could check with a friendly, fee-based independent financial adviser on this one), then consider freezing it (where you are unable to make any further payments to it and your previous contributions now make up the fund's total investment), and setting up something with a good chance of performing better somewhere else.

Have a look at the bottom line – how much do you have in your pension pot right now? Look at last year's figure, and the year before that, and the year before that. Has it been keeping up with the stock market (or, ideally, beating the market) or would you have done better putting the money in your local building society? To see how your pension fund and provider measures up against others, visit TrustNet (www.trustnet.com/pen/funds/perf.asp).

Order a pension forecast from your fund manager to see how your fund is stacking up for your retirement. They will let you know what sort of amount of money you can look forward to when you retire if you continue to contribute the same amount each month until that date. They'll give you two figures – the actual amount of money they expect you to have and the 'real' value of that money, that is, how much your money will buy you in real terms, taking inflation into account. Bear in mind that this is just an indication of what might happen based on various assumptions – the actual pension you can buy will depend on annuity rates when you retire, and the features you want from your pension.

IF YOU THINK YOUR PENSION'S RUBBISH ...

You can transfer the money in your pension to one from another pension provider, just as you can transfer an ISA, but you will probably be charged for it and you won't get to transfer the full amount. However, if your pension's performance has been very poor then it may be worthwhile moving it. In some cases it's better just to freeze it and set up another, better one instead.

If you've been paying into a company pension scheme for more than two years, you can leave the pension fund 'frozen' and start paying into a new one. If you 'freeze' your pension, you'll get your retirement benefits when you retire, as usual. It's just that the pension doesn't grow as much as it would if you were contributing to it each year. Bear in mind that when you transfer money from a pension scheme, the money can't go into your own bank account and sit there for six months while you think about what to do next. It has to stay within a pension 'wrapper' of some sort.

Moving a pension from one provider to another can be complicated and costly so it may be worth seeking (fee-based) professional advice.

Is My Pension Safe?

Well, some of it is – on the whole! There are some funds that protect pensions. You don't have to do anything about them; they are automatically there to protect your investments.

PENSION PROTECTION FUND/PPF (WWW.PENSIONPROTECTIONFUND.ORG.UK)

This is an insurance scheme that covers company pensions. It swings into action if your company becomes insolvent and the pension scheme doesn't have enough money to pay the benefits that have been earned up to that date. The PPF aims to pay 100 per cent of the pension for those who have already reached retirement age. For everyone else it will aim to pay 90 per cent of the pension earned subject to a maximum of £27,771 (see Moneymagpie.com for the latest figure). However, this scheme is thought of as a last-resort measure and so far it hasn't been tested.

FINANCIAL ASSISTANCE SCHEME/FAS (WWW.DWP.GOV.UK)

This is for people whose company pension scheme was unable to cover their pension benefits between 1997 and 2005. So this is only useful if your company had problems before April 2005. If your scheme is eligible, you get up to 80 per cent of your expected pension with an upper limit currently set at £26,000/year.

THE FINANCIAL SERVICES COMPENSATION SCHEME/FSCS (WWW.FSCS.ORG.UK)

This will provide some compensation if you lose money because the firm running your personal pension (including stakeholders and SIPPs) has gone bust. It's not clear how much they will cover but according to the Pensions Advisory Service (www.pensionsadvisoryservice.org.uk): 'If one of the plan providers were to go into liquidation, the level of protection for the pension plan member depends on the nature of their investment.' Mm, helpful!

Essentially, if your pension was provided by a financial advice firm that went bust, the scheme pays out *up to* £48,000 per person. The way they calculate it is complicated so here we go: the £48,000 maximum payout is made up of 100 per cent of the first £30,000 and 90 per cent of the next £20,000. If it was provided by an insurance company, the first £2,000 of an insurance claim or policy is covered in full, plus 90 per cent of the balance (but only the guaranteed benefits under the policy). There, clear as mud?

Which is the best pension scheme for you?

- **Company pensions** (including defined benefit and defined contribution schemes). If your employer offers a company scheme then you should seriously consider taking this option. You will almost certainly be better off than doing your own thing.
- **Personal pensions.** These are for self-employed people or for the more sophisticated investor who needs a wider range of funds. You can tailor investments in personal pensions to match your precise circumstances. This means you can end

up with a better projected pension at retirement than with a stakeholder pension but watch out for the charges. Many personal pensions have management fees that are far too high and could make you lose money over time.

- **Stakeholder pensions.** This is the starter pension for your average Joe (like me!) who is happy with an off-the-peg, relatively cheap option. Useful if you are expecting changes to your working life, but you are not sure in which direction, because stakeholders can easily be transferred. If you're unemployed, you can pay into any stakeholder pension scheme, so long as your maximum contribution is no more than £3,600 per year (including tax relief from the government).
- **SIPPs.** Suitable for the sophisticated investor who wants to control where their funds are invested. For example, the ethical investor who wants to invest in renewable hardwood forests; the company director who wants to use his pension to buy the company premises; the adventurous investor who wants to control exactly where their money goes; or just someone with huge funds who wants to spread risk across different companies …

So, that's pensions for you. Remember, though, pensions are not the only option you have for your future. There are many other products you could invest in as well as, or instead of, a pension. Move on to the next chapter to see what you can start to choose from.

chapter twelve

The Stock Market

This chapter will take you through some very simple ways to invest for big money down the line. It's about the stock market – but don't let that put you off! There are straightforward and easy ways of doing it as well as trickier ways for more sophisticated investors. In this chapter you will find out:

- *How to invest in an index-tracking fund (page 251).*
- *How to invest in exchange-traded funds (ETFs) (page 260).*

HOW TO USE THIS CHAPTER

- **If you're a real newbie** when it comes to investing in the stock market, start on this page. Read about tracker funds (page 251) and then either continue reading to the end of the chapter if you're generally interested in the stock market, or skip to the next chapter if you only want to dip your toes in.
- **If you already invest in the stock market,** read the whole chapter. Pay particular attention to the section on ETFs (page 260) if you haven't already invested in these.

- **If the thought of the stock market is just too terrible for you even to contemplate,** skip the whole chapter and move on to the next!

To make it easier for you, I've made a note where the options for investing are for beginners, for those who are growing in confidence and for those looking for something more challenging.

What is the Stock Market?

The stock market is just another market where you can buy and sell things. Think of your local street market where they sell fruit and veg and clothes – some people are selling and some are buying. The people selling want to get the best price they can; the people buying want to get the best bargains they can. Instead of buying and selling fruit and veg, though, on the stock market people are trading in bits of companies.

When you buy a share, or lots of shares, you are buying bits of actual companies. You can't see them but you get a receipt or an electronic record to say that you own these bits. Now, just as with a street market, you could go in and buy, say, lots of silver teaspoons at 50p each, knowing that in the next town you could sell them for £1 each. If you did that pretty quickly, you would make some cash then and there. On the other hand, you might have noticed that the price of silver teaspoons has gone up a lot in the last few years, and you think this trend is going to continue. You might buy 100 of them and put them in the attic and then sell them for a lot more five years down the line, making yourself an impressive profit.

Stocks and shares work a bit like that, on the whole. Unlike the silver teaspoons, however, they can also pay you some money back each year in the form of 'dividends' (your part of the profit that company makes in that year). Of course, you only get these if the company (or companies) you have bought bits of have done well in the year and are therefore willing and able to share some of their profit with you. You can either take these dividends, say 'thank you very much' and spend them then and there, or you can ask for them to be reinvested in the company, or the group of companies in the fund you have invested in, by buying even more shares in that company or that fund. Generally speaking, if you are going for growth, it is best to reinvest the dividends.

Investing for the Long Term

We *are* talking long term – at least five years – and that is the only way to think of investing in the stock market (otherwise known as the share market). 'Yes, but what about the *huge* crashes in the market?' you ask. 'Won't I lose everything?' Not if you're investing for the long term, no. On a daily – even hourly – basis, the stock market goes up and down. Sometimes – such as the Wall Street Crash in the late 1920s, the oil crisis in the mid-70s, just after 9/11, and in 2008 as a result of poor lending decisions – there have been big dives and everyone has been very frightened at the time.

However, if you put the newspapers aside, take a calm, deep breath and step back, you will see that the long-term view is quite different. Over time those ups and downs are smoothed out and the losses are more than made up for by the gains. In fact, over the last 100 years the general trajectory of the stock market index in this country (and in America) has been up. The diagram below shows how the stock market has moved over the last century:

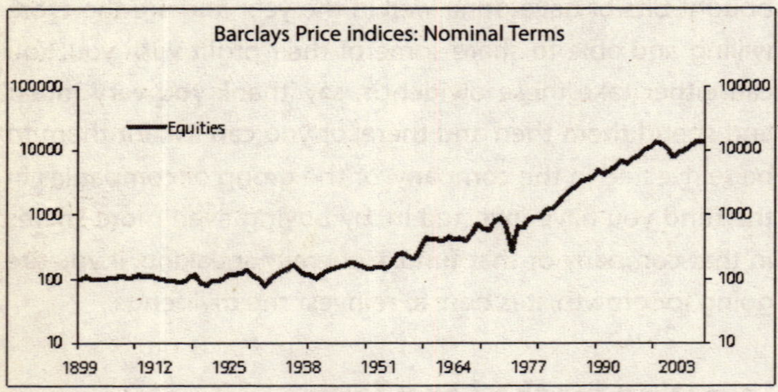

Source: Barclays Capital

Of course, no one can predict what any investments will do for definite over the next five, ten or a hundred years. None of us has a crystal ball. However, looking at the way the stock market has moved (or 'performed' as the investment commentators like to say) in the past, it's a fairly decent bet that it will continue to do something similar over time, that is, keep going up. Remember though, in the interests of you making your own decisions with full information, you should remember that nothing is a certainty. This is why I suggest that you put just *some* of your money into stocks/shares (maybe just 5 per cent of your investment money if you're unsure). The rest can go into other types of investments like property, pensions, bonds and cash.

Over the long term, the return you get from investing in the stock market is much the same, if not better, than the return you can get from investing in property (especially when you take the stress of being a landlord into consideration) and you don't have to stump up as much money for a share investment. So although you might feel safer with property because you can see it and touch it and watch TV programmes about it, you shouldn't think that it will be better than the stock market in the long-run.

> Spread your bets. We can't invest in certainties, but we can invest in probabilities. If you spread your money across various 'asset classes' (such as shares, property, commodities and collections) then if one of them tanks, you won't lose everything. In short: don't ever put all your eggs in one investment basket.

Also, don't be put off by the risk factor. If you just invest in low-risk, low-reward products, your money won't grow fast enough to keep up with, and beat, inflation, and you will have much less money to retire on. So, be brave. Don't listen to the scared, short-term thinkers. Remember to think for yourself, do your own research and be greedy when others are fearful and fearful when others are greedy. Look at the figures, read the arguments and instructions in this chapter and make up your own mind.

There are two main ways to invest in the stock market – either you buy individual shares (see page 264) or you invest in a 'fund', which is like a bag full of lots of different shares (see below). Investing in a fund is much easier (and theoretically less risky) than investing in individual shares, so that's what I'm going to talk about first in this chapter.

There are two main types of stock market funds you can invest in: managed funds (run by highly paid guys in expensive suits) and passive, Index-tracking funds, known as tracker funds (run by computers that don't need expensive suits). Some managed funds do well – very well, in fact – but the majority don't. In fact, 85 per cent of managed funds do worse than tracker funds over long periods. That means that only 15 per cent of managed funds do better than a simple tracker fund. This, and the fact that tracker funds are easy to invest in, is the reason why I'm starting this chapter with information on how to put your money into a tracker.

FIRST THING – DO IT IN AN ISA

You can invest a limited amount of money in shares each year without paying tax on your gains if you take out a shares ISA (see page 187). It's up to you how you put money into your shares ISA. You can put it into a tracker fund (see below) and ask for it to be wrapped in an ISA; or you can put it in a managed fund (see above), an ETF (see page 260) or individual shares (page 264). Just ask whoever is organising the investment to wrap it in an ISA for you.

Another option is to have a 'self-select ISA' where you get an ISA 'wrapper' and then choose either individual shares or a combination of funds to put inside it. However, if you haven't even started investing in the stock market yet I wouldn't worry about that. Just go for a simpler investment that can come pre-wrapped in an ISA, like the product I'm about to talk about – tracker funds.

INDEX-TRACKING (TRACKER) FUNDS

Skill level: Beginner

Tracker funds 'track' a particular stock market index (see below) by investing some of your money in *every single company* in that index. This means that as the index goes up or down (depending on how the shares of each of the companies in the index do each day), your investment goes up and down with it.

There are various 'indices' in Britain and around the world that are 'tracked' by tracker funds. For example, the 'FTSE 100' (the index you keep hearing about in the news) is made up of the 100 biggest companies in the country – the top 100 companies in the British stock market. They're 'listed' on the London Stock Exchange.

When a company gets 'listed' on a stock market it means that at least part of it has been sold to the public (you and me, if we have bought shares in it) rather than being privately owned. In other words, lots of people can own a little bit of each company by buying one or more bits ('shares') of it.

If you're considering a tracker fund, another index you should be familiar with is the FTSE All-Share. This measures how the majority of the companies (around 700) listed on the London Stock Exchange are doing. There's nothing to stop you investing in a fund that tracks one of the many other international indices – such as the Dow Jones or the Nasdaq in America, the Nikkei in Japan, the Hang Seng in Hong Kong or the DAX in Germany – but it's probably best to start with British funds, where you have easier access to information about them.

The Main UK Indices

There are three main British indices that you can choose to 'track'. The FTSE 100 and the FTSE All-Share tend to perform pretty similarly, but the third – the FTSE 250 – goes up and down a little more because it's made up of middle-sized companies, for which the prices can be a bit more volatile.

The FTSE 100

The FTSE 100 measures the largest 100 companies in the UK by value. The top 100 companies represent about 80 per cent of the value of the whole of the London-based market (the FTSE All-Share), so you can get a pretty good idea of what the stock market as a whole is doing from how these top 100 companies are performing. This is why they report on the FTSE 100 in the news – if the FTSE 100 is up a few points then the overall feeling is positive and companies are generally perceived to be doing well.

The FTSE 250

The next 250 biggest companies in size are known as the FTSE 250 – in other words, the companies ranked 101–350 in the market. Companies in this index are generally known as the 'mid-caps', meaning that they have a capitalisation (what they would be worth if you sold them) that is somewhere between the FTSE 100 and all the other tiddly little companies that are listed.

Interestingly, many of the traditionally 'British' companies, like manufacturers and house-building companies, are often found in the FTSE 250. For that reason, investors often choose to track this index if they believe the next few years will be bright for the British economy. They'll look for signals such as a falling unemployment rate, which means more people are holding down jobs and able to spend more on housing, travel and shopping.

The FTSE All-Share

The FTSE All-Share measures how the major part of the companies (around 700 of them) listed on the London Stock Exchange is doing. This includes each one that sells shares to the public, from the big household names like BT to the tiddlers, such as estate agents.

WHAT ON EARTH IS A FOOTSIE?

The FTSE (pronounced 'Footsie') stands for the Financial Times Stock Exchange. It's the common name for a set of British stock market indices that show how well companies listed on the London Stock Exchange (LSE) are doing.

The LSE is like a big marketplace where people (and companies) come together to buy and sell shares in companies. The FTSE All-Share is worth very roughly £1,000 billion altogether. (That is to say, if you sold all the shares for all the companies listed on the London Stock Exchange you would, in theory, be paid £1,000 billion.)

In the old days, the London market used to involve men coming together and yelling and waving their hands about a lot to buy and sell shares. Now everything is done 'virtually' using fancy electronic systems. With those systems in place, it's much easier for anyone with a computer, anywhere in the world, to access the market to buy shares.

The 'index' part of 'stock market index' is simply a way of showing us how a large number of companies' shares are doing on average. The more people that like a particular company, the more they want to buy shares in it. The more people want to buy shares, the higher the price goes.

If you have lots of people buying shares in companies that are represented in an index (say, the FTSE 100), then the combined value of that index goes up. That's what they mean on the news when they say, for example, 'the FTSE 100 has gone up by 30 points'.

How Do I Invest in an Index-tracking Fund (Tracker Fund)?
It's very simple to invest in an index-tracking fund. You can apply by phone, post or online. For example, you can just ring up a company that offers tracker funds (see page 257), tell them that you want to put some money in a tracker fund, and they will send you a form to fill in and sign. You send it back to them with a cheque (or even pay with a credit card over the phone) and you're done. They will ask you if you would like the fund wrapped in an ISA, so if you haven't already used up your ISA allowance this tax year, you can do that.

You can invest online as well. Just go to the tracker funds company's website (see page 257), look for the section on funds and search through for 'Index-tracking funds'. All the websites have different ways of displaying their information, so it might take a few minutes to find the part for index-tracking funds. Even if you want to deal with someone on the phone, it's a good idea to have a look at their website first to see what kinds of tracker funds the company operates. Most investment companies have funds that invest in different indices around the world. It's entirely up to you which one you invest in and how much you put in them.

Personally, I try to put in at least the ISA limit each year if I have it (currently that's £7,200 per tax year) and even more if possible (even though this extra won't be 'wrapped' by the tax-preventing ISA). It's a good idea to put money in different funds and different countries over the years to spread your investments around, but if you have never invested in a stock market before, then you might prefer to start off with a UK one.

> Think about how confident you are in the stock market long term. If you like the idea of it, and if you are planning to keep your money in a particular investment for at least five years (ten years is even better), then go for it.

There's nothing to stop you investing in one type of tracker (say, the FTSE 100) one year with one company (say, M&G) and then another type the next year (say, the FTSE All-Share) with another company (say, Fidelity) and so on. After three or four years, you could start getting adventurous with investments in an American index tracker or the FTSE 250 or the DAX in Germany. Your choice will depend on your research – on which market looks promising for the long term.

There's not a lot of difference in the performance of different companies' tracker funds in Britain; most do roughly the same. However, some charge more in management fees than others, so you're probably best off going for the ones with low annual management charges. The charges are based on a percentage of the money you put into the fund. Interestingly, economists say that the factor most likely to affect your investment is the annual management charges. The higher they are, on the whole, the worse your investment will do over time. So, as a general rule, if all other factors are equal, go for the fund or investment with the lowest annual charges.

MAJOR UK INDEX TRACKERS

Fidelity Moneybuilder
Index: FTSE All-Share
Annual charges: 0.10 per cent
Minimum investments: £500 lump sum or £50 per month, top-up minimum £250
Website: www.fidelity.co.uk
Tel: 0800 414161

Gartmore UK Index
Index: FTSE All-Share
Annual charges: 0.5 per cent
Minimum investments: £1,000 lump sum or £50 a month
Website: www.gartmore.co.uk
Tel: 0800 289336

HSBC FTSE All-Share Fund
Index: FTSE All-Share
Annual charges: 0.5 per cent
Minimum investments: £100 lump sum or £50 regular saver
Minimum additional: £500
Website: www.assetmanagement.hsbc.com/uk
Tel: 0800 289505

iShares FTSE 100
Index: FTSE 100
Annual charges: 0.4 per cent
Minimum purchase: 1 share
Website: www.ishares.net
Tel: 0845 357 7000

Legal & General UK Index
Index: FTSE All-Share
Annual charges: 0.52 per cent (0.5 per cent management plus extra expenses)
Minimum investments: £500 lump sum or £50 a month
Website: www.legalandgeneral.com
Tel: 0800 027 7169

M&G Index Tracker
Index: FTSE All-Share
Annual charges: 0.3 per cent
Minimum investments: £500 lump sum or £10 a month
Website: www.mandg.co.uk
Tel: 0800 390390

Sitting on Your Investment

Once you finish the application, you will be sent paper forms to fill in. You will probably need to show that you are who you say you are (to comply with anti-money-laundering legislation). That will mean sending them some household bills and a copy of your passport or similar, which they will return.

Then, once the money is in there, leave it, leave it and leave it until about five years before you are planning on retiring. Then you should start to move your money out and into more stable investments such as bonds. This is called 'lifestyling', where you take the gains you have made over the long term and look at short-term investing.

You need to have your money in something stable that won't suddenly drop right down just as you want to retire. There is nothing to stop you moving your money about before this time. You can take your money out and put it in something else any time you want. However, if you do, make sure it's for the right reasons, and that you have given your investments long enough to grow and take advantage of the upswings in the market as well as coping with the downswings.

Ensure, too, that you are not spooked by market crashes and take your money out of a tracker fund in panic when it is right at the bottom. If you did that, you really would lose out. Personally, when I see the market crashing, I look on it as an opportunity to buy into it, not to sell. When everyone else is selling in panic, that's when I decide to go in and put more money in my tracker fund, while it is nice and cheap.

WHAT IF MY INVESTMENT COMPANY GOES BUST?

If the management company that is managing your investments goes bust, such as a stockbroker, you are covered under the Financial Services Compensation Scheme. However, if the fund itself goes bust then you are not covered. This is part of the risk factor.

- Read all the above again to make sure you understand the concepts.
- Take a look at some of the websites of the fund providers. Get an idea of what they're selling.
- Once you are confident that it is something you want to do, ring them up, or go to the website, and put some money in.

So, if you're happy about everything so far and you're feeling bold, carry on reading about another pretty easy, cheap way to invest in the stock market without having to put too much effort into it.

EXCHANGE-TRADED FUNDS (ETFs)

Skill level: Beginner to intermediate

I like exchange-traded funds; they're cheap, pretty easy to buy and sell, and they work. They haven't been around for very long, so people are only just beginning to catch on to them.

ETFs are like traditional 'tracker' funds, meaning that they copy the performance of a market – such as the FTSE 100 – for their own value. Unlike tracker funds, though, they're actual companies in their own right and they're traded like individual stocks. So they're basically tracker-fund companies you can buy shares in. This means you can buy or sell a share in them, although you have to do it through a broker, just like you would if you bought shares in BT or Tesco. However, ETFs don't make money by making and selling things or services, like most companies do. Their value simply reflects the value of their underlying investment, usually one index or another. ETFs aren't managed by a fund manager ('actively' managed). As 'passive' funds, they're less expensive as there aren't any management fees or commission.

Why Are ETFs a Good Investment?

They're cheap: investment specialists say that one of the biggest factors affecting the health of your investments is the annual charges. Economists have worked out that when the charges are low it really helps your fund grow each year, mainly because less is taken out so you have more money in there to grow.

They are simple: there aren't lots of complicated layers and structures in them. They just invest directly into a stock market index or into a specific commodity (like oil, sugar or steel), or even into a particular country (like Brazil or India).

There are lots to choose from: as well as the British ones on offer, ETFs can be bought for exotic markets, such as Brazil, Eastern Europe, Taiwan or Korea, which have previously been rather hard to invest in for ordinary investors like us.

They work: ETFs are getting more popular because they have been seen to make money quite cheaply.

How do ETFs Work?

ETFs are like a bag into which you can put your choice of simple investments. This 'bag' is a company in its own right that is traded on the stock market. When you invest in ETFs you are effectively buying into the underlying index. You only have to buy one share to be involved in the fund (obviously the shares differ in price). They're very flexible too, and you can leave your investment in for as long or as short a time as you like.

Common Questions about ETFs

How Do I Set up my ETF?

First, you'll need to set up an account with a stockbroker. I suggest you go for an online one. It's free to register with online brokers and you don't have to buy anything immediately once you have your account. You can join now and wait for months before you invest in anything. However, once you do trade, it will be very cheap to buy and sell ETFs and you will have constant access to your stock.

Online brokers include:

- *TD Waterhouse: charge from £9.95 per online trade (www.tdwaterhouse.co.uk, 0845 6076002)*
- *Selftrade: £12.50 per trade – online, by telephone or via your mobile – and just £6 per trade when you qualify for its Frequent Trader scheme (www.selftrade.co.uk, 0845 0700720)*
- *Halifax Share Dealing: deal online for £11.95 (excluding international deals) or over the telephone from £15 (www.halifax.co.uk, 0845 7225525)*

Once you have an account, you can credit it with a money transfer, invest in your ETF and start to make some investments that will pay dividends!

How Do I Choose an ETF to Buy?

The ETFs that most people buy in the UK are those produced by iShares, which are index-tracking funds. In other words, they track a particular stock market index. If you look on the iShares site (www.iShares.com) and click on the 'iShares funds' button you will see a list of all the funds they offer.

The most common iShare in the UK at the moment is the iFTSE 100, which tracks the FTSE 100 index. Another one that people invest in a lot is iShares S&P 500, which tracks the S&P 500 index in the United States – the 500 largest companies listed on the New York Stock Exchange. If you were interested in investing in an economy like Brazil (it being fairly buoyant at the time of writing), you could consider the iShares MSCI Brazil fund. There are several different areas to choose from; it depends on what you are interested in. Once you have decided which one you want to invest in, make a note of the code for that fund and look for it in the list of the online broker you have chosen.

- Make sure you have understood what an ETF is. Read all the above again if necessary.
- Take a look at the iShares.com website and see what they're offering.
- Look at the information on investing in ETFs on Moneymagpie.com at www.moneymagpie.com/article/sfdsf/5

Once you have invested your money in a tracker fund or an ETF, you can pretty much forget about it, apart from when you get a report on your investment from the company – usually twice a year. Some years, your money will have increased; other years it will have gone down, depending on how the index itself did that year. Remember, you need to have your money in that investment for *at least five years* to get any real benefit from it. Over the long term these funds have historically gone up, even though at times they looked shaky. Hang in there!

There is a lot more that can be said about investing in the stock market. For example, there are managed funds that you could invest in – those are the ones run by guys in expensive suits that tend not to do as well as the computer-run tracker funds. Also, if you get really interested, you could look at investing in individual shares. Frankly, if you're going to do that properly you have to look at it as a job, or something that you take on as a serious hobby, because it really does take a lot of effort, research and thought.

Entire books have been written about investing in the stock market generally. If you're really interested, there are a few I would recommend (see Resources, page 399). Also, keep checking Moneymagpie.com for our investing features. For more in-depth articles about buying shares and funds, sign up to Interactive Investor (www.iii.co.uk) and the Motley Fool (www.fool.co.uk).

- Read this chapter again to get a really clear idea about how investing in shares works.
- Pick the kind of investment you're interested in and, as soon as you have the money, go for it!

So, you now have a couple more options to consider when thinking about how to invest your money. How are you feeling so far? Do take a break if you need a cuppa before we carry on looking at some rather more tangible options in the next chapter: property, gold and collectables.

chapter thirteen

Investing in Property, Gold and Collections

So far we've looked at basic investments such as pensions, the stock market and paying off your mortgage. However, there are many other things you can put your money into for the future. Some are much more fun and certainly more tangible, so they're a little easier to get your head around. I've come up with a selection of other types of investments you could consider, with their respective pros and cons. Read through the different options and decide whether any of them are the right place to put your hard-earned cash. In this chapter I'm going to look at:

- *Property in the UK as an investment (see opposite).*
- *Property abroad as an investment (page 274).*
- *Gold (page 277).*
- *Collections (page 280).*

Read through them all or just pick the ones you're interested in to find out more.

Investing in UK Property

Investing level: Challenging

Investing in property has traditionally been a really, really, *really* popular hobby for Brits. Since the 2008 economic crisis, though, we have fallen a little out of love with property as the market has been through quite a dip – something that came as a shock to many. Long term, though, property in the UK is a solid investment because:

1. We're a small island with limited space to build.
2. We're increasingly unable to live with each other, and the number of single households is set to continue rising at least until 2025, putting more pressure on the housing stock.
3. We're an ageing population and so more and more people are staying in their homes for longer, again increasing the pressure on the housing stock.
4. We are not building anywhere near enough properties each year to meet the increasing demand.

However, buying land, a buy-to-let flat or commercial property should be a well-thought-out decision, considering both the risks and the potential reward. It's definitely not right for everyone.

Contrary to popular belief – encouraged by television programmes and people at dinner parties – buying property doesn't instantly translate into cash. Like everything, there are arguments for and against taking this route. There are also all kinds of costs that you might not even have thought about until you get into it.

HOW TO INVEST IN PROPERTY

The point of investing in a property is either to buy something which will grow in value that you can sell or rent out when you come to retire or, if you want an income now, to get money in each month through rent. Because it is a business transaction, you need to approach it in a business manner. Think about the pros and cons of it as an investment (see page 270) and consider really carefully whether it's the right investment for you.

For example, do you have the time and energy to deal with complaints from tenants and to get the boiler fixed when it springs a leak in the middle of the night? Are you happy to have a large amount of cash, in the form of a deposit, tied up in this investment? Do you have a large amount of cash that you can stump up in the first place? If the answer to any of these question is 'no', then put off the idea of investing in property for a while. Maybe it will be right for you later or maybe never. If you're in any doubt, stick to putting money in your pension, stock market investments and, ideally, your mortgage.

Yes, I Really Want to Invest in Property

All right, if you think property is something you do want to invest in, make sure you take these steps before jumping in:

1. **Sort out your financial situation.** If you're in debt, get rid of it before investing in property. If you don't, any progress you make is negated by the debt sucking out money on the other side.
2. **Treat it as a business.** Buying property for investment

purposes is quite different from buying property to live in. You need to approach it dispassionately, looking at it from a profit point of view, rather than whether you personally would like to live in the place. Check out location, potential tenants, transport links and what the local government has planned for the area in the long term.

3. **Do the sums.** Look at the costs involved in buying and running a buy-to-let property. What would you have to pay each month for the mortgage? What do you estimate the annual costs for maintaining the property would be? What about letting agents' fees? You have to weigh up all of these against the possible rental income you would get. Also, how would you cope financially if the property were empty for a long time? Make sure you have funds in place to cover yourself if that were to happen.
4. **Swot up.** The first three rules of buying residential property are: location, location, location. Thorough research should help you avoid stagnant areas where things like crime, subsidence or finding tenants are a problem. You should also research the type of property that is likely to grow in value and likely to rent out well.
5. **Speak to the professionals.** Talk to local lettings agents about what kinds of property rent well and where is best to buy. They know what's hot and how to approach things. Always trust your instincts and seek out lettings agents with a good reputation. Contact ARLA (the Association of Residential Lettings Agents) through its website (www.arla.co.uk) to find out which lettings agents in your area are members.

Remember, there are many potential downsides to renting out a property, like bad tenants, periods when the place is empty or expensive maintenance emergencies. Think long and hard about your situation and decide if you can deal with the mental and emotional strain involved.

Benefits of investing in property:

- *Long term, prices should rise. Britain is an island facing property pressure from a variety of factors including people choosing single-person accommodation and the number of people coming into the country outweighing the number leaving.*
- *Property gives a double whammy of rental income – paying off your mortgage and potential capital growth.*
- *This is one of the few investment products for which it is acceptable – even advisable – to borrow money against, mainly because you can subtract the interest you pay on a mortgage against the tax you have to pay on the rent you receive. Some landlords who are comfortable living with risk make sure they borrow a lot of money, on an interest-only basis, because of the tax implication. It means you can, in theory, make money by using other people's (the bank's) money!*
- *There may be a ready market for resale. You might not get what you paid for the property – or even the face value – but you should get something.*

Downsides to investing in property:

- *There is no guarantee the value of your property will rise. Many people buy at the top of the market, yet are still shocked when their property's price falls. Property is a cyclical business (meaning prices go up and down every few years); you have to be very selective about the property you buy and its location, and time your purchase carefully.*

- *Property has generally risen in value over the past 30 years across the country, although it has been patchy. The growth is likely to be less steep in the next 30 years.*
- *Doing a place up can do your head in. There are a lot of unexpected costs in revamping an old property. Plus, there's no way of knowing if you will make back the money spent.*
- *Property is hard to convert to quick cash. It's an investment that should lock up your money for five years or more.*
- *You'll need a big deposit – at least 25 per cent. As prices get higher and higher, lenders need larger and larger deposits. This means you can be married to the bank for the majority of your adult life.*

Financing a Buy-to-let Property or Portfolio

As with buying property to live in, you will need enough money to put down as a deposit on your buy-to-let place, together with enough to cover arrangement fees, legal fees, the survey and all the other bits and pieces (see Chapter 8). However, you will probably need to put down even more as a deposit than you would for your own home. You will certainly need to stump up *at least* 25 per cent of the value of the property. Then, of course, you should go for the best-value mortgage you can find. As with finding a mortgage for your own property, it's best to shop around and speak to brokers (see page 148). A buy-to-let mortgage is offered on the basis of the property's potential rental income, not on your personal ability to pay it back as with an ordinary residential mortgage.

Seek out advice from professionals and other experienced investors. It's worth going to property investment exhibitions and shows (but make sure you avoid the seminars that get a heavy sell on radio and in magazine ads). There you can meet people who are already investing in property and talk to them. You're not the first, and won't be the last, person to look into buying a rental property. Sieve out the drivel and you can learn something by listening to other people's experiences. What kind of mortgage did they favour? How much did they budget for annual home maintenance? Speak to the Association of Residential Letting Agents (ARLA) (www.arla.co.uk, 0845 3455752) to find out all about these sorts of details from them.

Mortgages for buy-to-let properties are seen as riskier than those for people's own homes, so the interest rates and fees tend to be a bit higher. Make sure, if you get offered a mortgage, that you could cover the repayments with a margin of at least 20 per cent on top. This is because your mortgage interest rate could increase at any time, or the rent you get on the property could decrease or disappear at any time. You need to give yourself enough of a margin to cope with either of those eventualities.

Also, think about the type of mortgage you want to get. As landlords only get tax relief on their mortgage *interest*, and not on the capital, many property investors go for interest-only mortgages. They maximise their tax incentive and bank on the idea that they will keep the property for long enough for it to increase in value so that when they sell they can pay off the mortgage and keep what's left of the equity. Interest-only mortgages tend to have a lower monthly outlay too, so that can help if other costs are high.

On the other hand, if you would like to own the place outright one day, you could either take out a repayment mortgage (only getting the tax advantage on the interest part of the loan) or, if your rental income is a lot more than your expenses, you could use some of the rent to pay off the capital of your interest-only loan as well as the interest.

Get your sums right

- You'll need to keep some cash spare to cover periods when the property is empty and for repairs – this should be at least six months of rent. Tenants who fail to pay their rent are a real problem – not only does it mean you're subsidising their housing when they don't pay up, but it's also an expensive and difficult business to have them evicted.
- Property, like all other investments, is subject to tax and other expenses. If you're looking to make some money by waiting for the value of the property to go up and then selling, remember that most of the profit you make on the sale will be subject to capital gains tax, which is 18 per cent. Property also costs money to buy and sell, to maintain and to rent out. Do your sums before committing your hard-earned cash to a deposit.

Investing in Property Abroad

Investing level: More challenging

If you think that investing in buy-to-let property in the UK is complicated, just try doing it abroad. As a rule of thumb, the further away your property is, the harder and the more expensive it is to run. So if you buy something in another country – particularly one with another language, a very different culture and certainly different laws – then you really are piling on the potential problems and costs.

These, as I see it, are the pros and cons of investing in property abroad:

Pros:

- *You are investing in a tangible asset that you can actually live in sometimes and that you could retire to later on.*
- *You will (I assume) be buying in a country that you like, know and enjoy visiting.*
- *If you pick the right country at the right time, you could grab yourself a bargain. Some places in underdeveloped areas could almost be bought with a credit card!*

Cons:

- *It can be a lot more expensive than you would expect, particularly if the country you buy in has laws insisting on excessive taxes and payments when you buy. For example, if you buy in France, you have to allow for a whacking 12–15 per cent on top of the purchase price in expenses. In Spain, Italy and*

Portugal, you should allow for 10–11 per cent in fees and expenses, including essential legal advice.

- *Different laws on inheritance mean that you may not be able to leave your property to whom you wish when you die (see overleaf).*
- *All properties need to be maintained, particularly in emergencies, so you will either have the expense and nuisance of flying out to the property to deal with it or you will have to pay someone out there to maintain it for you.*
- *It's even harder to rent out a place regularly abroad than it is in the UK. You could have months and months in which you get no rent at all.*
- *Can you speak the language? Dealing with the local customs, tradesmen and power brokers will be less difficult if you can.*

If you do go ahead and buy a place in the sun, keep these points in mind:

- *If you're looking at buying a home as an investment as well as a place to escape to, you need to research the market before jumping in. Prices of property in France, for example, vary wildly. Buying in popular areas like Paris or the Côte d'Azur might be better than buying a cheap farmhouse miles from anywhere that will be hard to resell.*
- *Think carefully (and research thoroughly) whether you should get a mortgage in the UK or in the country in which you are buying. UK mortgages can be cheaper and easier to arrange, but you could lose out if exchange rates change wildly. Plus, in some countries you'll be allowed tax relief against rental income for the interest on a local mortgage, which may not be the case with a UK mortgage.*

- *Get a preliminary mortgage agreement before you start looking at properties. In some countries, if you pull out of a sale because you can't get a mortgage, this can put you in breach of contract.*
- *Even 'preliminary' or 'reservation' mortgage contracts should be checked by an independent local solicitor before you sign them.*
- *If you want to let the property or alter it, find out beforehand if you will need permits to do so. These can be hard to get in some countries.*
- *Decide who should own the property – you, you and your children, a trust or just you as a couple. There are usually tax implications for all of these options, so get it right before you sign the contract.*
- *What would you like to happen to the property if you die? In some countries, you're not allowed to leave your property to whomever you choose. Make a local will at the same time as you buy the house – don't just trust your UK will.*
- *Get a full structural survey done, particularly if the property is quite old.*
- *Get advice from a local independent lawyer and listen to the experts on the ground – so long as they are not connected to the sale of the property.*
- *Does the property have the necessary permissions and licences? More importantly, is the property allowed to be sold? Horror stories recently show that it's quite possible to buy a villa in Spain built on land that wasn't owned by the vendor.*
- *Always give yourself a 'cooling off' period if you see a 'must-have property' and are tempted to put down a deposit there and then.*

- *If you rent out or sell your property abroad, income will have to be declared to the British taxman. Check out the tax laws of the country you're buying in. Many countries have reciprocal tax agreements with the UK so that you don't end up paying tax twice.*
- *Set up standing orders in a local bank account to meet bills and taxes. Failure to pay your taxes in some countries, such as France, Portugal and Spain, could lead to court action and possible seizure of your property.*

Gold as an Investment

Investing level: Medium to difficult

Gold has been popular as an investment for centuries. It's not surprising really. It's pretty; it's relatively rare; it has retained a sense of value for thousands of years; it's useful and you can hold it in your hands. Even when all other investments seem to be going down and everything is uncertain, gold is seen by many as a safe haven for money.

Gold has performed very well in recent years; people feel safe with it, and you can buy it in different forms such as gold bars, jewellery, sovereigns or coins. Be warned, however: initial dealing costs for buying basic gold are high – sometimes 5 per cent or even higher every time you buy or sell. There is no annual charge to hold the gold after that, but you will have to keep it somewhere safe, which could cost you. Actually, you don't have to buy actual physical gold. There are various ways to invest in it – some of them where you never even see it!

WAYS TO INVEST IN GOLD

Bullion

Small bars and bullion coins can be bought from dealers, such as Spink (www.spink.com), at about 5 per cent above metal value and sold back at the same rate below value. Dealers tighten margins (make it cheaper) for customers who buy or sell in bulk.

Collectable Coins

Gold coins (antique ones, as opposed to standard ones) with a value above their bullion content are an interesting option, but not one recommended by the dealer Spink. It says that the market is notoriously difficult for non-collectors to second-guess. If you do decide to buy, rare coins in excellent condition are the safest.

Jewellery

Jewellery has the advantage of being both decorative and wearable. Also, it's easy to get – you just walk into a shop. However, bog-standard new items come with a mark-up of as much as 300 per cent on the price of the actual gold content. Collectable items – either vintage jewellery or new pieces from top designers – have greater investment potential and a value well above their actual gold content, but they are a risky buy. Their value could go up or down depending on the current fashion. Like most investments, in order to get a good price you need to research this market, find out where the best deals are and go there.

Exchange-traded Funds (ETFs)

Gold ETFs track the gold price and offer the easiest way to invest in pure gold as a commodity. ETFs are listed on the stock market, like shares, and can be bought through a stockbroker, and charge much smaller fees than managed funds. (See Chapter 12 for more information on ETFs and how to invest in them.)

Mining Shares

Shares in gold-mining companies provide 'geared gains' over the price of gold itself. This means that a rise or fall in the price of gold translates into a greater rise or fall in the share price. So you could make a lot more money but you could also lose more. Several funds invest heavily in the gold-mining, particularly the Black Rock Merrill Lynch Gold and General Fund. This has returned a whopping 2,026 per cent since its launch in 1988.

Gold Futures

These are high-risk investments available from stockbrokers. A futures contract is a tradable promise to buy or sell at a set price on a future date. Investors put down a deposit of only 10 per cent, so they can buy 100oz of gold – the size of a futures contract – for the price of 10oz. Huge profits, and losses, can be made. I wouldn't bother with this option, though, unless you're a really, really, *really* experienced investor.

An Online Option

BullionVault.com offers the chance to buy and sell shares of gold bars held in secure vaults in Zurich, London and New

York. The metal is held in your name. Transaction costs are nice and low, as are the charges for storage and insurance costs. New users can sign up for a free gram of gold to get a feel for the site. Again, though, don't touch it unless you're a confident investor and happy to trade online.

Collecting

Investing level: Medium to hard

There's nothing to stop anyone using one of their collecting passions as a possible money-earner as part of a portfolio of investments. Once upon a time, people bought paintings, wine, antiques or classic cars because they liked them. Now all these things, and more, are seen as serious investments. In fact, nowadays people make sensible money selling their collections of children's books, designer clothes and even top-of-the-range Barbie dolls! It's amazing what you can collect as an investment today.

Of course, there are many pros and cons to using collections as an investment vehicle:

Pros:

- *This is an investment you can actually enjoy. Share certificates aren't much to look at, but a Rembrandt or a classic Jaguar certainly is.*
- *It's a great excuse to spend money on things you love.*
- *It's something you can control, unlike pension funds or equity funds. It's up to you what you buy, when and at what price.*
- *Rarity. With some types of collecting – great art or sculpture,*

for example – there is a very limited number of certain items. This very rarity means they have the potential to increase in value over time.

- *Collecting is big news in several Western countries and increasingly in Asian countries too, so if you happen to pick the right items to buy, you can be confident of a growing global market for them.*
- *Some collections that are popular now can be very cheap to start (see overleaf).*

Cons:

- *Collections of all types are vulnerable to the whims of fashion. You could have a fabulous collection of silverware, for example, but when you come to sell it, it could suddenly be out of fashion and, therefore, not as valuable as it once was.*
- *Storage, maintenance and insurance costs can be steep. In some cases, these costs can be much greater than the annual management fees charged by equity funds.*
- *There's no guarantee that the value of your collection won't go right down to the floor. In fact, there is nothing to stop a poorly thought-out collection losing its entire value.*
- *It can be very hard to find, and afford, individual items for your collection, particularly if your passion is old masters, classic cars or Louis XIV furniture. If it is a serious investment, you need to factor in costs such as transport and internet access when looking at profits.*
- *Collections are vulnerable to burglary, fire and other forms of destruction.*
- *Unlike shares, cash or property, most collections don't produce*

any sort of income, only potential or capital growth. Capital growth is growth in value of the product itself.

- *You could love the things too much to sell them when you need the money.*

WHAT CAN I COLLECT?

What you collect depends on your tastes and, importantly, how much money you've got to spend. People with lots of money will collect top-of-the-range classic cars, rare antiques and art, gold, rare stamps, top wines and first-edition books. Even if you have little money to play with, though, you could still develop a decent collection of slightly less rare first editions of books and stamps, more affordable art and perhaps a classic MG.

Collections of off-the-wall, cheaper items have been rising in value recently and, if you pick the right things, you can make money out of kitsch after just a few years. Barbie dolls, Elvis memorabilia (even things produced now), Bakelite products, Ladybird books and electric guitars half-trashed by a rock star are just a few of the more bizarre collectables that are finding a growing market.

If you don't have thousands to invest right now but you'd like to start a collection that could make money later on, professionals advise you to buy things that today's teenage boys want but can't afford, like Game Cubes, BMX bikes or a girlfriend (no, not really!) The idea is that in 20 years' time, when they're old enough to afford these things, nostalgia will kick in and they'll pay over the odds for something they've yearned for since they were 13. Just remember to keep them in mint condition if possible and in the original packaging – that's what collectors love.

TIPS FOR BUILDING A COLLECTION

- Only collect things you love. You can't guarantee that they will be a good investment, but if you love them you'll have had all that enjoyment of them over the years anyway.
- Go for the best you can afford – quality is better than quantity.
- Study your subject thoroughly so that you know what's a good investment and what isn't.
- Stick within the realms of reality. Unless you're passionate about underground train tickets or Smurf memorabilia, try to collect things that already have dealers and a decent group of other collectors interested in them. To find out about the types of things people collect, have a look at the collectables section on eBay (www.ebay.co.uk).
- Make sure you have the physical space to store the items, keep them from danger and protect them from deterioration.
- Budget enough money to cover maintenance and insurance costs.
- Don't skimp on insurance for your collection. This is an investment and needs to be protected as much as anything else. If it got burnt, stolen or flooded, you could potentially lose thousands.

We've got all sorts of ideas on things you could collect and grow into a really impressive investment on Moneymagpie.

com. Make sure you sign up to the newsletter to get some of the regular articles we produce about fun and lucrative things you could collect.

part four

MAKING MONEY

chapter fourteen

How to Make Extra Cash

Once you've made sure that you're not paying out any more money than you have to each day, the next step is to make some extra cash. This could be used to turbo-charge your debt repayments or, if you're out of debt, to add to your savings and investments. There are hundreds of ways you can make some extra cash on the side and you will find all kinds of easy and fun ones. In the next two chapters I've put in just a few to give you an idea of some of the ways you can make money with what you've got including your things, your space, your time and your talents. In this chapter you will find out:

- *How to make money with what you've got (see opposite).*
- *Quick ways to make cash (page 302).*

We could all do with making some extra money here and there, and there are lots of ways that you can do it without too much effort. Some of these activities also give you new experiences and enable you to make friends and find talents you didn't know you had.

There are step-by-step instructions in the 'Making Money' section of Moneymagpie.com for literally hundreds of different money-making ideas so look there for more detail. Also make sure you are signed up to the newsletter because we come up with new money-making ideas each week. However, here I'm going to give you some ideas to get you going, starting with using what you've got. There's bound to be something in this list that interests you or matches your situation.

How to Make Money with What You've Got

You don't have to invest a lot of money on crazy schemes or get a second job if you can use what's already at your disposal to make money.

Obviously, the first thing everyone thinks of when it comes to making a bit of quick cash is to sell their junk. I'll be covering ways you can sell that (and other people's junk) on page 293, but I thought I'd start with a new approach to making money with your stuff which is to rent it. Really, it's the new thing!

RENT JUST ABOUT ANYTHING!

Some websites will let you advertise everything from video cameras and chainsaws to bouncy castles and massage tables. Whilst www.rentrino.co.uk charges 5 per cent on anything you successfully rent out, www.RentNotBuy.co.uk does it absolutely free! Renting not only saves you money, but helps the environment too by encouraging people to share and reuse instead of buying new.

This table gives you a few ideas of what you can make from renting:

Item	Weekly Revenue	Website
Baby bath	£8	RentNotBuy.co.uk
Triathlon bicycle	£60	RentNotBuy.co.uk
VW Golf	£140	Rentrino.co.uk
Underground parking space in London	£100	Parklet.co.uk
Trampoline	£60	RentNotBuy.co.uk
Spare room in London	£150	EasyRoomMate.co.uk

Rent out Your Driveway/Garage

If you have a driveway or garage but no car, this means you could potentially rent it out for others to park in (if there is a demand for spaces). Let thousands of people know about your available space by registering with www.parklet.co.uk or www.parkatmyhouse.com. Both are free to advertise on and charge a 10 per cent commission. If you live near a station, see if they will let you put a notice up there. Then see how much the station car park charges per day and try to undercut them – crafty!

For Londoners, there are also websites like www.london-garages.com that deal solely in garage rental if you want to work through an agent. If you live near a sports stadium, airport or congestion charge zone your parking space could be worth even more!

Sort out your written agreement, make sure the locks are secure and get a second set of keys cut. These are the only extra costs apart from the advertising that you have to pay for. You could be making anything from £10 a day from a driveway in, say, a Manchester suburb to up to £17,000 a year from a garage in central London. Amazing!

Rent out Storage Space

Of course, cars aren't the only thing you can keep in a garage. People will pay to use not just your garage but also your cellar or attic space for storage. To advertise your space for free, visit www.spareground.com.

Rent Your Garden

Although municipal allotments cost relatively little, the waiting lists for them are often very long. There is bound to be someone eager to use your garden for growing their vegetables and you can charge as much as you like. All you need is a large garden which is easily accessible and then you can rent it out. You can make as much or as little of it into allotment plots as you want.

Advertise through word-of-mouth or by putting up a card in your local newsagent's window or library. Once you've found someone who wants to use your garden, make sure you draw up a written agreement (again, see Moneymagpie.com for a suggested template). This doesn't have to be anything complex; just some straightforward rules stating exactly when the garden can be used, and for what purposes.

On average, allotments in Britain cost between £10 and £30 a year. So with three or four plots, that's about £80 a year or more without you having to do anything! It's also a fairly certain source of income. If you have any more questions, contact the National Society of Allotment and Leisure Gardeners (www.nsalg.org.uk). It's also worth looking at the Communities and Local Government's Plot Holder's Guide (www.communities.gov.uk).

You can also rent out your garden as a camping space. This isn't as crazy as it sounds. If you are near a festival or a national park or tourist centre then paying you £5 for a safe night's pitch is a good deal for the would-be camper. Once again, take advantage of the free advertising offered by www.sparegound.com.

Rent Your Spare Room

If you have a spare room, renting it out on a temporary or permanent basis is the most obvious way of making money out of it. It's a particularly good idea as you can make up to £4,250 a year from renting a room before you have to pay tax on it.

You can use any of the following websites to advertise your room. For a basic advertisement you can list your room for free, or you can pay a charge to list it in the top categories:

- *www.gumtree.com*
- *www.easyroommate.com*
- *www.roomsforlet.co.uk*
- *www.torent.co.uk*
- *www.letsdirect.co.uk*
- *www.rentomatic.co.uk*

If you prefer, for a small fee you can advertise in your local paper or put an ad in your newsagent's window. And if you don't mind paying a bit more, you can hand the advertising over to a managing agency – find these in the Yellow Pages.

Ask your prospective tenant for – and check – at least two references, ideally before they haul their bags through the front door. This can be a bank or utilities statement and a passport or driver's licence. As well as writing up a contract, you should also ask for a deposit in case of damages. It's reasonable to ask for about a month's rent in advance and to give each other a month's notice to leave.

If you're not sure about having someone permanently renting a room in your home, renting it to foreign students or lecturers visiting a local university or college can provide a gentle introduction. You can choose between hosting students learning English as a foreign language, who usually stay for only about six weeks; or university students and lecturers who can be in the country for up to six months at a time. It is a great way to meet new people and experience different cultures.

If you want to start hosting students, contact the accommodation officer at any local language schools. Idiom.co.uk has a list of English language schools in the UK as does the International Association of Language Centres (www.ialc.org) and English UK (www.englishuk.com).

What you can charge depends on where you live, what your home is like and the facilities you include as part of the rent. In London for bed and breakfast you can charge around £100 a week, or about £150 with dinner. If you offer a posh house with an en suite bathroom you can charge more –

around £200 a week. Outside the bigger cities, the going rate can vary from about £35 to £80 per week.

Stop! Do this first

When you rent out your property to strangers, the first thing you must do is write up an agreement. Check the article on 'Renting out a Room' on Moneymagpie.com (www.moneymagpie.com/article/renting-out-a-room/24) for a template agreement that you can print off. Your contract will differ according to what you are renting, but the basis is the same. You need to have the name and contact details of both parties, what is being exchanged, how much the rent is per week/month/year, the period of rent, any damages that may need to be assessed (such as lost keys), and how much notice needs to be given to end a contract. Also, if you're going to rent your property out permanently, you should let your mortgage provider know.

Rent Your Whole House

This may seem extreme, but your house is probably the most valuable thing you own and renting it will bring you a lot more money than just a room. While renting, you can either move in with friends or family, or rent somewhere smaller using part of the income from your house.

Rent out Your House as a Film Set

If you don't want to rent your whole house all the time, consider renting it out for short periods. If you live in an interesting house or flat in the right location, you could make serious money by renting it out for filming. With day rates starting at £1,000 you could be sitting on a goldmine without even knowing it. Not every home is of interest to production companies, and it helps if you have a large, posh pile within easy reach of Bristol, Manchester, London or another major filming city, but location managers are often on the lookout for small or unusual homes for different projects.

Make sure your house is clean and tidy, and apply to one of these companies:

- *Sarah Eastel Locations: www.film-locations.co.uk*
- *Lavish Locations: www.lavishlocations.com*
- *The Location Partnership: www.locationpartnership.com*
- *Location Works: www.locationworks.com*
- *BBC Locations Department: www.bbc.co.uk*
- *Amazing Space: www.amazingspace.co.uk*
- *Film Locations UK: www.locations-uk.com*

Make Money by Selling your Stuff

CAR BOOT SALES: TURN YOUR TRASH INTO CASH

Not only is it a fun day out for the whole family, car boot-selling is also a great opportunity to sell all your unwanted items – and possibly more.

Step 1: Find those Items

Start raiding all those cupboards, drawers and boxes that haven't seen the light of day for a while. If you don't have many items consider sharing a pitch with a neighbour or friend (but agree to either split the profits or only take money for your own items).

Step 2: Find a Place to Sell

Use a search site like Carbootjunction (www.carbootjunction.com) or Your Booty (www.yourbooty.co.uk) to find your nearest car boot sale or check the local papers. Carbootjunction has over 955 local car boot sales listed in their directory. They recommend Sundays as the best day for a sale.

Once you've organised a place to sell make sure you arrive extra early to get the best pitch. It's a good idea to phone ahead and get some advice from the organiser.

Step 3: Do Your Homework

Visit your local car boot sales to see how other people sell their goods and what sells well. For bigger items you're planning to sell look on eBay (www.eBay.co.uk) and Amazon (www.amazon.co.uk) to see how much they cost there. This will give you a rough price guide and will alert you to anything you have that might be collectable.

Step 4: Be Prepared

Bring along a table – a decorating table is perfect. Also, remember to take lots of loose change and refreshments. Bring lots of carrier bags and a few small boxes for buyers to take their goods home in, and a plastic sheet to cover your table if it starts to rain. Rope in your children, husband or a friend to help. An extra pair of hands is indispensable and makes the day much more enjoyable, plus it'll mean that you can take toilet breaks!

Step 5: Presentation

Place your most eye-catching and attractive items in front. Take the time to make things look as appealing as possible and try to group items in some kind of order or theme, such as kitchen items, music, toys and decorative pieces. Use a clean, colourful cloth on the table to attract the buyers' attention.

Items that are less likely to sell can be put into a box at a set price, such as 50p per item. People like a good rummage. If you put toys low down where kids can see them they may be more likely to sell. If you're selling clothes try to bring along a mirror. People will be much more inclined to buy something they can try on.

Step 6: Keep the Pricing Simple

Perhaps choose three amounts and label the smaller items the night before. For example, you'll have things that cost 50p, things that cost £1 and things that cost £5. It keeps it easy and straightforward for both buyers and yourself when trying to remember prices. You may want to leave bigger items without labels and see how much you can get for them.

Remember that people love to haggle. Be prepared to either stick to your guns if you know the item is worth more, or be flexible if it's towards the end of the day and you just need to get rid of it. Dealers may make you an offer early in the day BUT only accept this if you are happy with the price.

Tell them to come back later – if they are serious they won't mind doing this.

Consider copying some supermarket tricks towards the end of the day to get rid of the last items. Try buy-one-get-one-free offers, or dropping the price of everything to £1. It should bring in the last few customers still searching for bargains. Be prepared for major haggling by the end of the day and remember that 20p for an item you no longer need or want is better than leaving it to clutter up your house!

You don't have to stop at just selling your own junk at these sales. There are all kinds of money-making possibilities once you get into the swing of selling. You could be making cakes and sweets and selling those or propagating seedlings and selling the plants or buying up cheap job lots of toiletries from factory outlets and making a profit on them. Car boot sales are a good place to start small. If you're successful you could then move on to selling from a market stall or online.

HOT TIPS FOR CAR BOOT SUCCESS

- *Bestsellers:* Perfume, smellies, plants, children's toys and kids' clothes always sell well so take as many of these items as you can. Another great tip is to bring along some homemade breads, cakes and biscuits which sell brilliantly and don't take much effort or money to make.
- *Safety first:* Keep expensive items near you at all times. Car boot sales can be magnets for thieves so be careful and always lock your boot after you've unloaded your items.

- *Know the law:* As a one-off, income from a car boot sale is fine and does not need to be declared. However, if it becomes regular, or you start selling items that aren't your own personal property, it's very likely that in legal terms you would be considered a trader. This means you must follow 'good practices' requiring you to give refunds, replacement or partial refunds if something you are selling is not to standard.
- *Alternative ways to make cash from trash:* If the idea of packing up all your things and lugging them around doesn't take your fancy, try an online car boot sale like iBootSale (www.ibootsale.co.uk). Sell books online at Green Metropolis (www.greenmetropolis.com) where all the books sold make the seller £3. There's no charge for listing books, so it really is the ideal way to make money and recycle your old books.

Set up and Run Your Own Car Boot Sale

You could earn a regular income by setting up your own car boot sale. Anyone can do it. You just have to find a space that you can rent (you could do a profit-share deal with the owners to start off with) and then put the word out that you're in business. Good spots for car boot sales include school playgrounds, car parks that are not used at the weekends, fields or even the odd patch of wasteland that's not too hard to get to by car (and doesn't have resident travellers). In some cases you will need to seek permission from your local council's licensing and/or planning department. You will also need public liability insurance (see Moneymagpie.com for the best one) to protect you if someone hurts themselves while at your event. Insurance varies in price but expect it to be at least £50 per sale.

Add your sale to the list on Carbootjunction (www.carbootjunction.com) or Your Booty (www.yourbooty.co.uk). Use other free 'advertising' places, such as community slots on the radio, before considering running a small advertisement in the local press and leafleting the neighbourhood.

Need more info? See The Car Boot Sale (www.thecarbootsale.co.uk) for contacts, links and help setting up your own operation.

BUY BANKRUPT STOCK

Many businesses go bankrupt during a downturn. It is a tragedy for the people who owned the businesses but it can create an opportunity for you. The stock, furniture, machinery and equipment that these businesses had need to be sold – and usually they need to be sold fast. That means they can go very cheaply.

There are two ways you can profit from this. First, you could get friendly with local receivers and insolvency practitioners (you can find out about local ones through the organisation R3 at www.r3.org.uk which covers all bankruptcy professionals). That way, you can be the one to bid directly for what is left of the business's goods. It's then up to you to sell them to make a profit. You could do so through an auction, at a car boot sale (see above), on a stall (see opposite) or through direct contacts.

Alternatively, you could attend the auctions of bankrupt

stock and buy up the goods cheaply for your own use. There are auction houses all over the country that sell bankrupt stock. All you have to do is find your nearest one and get there quick! Charles Taylor (www.charlestaylor.co.uk) in Manchester update their site every week with new information on forthcoming auctions, as do Frank G. Bowen (www.frankgbowen.co.uk), London, and Walker Singleton (www.walkersingleton.co.uk) and (www.halifaxauctions.co.uk), Halifax. For other auction houses, such as Crossgar Auctions in Belfast (www.crossgarauctions.co.uk), you just have to pop along and see the stock for yourself.

If you don't fancy the high-pressure atmosphere of the auction room, Centaur Auctions (www.centaurauctions.co.uk) has set up an online auction house. You email your bids to them, which they accept if they consider them to be high enough. The waiting time on your purchase is dependent on whether they think they'll get a better bid. If they think your bid is high enough, they'll usually email you back right away.

RUN YOUR OWN MARKET STALL

Street markets are the oldest and most successful form of exchange. There are more than 1,700 markets in the UK, at which shoppers spend an estimated £1.3 billion a year. In tough economic times there's often a higher demand for second-hand goods, which makes outlets like markets good places to sell your old items. As with everything else, however, you must do your homework. The market stall is a very competitive place to operate.

Have a look at various markets and see what sells well.

If you notice, for example, that there is a cake stall in a market 30 miles away doing well but no such stall in your local market then you might be on to something. Make sure, though, that your local residents are the sort of people who would buy cakes (or whatever gap you have spotted).

Most local councils will require you to have a street trading licence, and it's illegal to trade without one. A licence in busy places such as central London will cost from £15 to £35. Some smaller towns don't ask you to pay for the licence.

The income from your stall depends entirely on what you sell, where your stall is positioned, and how much time you put in. A stall takes a lot of time (most people can't do it as a part-time job) and requires commitment. As a reward for your hard work, you can make as much as £2,000–£3,000 per day, but bear in mind that weather, the time of year (Christmas is good) and the location of the market and your stall can all make a difference. You must aim to at least cover your market rent, which will probably be about £50 per day or £200 per day for shows lasting two to three days.

Tips for Setting up a Market Stall

- Decide what you're going to sell and buy. *Will your stall sell general second-hand goods, or do you want to concentrate on one type of product, such as antiques or vintage clothing? Specialising is usually better although it helps to have specialist knowledge. Once you've decided what you want to sell, find the best suppliers for the right goods at the best price. You need to buy good-quality stuff as cheaply as possible to make the most profit. One way to source things is by buying bankrupt stock (see page 298).*

- Choose a good market. *You will probably know the good markets in your area, but if you don't, the National Market Traders Federation website (www.nmtf.co.uk) has a comprehensive list. If you're just starting out you could try car boot sales to get used to the whole idea of stalls, selling, dealing with the (often very strange) public and working out how to get a good sale (see page 293).*
- Set up your stall. *Markets often provide stalls, but second-hand market stalls can be in bad condition, so it might be better to buy a new stall that will last you for years from Gavin Kenning Engineering (www.market-stalls.co.uk). To start with, though, try a basic trestle table that's cheap and sturdy while you get used to the whole market-trading thing!*
- Haggle. *This can be a challenge when you first start, but keep going and you'll soon get into the swing of things. See haggling as a game and enjoy yourself. The important thing is to decide the lowest price you will sell for in advance and stick to it. Don't give away your lowest or highest price and you may come away pleasantly surprised with the profit you get.*

Need more info? See:

- *www.market-stalls.co.uk/resources/setting-up-a-market-stall.php*
- *www.nmtf.co.uk/index.php?id_cpg=7*
- *www.market-stalls.co.uk.*

THREE WAYS TO MAKE QUICK CASH

1. Ads on Your Car

You could make £200 a month without lifting a finger. Just go to the Adsoncars website (www.adsoncars.com), fill in the online form and wait for them to contact you to match you with a product or service. You then have to choose an advertiser you're happy with, and your car will be taken into their workshop to have a special 'skin' applied that doesn't wreck the paintwork. It will stay on for the length of the contract (3–12 months), and you are paid or offered free petrol for every full month the ad is on your car.

The amount you get paid depends on the car, your average mileage and the size of the advert, but expect to get between £70 and £200 a month. This can at least cover your petrol costs.

2. Recycle Your Old Mobile

Instead of chucking your old mobile phones in the bin, get paid to send them off to a company that will recycle them. Go online to Mopay (www.mopay.co.uk) to find out how much your phone is worth. If you're happy with the price, accept it and they will send you a freepost envelope. Pop your phone in it and send it off. Then all you have to do is wait for your cheque.

What you get for your phone depends on how new it is and its condition. Payouts range from £1.80 to £160. Basically, the newer the phone, the closer to its market value you'll get. See the Moneymagpie.com article that reviews the different mobile phone recycling companies.

3. Find Your Friends a Job

You can make up to £4,000 just by referring someone you know for a new job. Sign up for free with Zubka (www.zubka.com) and browse the jobs on offer. If you think any of them would be right for someone you know, you stand to make some serious cash.

SELL YOUR JUNK ONLINE

Try selling books, DVDs and CDs on Amazon (www.amazon.co.uk) or eBay (www.eBay.co.uk). Don't forget the other online auction sites like CQ Out (www.cqout.com), eBid (www.ebid.net), Tazbar (www.tazbar.com), Preloved (www.preloved.co.uk) and Auction Air (www.auctionair.co.uk).

TIPS FOR SELLING SUCCESSFULLY IN ONLINE AUCTIONS

These tips come from Moneymagpie.com eBay blogger, Nicky Peckham:

- Maximise your chances of a sale by including a good photograph of your item. Take the photograph against a plain background, such as a sheet or white paper, with plenty of (but not too much) light.
- Make sure your item is listed in an appropriate category. For example, if you have a book on fly-fishing you may well be better off listing the book under fishing than books.
- Listing in just one category is fine. eBay will try to persuade you to use more than one but beware – this costs more and is generally unnecessary.

- Get the description right. This is your opportunity to entice a buyer. Make sure you use the key words that describe your item, including brand name, colour and size, if relevant. You are given 55 characters; if there's room you can put in a 'gorgeous' or 'stunning' but these aren't words that potential buyers will be searching for. If your item is brand new and still in the box then add BNIB (brand new in box). Or, if you are selling something new with labels still attached, add BNWT (brand new with tags). Many buyers will use these terms to search for items. There are loads of these eBay abbreviations and you will come to recognise them as you get more familiar with the site.
- Add a subtitle if you are really struggling to say everything you want in 55 characters. Again, though, this is an additional cost and one I always try to avoid. You really don't want to see all your profit disappearing when those selling fees come in at the end of the month!
- Decide on a clever starting price. Look at similar products on auction and compare the starting price and final bid. As a general rule, a lower starting price will generate more interest and more bids but be realistic – if your item is a big designer label, start higher.
- Be careful what you put in for postage. Buyers will be put off if you are charging excessive postage. It's important to get it right and don't allow yourself a lot of extra to cover the cost of packaging.
- Offer your item on a 'buy it now' basis alongside the auction price. Lots of buyers prefer to buy in this way.

- Keep track of your auctions and respond to questions from buyers. Send items out as soon as you receive payment or leave four days for a cheque to clear. Do everything you can to ensure good feedback.

Sell for Others Online

If you are a major eBay enthusiast – or know your way confidently around the site – you could make money by selling other people's things for them. Why? Because many people would happily pay a percentage to someone who is willing to do all the above things. You should look to charge about 30 per cent of the sale price to make it worthwhile for yourself and for the people you're selling for.

- *Research other auctions so that you know what sells and for how much.*
- *Consider specialising in one or more categories that will help you make the most profit possible. On the other hand, if friends and neighbours use you as an 'agent' for them on eBay you will have to get to know all sorts of categories.*
- *Advertise your services by telling friends and also signing up to eBay's Trading Assistant Directory. To become a trading assistant you need to have sold at least four items in the last 30 days and have a feedback score of at least 50. At least 97 per cent of your feedback needs to be positive.*
- *Agree terms and conditions beforehand with your clients. eBay won't mediate so you're on your own. Agree who does the shipping, what sort of prices should be charged, how things should be described and so on.*

- *For more information visit http://pages.eBay.co.uk/trading assistants/hire-trading-assistant.html and http://pages.eBay.co.uk/tradingassistants/learnmore.html.*

MAKING EXTRA MONEY – DO I HAVE TO PAY EXTRA TAX?

Reading this chapter you have probably started to ask yourself how your tax situation could be affected by making extra money. For most small earnings (and getting cash for your old junk) you won't be affected at all – you won't need to pay more tax and your tax credits won't be affected. However, if you make regular, good money you will have to take tax into account. Here are a few of the main points:

- Don't be afraid to declare your extra money to the taxman. Everyone can earn a certain amount per year tax-free, but if you exceed this amount, you need to let the tax office (HMRC) know.
- You need to register any new business within three months with HMRC, or you may be fined.
- If you are selling on unwanted items every now and then, you may be taxed on any profits but usually small earnings will be ignored. However, if you start to buy products to then sell on, or you are regularly selling large amounts of your possessions, the rules change. For a complete guide to selling online or through classified adverts see www.hmrc.gov.uk/guidance/selling/index.htm.
- You may have to pay capital gains tax if you are selling any belongings that have increased in value whilst in your ownership, such as a piece of art or an antique.

- Renting space, your house or your drive is always taxable.
- If in any doubt, consult your local tax office – they will be able to advise you fully (www.hmrc.gov.uk/local/index.htm).

So, we've looked at ways to make money from what you've got in and around the house; now let's see how you can use your talents and your time to boost your income.

chapter fifteen

How to Make Extra Cash with your Talents and Time

You'd be surprised what talents you have and what possibilities there are of making extra money here and there in your spare time, particularly if you have a computer. You could even come up with a money-earner that will keep giving for years to come. In this chapter I will cover:

- *How to make money with your talents and time (see opposite).*
- *Money-making ideas for the over-60s (page 322).*
- *How to make money from your computer (page 324).*
- *How to make money in a downturn (page 341).*
- *How to make money while you sleep – setting up passive streams of income for your future (page 342).*

How to Make Money with Your Talents and Time

There is always something that you'd rather be doing than work, but how about using some of that free time you have, or one of your hobbies, to make a bit of extra cash? In a tight economy, people tend to 'make do' more often, repairing or reusing things so that they go further. This provides lots of opportunities for people who are good with their hands. Think about what people need to have done – or would like to have done – but don't have the money to pay a professional.

MEND COMPUTERS

Are you good with computers? Offer your services as a computer trouble-shooter at a knock-down rate in your local area. People traditionally throw away their computers when things go wrong, but, when times get harder, they start to get things mended.

CLOTHES: MENDING AND ALTERATION

When we want to save money, new clothes are often the first thing we cut back on, but these days few people have the time, energy or know-how to mend or update old outfits. If you have a talent for this then now is the time to turn your knowledge into cash. Stick to simpler jobs like changing buttons, fixing tears and holes in pockets and mending hemlines. These will take minimal work and bring in maximum return. If you want to try your hand at more complicated jobs like changing zips or altering clothes, make sure you charge enough to make it worth your while.

> Changing buttons is an easy and effective way to update an outfit, so collect buttons wherever you find them. Charity shops are a good place to start looking.

Try these websites for advice on how to do just about anything with a needle:

- *Start Sewing (www.startsewing.co.uk)*
- *Sewing Support (www.sewingsupport.com)*
- *The Sewing Forum (www.thesewingforum.co.uk)*

DIY

Painters, decorators and handymen can be pricey, so undercut the professionals and use your DIY skills to earn some extra cash. Stick to things you know you can do well such as painting and small repair jobs. Don't do more complicated work such as plumbing, electrics and gas fitting unless you are qualified. These are highly skilled jobs, and in the case of electrics and gas can be very dangerous if done wrong. With gas, only a CAPITA registered workman is allowed to fit or service a boiler, so don't even go there.

Try these websites for DIY tips:

- *DIY Doctor (www.diydoctor.org.uk)*
- *Ultimate Handyman (www.ultimatehandyman.co.uk)*
- *DIY Fix it (www.diyfixit.co.uk)*

SELL CAKES AND JAMS

If you're good at making cakes, jams or sweets, you can earn some extra pocket money selling them at local fairs and car boot sales. Take a trip to your local car boot sale or farmers' market and look for which food stalls are the busiest. Ask a wide range of people what they would like to see on offer. Also, speak to any cake sellers you see at fairs and markets and ask them which cakes sell best.

It's important to research the food safety standards you'll have to meet to keep on the right side of the law. All food businesses must register their kitchens with their local authority unless they operate on a 'casual and limited' basis only. If you're regularly selling food produce, it's highly likely you'll need to take a course in food hygiene. You can do this over the internet and it'll cost you about £30. The course is mostly just common sense so it's reasonably easy and you can complete it in your own time. For more information visit LearnDirect (www.learndirect.co.uk).

Try out a stall at a car boot sale first as it will only cost you £5–£15 to set up there (find your nearest car boot sale on Carbootjunction.com). The Women's Institute (www.womens-institute.co.uk), which runs country markets around the UK, will let you sell your goods (for just 5p to join) and they'll take about 10 per cent commission on sales to cover the costs of the market. See also Country Markets at www.country-markets.co.uk.

To find your local farmers' market, search the Certified Farmers' Markets websites (www.farmersmarkets.net and www.scottishfarmersmarkets.co.uk). You're not likely to sell a lot at farmers' markets unless you use local, organic ingredients. People who go to these events look for traditional homemade foods. Stallholders should be prepared to give honest, credible answers to customers about where the food came from and how and with what it was made.

If you make cakes, you can advertise the fact that you bake to order for parties and events (if your kitchen can take the strain!) Pop into local cafés and coffee shops (not the chain outlets), hand them your card and make your services known – maybe even provide them with a few samples.

BE A FILM OR TELEVISION EXTRA

If you have time to spare during the week, live in or near a major city and would like to rub shoulders with famous actors, then being an extra, or 'supporting artiste' (the new politically correct term for it), can be a great way of making some extra cash. You don't need any acting experience at all, but you do need to be punctual, reliable and able to take direction. Although getting picked as an extra does depend on how you look, most of the time film-makers just want normal everyday people. You can look a bit scruffy, overweight or unusual and still have a good chance of being chosen.

Extras agencies work like temping agencies – you can join as many as you like. Try contacting:

- *The Casting Collective (020 8962 0099, www.castingcollective.co.uk)*

- *Ray Knight Casting (020 7722 1551, www.rayknight.co.uk)*
- *2020 Casting (020 8746 2020, www.2020casting.com)*

You will also find a list of UK agencies at www.ukscreen.com. The back pages of *Screen International* (www.screendaily.com) list all the films in production, and sometimes in pre-production. Your local film commission will usually have an idea of what major projects are coming up and where extras will be needed (find them through the UK Film Council, www.ukfilmcouncil.co.uk). Look in the local papers, watch out for film festivals and try the local university's film department. Once you find and sign up to the right agency, you need to be patient and wait. Calls can be rather sporadic, depending on the number of extras needed and whether filming is happening nearby.

BEWARE!

There are many unscrupulous people out there so check and double-check any agency before you sign up with them. If they ask you for money straight away, move quickly to the door and keep running. Have a look at Clive Hurst's webpage (www.anactor.net) about dodgy agencies before signing up and, certainly, before handing over any money. Remember: it's not normal to pay for work you are supposed to be paid for. Ask the casting office for a list of shows they've worked on and cross-reference that with the actual television show or film credit; or contact the Broadcasting Entertainment Cinematograph and Theatre Union (www.bectu.org.uk). If the business looks dodgy, it probably is.

The basic rate for films is £76.85 per day plus travel money. For overtime (payable after nine hours) you can expect £6.74 per half hour. For television you can expect £90 for a 10-hour day if you're in the background of a commercial and £200 for a proper walk-on part. The BBC pays around £73 per day; ITV pays slightly less. The Film Artists Association set fees of £69 per day with extra for a walk-on part, overtime and wearing your own costume. Most of the time you will get free meals.

SELL YOUR OWN PERFUME

If celebs can do it, so can you. Make money by inventing your own scent for perfume and perfume-based products. If you learn to make soap, candles and creams, you can supply a range of products in one particular scent which you can also market as gift boxes. It's not that hard or expensive to do, and you can almost always find what you need at a health food store.

You will need:

- *Your favourite pure essential oils (such as rose, lavender or sandalwood)*
- *Specialist alcohol for cleaning*
- *Fixatives*
- *Eye-droppers*
- *Small vials*
- *Bottles or jars*
- *Good packaging – pretty printed labels and possibly extras such as ribbons, dried flowers or coloured plastic wrapping and boxes*

- The Chemistry of Fragrances *by D.H. Pybus and C.S. Sell – a must if you are serious about perfume-making*

It's important to work out your marketing concept before you finalise your fragrance. You want the concept – the image of the fragrance – to work in tandem with the scent. Don't go overboard on frills. Try to find a theme and express it in a simple yet creative way.

There are many ways to market your product:

- *Local gift shops and chemists. Stick to independent stores at first as the chains won't take you seriously until you've established yourself at least on a local level.*
- *Craft fairs and local markets.*
- *Gift fairs such as Top Drawer (www.topdrawerspring.com), which takes place annually at Earls Court in London.*
- *Set up your own website and sell your products direct to the public.*
- *Set up your own perfume-selling marketplace on eBay.co.uk.*

The mark-up on perfumes is very high, so if you are successful you could earn thousands a month, but it will take a while to build the business up to this kind of level. Make sure you start with a modest range. You will have to spend a lot on raw materials, bottles, labels and packaging. There will also be advertising, travel and marketing costs, including the cost of web design and hosting, if you sell that way, and fees for exhibiting at fairs or markets.

MARKET RESEARCH: EARN BY ASKING QUESTIONS

Market research is a great job once you get into the swing of things. It basically involves talking to strangers and getting their opinions about products and services on behalf of companies wanting that information to improve what they offer. You need to be interested in what everyone has to say; so listening skills and people skills are essential.

Most interviewers are employed on a part-time basis by market research agencies. Other employers include government departments, research institutes and opinion pollsters. Researchers are paid per completed interview, but your pay will be topped up in the first few weeks as you learn the ropes. A national average is around £8.75 per interview, but those living in London and the Southeast should expect to earn £9.25 each. Some companies will also reimburse fares and mileage. At the most, you could earn a couple of hundred pounds a week. There are also bonuses available for those who meet their quotas.

Once you get through the interviewing process, you will receive a few days' training. On your first outing into the big wide world of market research you'll be accompanied by an expert to make sure you're okay. Workshops and courses are often run to improve and update skills, and there are many networking events to help develop careers.

The Market Research Society (www.mrs.org.uk) is the professional association for the sector. They publish the industry magazine *Research* (www.research-live.com), which lists job vacancies. You can also look at graduate recruitment websites, and weekly magazines like *Marketing* and *Marketing*

Week. The IMRI (www.imriresearch.com) is a comprehensive directory of market research agencies, publishers and associations in over 100 countries.

Useful Websites

- *Research and Marketing Plus (www.rmltd.net): provides research services throughout Wales and Southwest England. They have vacancies for telephone interviewers in their Cardiff offices (full- or part-time work, no experience necessary as full training is given) and field interviewers, particularly within South Wales (flexible work on-street and in-home).*
- *Research247.com: exists solely for the market research industry to ensure that employers and researchers can access and advertise a wide selection of local and international vacancies.*
- *National Centre for Social Research (www.natcen.ac.uk): the largest independent social research institute in Britain. It has a national panel of over 1,000, and all receive paid training and reimbursement of transport costs. You can get around £15 for a 35-minute interview, and around £5.50 for every hour spent travelling.*
- *Criteria.co.uk: a qualitative market research agency based in North London. Check the website for vacancies.*
- *ACNielson.co.uk: one of the biggest marketing information providers around the world. Check out their job vacancies in the UK.*
- *Ipsos-MORI.com: a global research company.*

HOST A PRODUCT PARTY

The role of a consultant is to book and organise parties to demonstrate products to the host and their guests. Being a consultant is a great way to earn money flexibly because you can choose how many parties to book. You can do it part-time or full-time. Many mums do it in the evenings for some extra pocket money. You'll be working for yourself so you can be your own boss. It's also a brilliant way to boost your social life, and the stress levels involved are minimal. Ideally, you need to have a talkative, confident and organised nature. If you don't have a strong social network you may find it difficult to get the initial party bookings.

All consultants are assigned a mentor and receive training on all the products and/or beauty treatments. You also get free advice on how to maximise your bookings and business. Your training will be specific to the company. For example, as a Body Shop at Home consultant you'll be taught all the ethics that The Body Shop products endorse such as fair trading, protecting the planet and anti-animal testing. At Ann Summers (www.annsummers.com) you'll be taught saucy party games and so on, so that you know how to tailor the party to your customers. It's important to remember that you aren't guaranteed to cover your costs. You might make a tenner one night and £100 the next.

The Body Shop at Home

The amount of products that are sold at your demonstrations will determine your wage per party. The Body Shop says that the average party makes £200. Consultants get 25 per cent commission so you can expect to earn roughly £50 a party. There are tons of incentives for you to do well, like earning 2 per cent bonus commission when you reach sales of £1,200 in a calendar month or 5 per cent when you sell over £1,600 worth of products. There are also chances to get whisked away on all-expenses-paid trips and the like, providing you meet a certain number of sales. Unlike other direct sales companies, there are no minimum sales levels. To start up as a consultant, it will cost you £95. This pays for your starter kit which includes over £500 worth of products. For more details, visit www.thebodyshop.co.uk.

Virgin Vie

Consultants earn 25 per cent commission from party sales, plus additional financial bonuses if they reach certain sales and recruitment targets – and can also qualify for five-star luxury holidays around the world. On average, each party sale is around £250, which means the consultant takes home £62.50 per party. Hold three parties a week and you could be taking home around £750 a month as an income. There are three starter kits to choose from: cosmetics, home ware or jewellery kits, each costing £120. For more details, visit www.virginvieathome.com.

Other opportunities exist with the following companies:

- *Just Trade (www.justtrade.co.uk/party)*
- *Shoes Galore (www.shoes-galore.co.uk)*
- *I Am Natural (www.iamnatural.co.uk)*

BE A VIRTUAL ASSISTANT

Virtual assistants (VAs) are like PAs but they work from home. They help small businesses that can't afford full-time secretarial support or need to delegate occasional typing or admin work. If you've got a good background in secretarial or administration work in an office environment then this could be an ideal way for you to make extra money in your spare time. The job can involve a wide range of tasks, from simply answering calls and sending emails to bookkeeping, business planning and desktop publishing.

How much you make depends on the level of service you offer, with clients being charged a fixed hourly or daily fee (not including phone calls, postage costs and so on). Agencies charge up to £150 per client per day, but typically you would charge between £15 and £25 per hour for routine admin work done by phone or email. VAs can make more money by increasing the skills they offer.

By far the best qualification for this job is experience, ideally at least five years' office experience. There are also courses you can do. Christine Richmond, who runs her own VA business (Assistyourbiz.co.uk), took the online VA course at VirtualAssistanceU.com and recommends it to others.

Register your business with your company name with Companies House (www.companieshouse.gov.uk). A business name is really important for first impressions. Check that your business name is unique at the National Business Register (www.start.biz). You'll also need to register yourself as self-employed with the tax office (ww.hmrc.gov.uk). See if your house insurance will cover you as a self-employed person working from home, otherwise you may need to upgrade. Business link.gov.uk provides a handy tool for working out what kinds of insurance you'll need.

To get started, you will need a dedicated work space with a phone, office stationery, internet access and computer – packed with all the usual software applications. Your first step to getting customers should be to sign up to a decent agency. Don't pay any agency and avoid anything that advertises 'get rich quick' offers. Your best bet is to sign up with an agency such as VOT (www.virtualassistantjobs.com). This doesn't charge you a penny to sign up and will offer your services to companies all over the world. The Society of Virtual Assistants (www.societyofvirtualassistants.co.uk) supports virtual assistants of all levels of experience and is completely free. You also must be prepared to generate leads one by one. It will sometimes be a case of getting out the Yellow Pages, calling all your friends and pulling out all the stops to find some decent clients. It's a good idea to list your business on a VA directory such as the one on Virtual Business Solutions (virtualbusinessstartups.com), which also offers a package to help develop your own VA business.

Useful Websites

- *The Alliance of UK Virtual Assistants – hints, tips and a localised bulletin board to promote your services (www.allianceofukvirtualassistants.org.uk/)*
- *The International Association of Virtual Assistants – largest group of virtual assistants in the UK (www.iava.org.uk/)*
- *VA4U.co.uk – an online agency for virtual assistants*
- *The Society of Virtual Assistants (www.societyofvirtualassistants.co.uk/)*

SIX MONEY-MAKING IDEAS FOR THE OVER-60S

You don't have to be in your golden age to do these money-makers but they are particularly good for more mature people.

1. Be a Doula: Sorry men – this one tends to be for women only. Basically, this involves using your experience as a mother (or grandmother) to help families with a new baby. You support the mum-to-be during her pregnancy and often after the birth too. Sign up to an agency like BritishDoulas.co.uk which will train you and place you with families. Doulas in Britain make, on average, about £10–£12 per hour for post-birth work and £200–£400 for a birth.

2. Tutoring: Whatever your skill, you can make money from it by tutoring people or groups and charging by the hour. Post an ad on Gumtree.com or advertise locally.

3. Ironing: Providing an ironing service could be the answer to your cash flow problems. Best of all, you can do it all from your own home and the set-up costs are minimal.

4. Join a Focus Group: Market research companies are always looking for people to join focus groups, where people sit round and respond to questions on their views and experience of a particular product or service. Most will only be asking you to work for an hour and the pay won't be much (probably £10–£20) but it may be quite interesting and could lead to more work. Here are some market research companies you may want to contact: Researchbox (www.researchbox.co.uk), Category Consulting (www.surveyshack.com), Focus4people (www.focus4people.com).

5. House-sitting: Older people are usually more in demand as house-sitters than younger people. This is because they tend to be seen as more trustworthy and have more experience running a home. They also have the flexibility to sit during holidays and weekends. This is a job that you can do as a couple, so it's a fantastic way to spend some time together and make a little extra money.

You can start by joining an agency like Homesitters (www.homesitters.co.uk), who will match you up to suitable clients. Working with an agency may be the best option if you're a little nervous about house-sitting for a stranger. They will often arrange a meeting between client and sitter to make sure you know exactly what is expected of you. They should also have insurance to cover you should anything go wrong.

6. Dog-walking: If you love the companionship of dogs but don't want the responsibility of owning and looking after one full-time, dog-walking could be the perfect way for you to earn some extra money. Register yourself with a dog-walking company like Nards (www.nards.co.uk), or keep it simple and look after the pets of people you already know. Expect to make around £6–£10 per walk. You could also take it a step further and actually look after an animal in your own home while the owners are away. Join a company like Barking Mad as a 'host family' (www.barkingmad.uk.com).

Making Money from Your Computer

I'm going to begin with some of the easiest ways to make money from your computer, moving on to increasingly sophisticated methods. There will be something for everyone who owns a computer.

BEFORE YOU BEGIN: TOP TIPS

Get a New Email Address: It is a good idea to get yourself a new email address just for your online ventures. It's common to get a lot of junk mail with some of the things you sign up for, so a different email address lets you keep your personal mail separate.

Click on the Link: When you first register with a new site, most of them will send you an email to confirm your details. This is their way of ensuring you are not signing up with someone else's email. All you have to do is click on the link highlighted in blue in the email and you will be taken to a page from the website that will thank you for registering and accept your email into their system. Then you are ready to begin using the service.

Record Your Password and Login: On some sites you just need to enter your email address as a login, while others offer a separate login. Either way, you need to keep a note of them so that you can log in quickly. The best way to do it is to create a word file listing the survey website, your user name and password. Keep this file on your desktop so it's nice and easy to find.

ONLINE SURVEYS

Skill level: Easy

If you're stuck at home and you like surfing the net of an evening, or you have some free time in your lunch break, why not fill in a few surveys and make some cash while you're at it? You can make regular pocket money and you have the possibility of winning cash prizes every now and then.

BEWARE!

There are a lot of sharks in the business and you have to be careful what you sign up for. Some even have the cheek to try to get you to pay to join – ignore these companies. As a rule of thumb, the more lucrative or tempting it sounds, the more likely it is to be a waste of time.

You can sign up to as many survey companies as you wish (I've listed a few below). Once you get an idea of how each company works – how often they send you emails, how much you make from them or even how visually easy they are to complete – it is a good idea to focus on one or two companies that appeal to you. Survey companies are after a 'sample group', which means they look for a particular number of people within a specific age range or area, or who use a certain product. This means you will get sent surveys that you cannot complete because you don't fit the required profile. It's also called being 'screened out'.

One of our readers on Moneymagpie.com says that although doing surveys can't replace a full-time income, they can certainly add a small but steady amount of extra cash, particularly if you fit the right demographics. She earns about £50 a month plus a regular supply of products to test. Another reader has made £150–£200 in four years of doing surveys and enjoys Ciao the most (see opposite). With most companies you begin by earning points which can then be converted into cash or vouchers for some of the major high street retailers.

Most surveys are sent to you via email at random times. Some will close by a specified date or when enough people have taken part so get your skates on or you'll miss out! Surveys can take anywhere from 10 to 45 minutes to complete. When you receive the email it will tell you roughly how long the survey will take and give you a link to a new window where the survey will begin.

Below are my favourite survey sites:

Panelbase (www.panelbase.net)

Panelbase will talk you through the whole process. It has turned many survey drawbacks into a positive experience for its users. For example, all respondents who are screened out of a survey are put into a monthly prize draw to win £50 cash. Each survey pays between 50p and £3. Some surveys include entry into special prize draws where you could win a box of wine or a flashy new widescreen television.

Toluna (www.toluna.com)

With Toluna you can earn between 1,000 and 20,000 points for each survey, depending on its length, and these are sent to your inbox. You earn a bonus 2,000 points to complete your profile, which will tell the company what surveys will suit you. You need 60,000 points to convert to the lowest £10 voucher from places like Amazon (www.amazon.co.uk).

Lightspeed Panel (http://uk.lightspeedpanel.com)
You can earn between 50 and 150 points for each Lightspeed survey and these are sent to your inbox. You need a minimum of 1,100 points to convert your points into vouchers. Completing mini polls on the website enters you into cash prize draws of up to £2000.

Valued Opinions (www.valuedopinions.co.uk)
You can earn between £1 and £5 to complete surveys that are sent to your inbox. You can also earn up to £50 for specialist surveys. Once your account reaches £10 you can redeem your points for vouchers or you can choose to donate your rewards to charities like the World Wildlife Fund and World Vision.

My Survey (www.mysurvey.co.uk)
Surveys are sent to your inbox, and you must have at least 1,000 points to be rewarded with vouchers. Your points can also be converted into Nectar points if you have a Nectar card.

Ciao for Surveys (www.ciao-surveys.co.uk)
When you fill in the profiles it gives Ciao enough information to select you for more surveys, which are then sent to your inbox. Each survey you get will tell you how much it is worth, and once you've reached £5 or more you can request a payout into your bank account.

Ciao for Product Reviews (www.ciao.co.uk)
You write reviews for Ciao and earn money when people read them. Different reviews are given different rates of pay. The rate for each review changes monthly because of how Ciao is financed. Reviews are worth 0.5p per rating, 1p per rating or 2p per rating and you earn more if you write a first review of a product or very high-quality reviews. You can invite friends to join and earn a commission equal to 50 per cent of your friend's earnings for the first six months of their membership. Once you've reached £5 or more you can request a payout into your bank account.

MAKE MONEY SURFING THE NET AND READING EMAILS

Skill level: Easy
If you spend a few hours a night surfing the internet it is worthwhile signing up for some sites that will pay you for what you are already doing. The following websites will let you earn a percentage of the advertising revenue just for using them. The way it works is this: the website gets paid to advertise; you get paid to read the advertisement; you tell your friends you get paid so they sign up; the more people who sign up increases the popularity of the website, and the advertisers will pay more for a larger audience.

Win Prizes for Searching the Internet
Winzy (www.winzy.com)
Instead of using Google to search the net, use Winzy – they give prizes for searching with them. Each time you use the search engine you collect points or have the chance to win

instant prizes. With all the points you collect, you go into a monthly draw to win big prizes, so the more points you have, the more chances you have to win.

Register with Winzy and you're ready to begin. Make Winzy your homepage, and download the Winzy toolbar to search with. You can also increase your chances of winning by inviting your friends. You can earn 250 bonus points for each new friend who joins, and you will be automatically entered into the iPod giveaway sweepstakes. Prizes include iPod Nanos and Shuffles, cash and Amazon gift cards, but you've got to be in it to win it!

Get Paid to Surf the Net

Moneymagpiesearch (www.moneymagpiesearch.com)

Moneymagpiesearch.com is a search engine (powered by Myhomepagesfriends) which operates on the same concept to Winzy (see above), except you get paid in cash. You need to go to the homepage and register. You can then download the search toolbar and make it your homepage, so you can start surfing more profitably.

You get paid 50 per cent of the revenue that Myhomepagesfriends makes. Searches are paid about 1p per search. The idea is to search as you normally would (note, though, that unusually high volumes of 'search fraud', such as repetitive searches or searching for known websites, will not count). You need to use the search engine with the intention of using the results you are asking for.

Calculate how much you can make: There is even a fun calculator that gives you an example of how much you can earn for yourself, and how your friends can earn more for you.

One of Moneymagpie.com's readers has been searching with this facility for three months and has so far been paid £27.

Get Paid to Read Emails

HTMail (www.htmail.com/meminf.html)

HTMail sends you emails from their advertisers. When you click on a link in the email you are taken to a feedback page and then forwarded to the advertiser's homepage. Good feedback helps ensure advertisers benefit from HTMail's service. When you complete the short form and send it back your account is credited.

HTMail is currently one of the highest-paying sites for marketing emails. You get 5p for each email you give feedback on, 3p for direct referrals (when you refer a friend) and 1p for indirect referrals (when your friends refer their friends). Typical earnings are £1–£3 per month. HTMail pays out every three months once you have a minimum balance of £15 if you wish to receive a cheque, or £10 if you wish to be paid by PayPal.

You can receive 3p for every item of postal mail you refer to, but if you can't stand junk mail coming through your door it's a good idea to opt out of receiving mail when you register.

Get Shares for Receiving Emails

SendMoreInfo (www.sendmoreinfo.com)

When you register with SendMoreInfo, every time you receive an email that you open, read and click on, you are credited with one share. At the end of the month those shares are converted into cash. The share value changes monthly and is determined by the amount of ad revenue the site receives. They are quick to get you started, sending emails within 24 hours of you signing up!

The catch with this one is that it is in American dollars and it comes to you as a cheque. However, you can put your money on to a prepaid card in American dollars and then simply either save it for travelling or take it all out at a UK cash machine. This means you only get charged a 2.75 per cent exchange rate and no fees. For details, see the section on prepaid travel cards on Moneymagpie.com.

Get Paid to Social Network

Yuwie (www.yuwie.com)

Yuwie is the first social networking site that aims to share its profits with users. Social networking is a space on the internet where you and your friends get together and share your photos and videos. You can email each other and set up a profile page about yourself, and an online diary where you can write about your day or the things that interest you. Best of all, Yuwie will pay you!

To make good amounts of money, you need to have friends who will join and refer their friends, who will then refer their friends and so on. When you sign up, a lot of people on the site are keen to become your 'friend' for the sake of referral money, which is a good start. You also need to be an active social networker. This means that you spend at least two hours a night on the site looking at other people's pages or uploading your own new information.

The potential to earn thousands of pounds exists if you stay chained to your computer day and night referring new friends, but the reality is that you may only make a few pennies or $5 a month if you're lucky. You can get paid by PayPal or by cheque. As with SendMoreInfo, you can convert the American dollars on to a prepaid credit card (see above).

MAKE MONEY BY ANSWERING QUESTIONS

Skill level: Medium to difficult

The UK has a range of text-answering services that are constantly looking for more researchers to answer the thousands of questions they receive per day. Customers can text a question 24/7 from anywhere in the world and can ask absolutely anything – fun or serious, or just challenging.

If you're willing to spend the time on being a researcher, you can make a lot of money. These services receive on average 20,000 questions a day. You can work from wherever you want, and you get paid for each question you answer. Some people do it as a full-time job, while there are many who just log on when they can to earn a bit of money. Students, mums and retired people benefit strongly from the flexibility of the job.

You need to be fluent in English, with excellent writing skills. You must be able to use your own knowledge and internet skills to help you come up with great answers for the multitude of questions customers are going to ask. You will be working on a self-employed basis, conducting research from home at times that suit you – all you need is your own computer with a broadband internet connection. Other resources such as reference books or magazines on various topics can also be helpful.

The three main text-answering services in the UK are AQA (Any Question Answered) 63336 (www.63336.com), ANSA 87199 (www.ansanow.com), and Texperts 66000 (www.texperts.com). On average, about one in ten applications are accepted by the companies, usually after an aptitude test. With AQA, you make 30p per question you answer. ANSA pays 10p per answer and a further 5p for each time your answer is used. Texperts pay 30p per answer. The amount you make depends on the time you spend answering questions but about £10 an hour is average. Dedicated researchers tapping out answers on a full-time basis can pull in up to around £25,000 a year. You are paid directly into your account, on time, at the end of each month.

SELL YOUR PHOTOS

Skill level: Medium to difficult

If you have an eye and a passion for photography you can submit your best digital photos to online agencies and sit back as the money comes in. Stock libraries look for photos that cover many different subjects, ideas, cultures and issues, and will provide lists of what they are looking for. Each website also has a release form for you to download if you need it. In theory, you need to get every person who is recognisable in your photos to sign a release form saying you can sell the image. It can be a little tricky, but it's good practice. If you're not sure what to write, get a free 'Sellers' Pack' from Picture Nation (www.picturenation.co.uk) for an example.

There is nothing stopping you from registering with more than one company. Most sites need photos to be RGB JPEG saved at a high setting (such as Photoshop level 10) and they must be uncompressed file sizes. The higher the image resolution, the higher the ceiling price for your images.

These are four top stock photo sites:

- *Picturenation (www.picturenation.co.uk)*
- *Fotolia (www.fotolia.co.uk)*
- *iStockphoto (www.istockphoto.co.uk)*
- *123RF (www.123rf.co.uk)*

When you register your details the sites will ask you to send between five and ten photos so it can test their quality and type. If your photos don't conform to the site's requirements, they will be rejected. That's fine; just try again, taking their comments into consideration. Sometimes they may already have too many of the type of photo you are sending.

One of Picturenation's newest photographers made £390 in commission in his first five weeks, and it has several members who are earning hundreds of pounds a month. Of course, it depends on the quality and saleability of your photographs. The websites also sell the photos on your behalf at different resolutions, which means different pay structures.

MAKE MONEY BY LISTENING TO MUSIC

Skill level: Difficult

For all music enthusiasts, making money while listening to a couple of tunes sounds too good to be true, but a site called Slicethepie (www.slicethepie.com) helps you do exactly that. Once you have registered, the scouting room is where all the reviewing takes place. Bands upload their tracks into the room and then Slicethepie selects them at random for you to listen to. All the tracks are anonymous until you've reviewed them, which means you can't be picky about what you review or favour a particular band.

You get to listen to a track and after 60 seconds you can start writing your review. Once you've listened to the sound clip as many times as you want, you have to rate it from 1–10 and then submit your review in order to start another one. The tricky bit is how to get the maximum amount of money for your review. Rather than a flat rate, Slicethepie pays you depending on your star rating, which in turn depends on the quality of your reviews. The maximum rate you can get is 25p per review.

If you're a bit more daring and think you might try your hand at a bit of market trading, Slicethepie encourages you to stick with the bands you like, to help finance the recording of their album by investing in them, and then eventually take away a proportion of the profits made from their album.

SELL YOUR VIDEOS

Skill level: Difficult

The immensely popular YouTube site allows users to upload and view videos for free. Now, however, people with popular videos should be able to make some money from similar sites that will pay a share of the revenue they get from advertising.

The first step is to find the site (described overleaf) that best matches your talents:

- *If you can make a really entertaining video, see Revver*
- *If you have original videos for people to watch, see Spymac*
- *If you can make good video reviews of hotels, see Tripr.tv*
- *If you can make videos that are funny and inspiring, see Metacafe*

Making and uploading a video is easy-peasy. All you need is a camera that you can take a video with. It doesn't have to be professional quality, but you'll be likely to get more views if the quality is decent (not blurry or obstructed). You need to get the footage from your camcorder on to your computer. From the video file you can do some rough editing if needed, and then upload the footage straight to the internet for all to see.

Revver (www.revver.com)

At Revver you can share your videos for free and get rewarded for doing it. It helps by connecting the videos you upload with targeted advertisements, so the people who view your videos are more likely to click on the ads. Revver then splits the ad revenue with you 50/50. In the last 12 months Revver has paid $1 million to more than 25,000 people, according to *USA Today*. The biggest pay cheque – $50,000 for 15 clips – went to two guys from Maine who inserted a Mentos mint into a bottle of Diet Coke and watched it explode. You can track your video's performance through your Revver account, and when the amount hits $20 you will be paid into a Paypal account 30 days after the end of the current month.

Spymac (www.spymac.com)

Spymac is a bit tacky, described by bloggers as an 'online *American Idol* without the Simon Cowell' but it has more than a million users and has given away more than $1 million. Users are encouraged to focus on uploading a few really good-quality original videos rather than lots of average ones. Spymac pays out internationally with a minimum of

$25 (however, there is a $5 fee to cover costs unless you are withdrawing more than $50 – a good base to aim for). You can upload videos, pictures and audio for people to rate, and users make 50 per cent of the profits.

Tripr.tv (www.tripr.tv)

Tripr.tv is best for hotel reviews. It's so easy – stay in a hotel and make a video review including important information and pictures of the hotel and surrounds. You can then publish your video review and, when the video results in a booking from a customer, you receive a fee. Tripr.tv makes its money getting commission from online travel agents, which it then shares with the users who upload their video.

A normal hotel booking costs around €400. The average commission Tripr receives is 7–10 per cent, of which the film-maker gets a third. If that was the case, you would receive €9.32 per booking placed through your video. You are then paid 30 days after the end of the month.

Metacafe (www.metacafe.com)

Attracting 25 million unique viewers a month, Metacafe is about entertaining large audiences with videos that amaze, inspire and make viewers laugh. You won't get just any old clips on this site; featured clips are good quality and it's easy to find interesting ones to watch and enjoy. There are no full-length television episodes or movies chopped into pieces. Copyright is strict and your video must be suitable for a mainstream audience.

You are paid $5 for every 1,000 views your video gets. Payment starts after your video reaches 20,000 views and has a rating of 3.0 or higher. The minimum payout is $100. You can get paid into a US bank account, through Paypal or via a Metacafe prepaid MasterCard.

SET UP A BLOG

Skill level: Intermediate

A blog, which is short for 'web log', is a type of online diary or opinion website or web page. All you need to start blogging is a blog address and something to say. Don't worry if you're a first-time blogger: setting one up is quick, easy and free. There are a few free blog-hosting services that provide a template, web address and rich text editors so you'll be up and running in no time. One of the easiest services is Blogger (www.blogger.com). This requires no technical expertise at all and provides simple steps to help you create your blog. You might also like to try Wordpress (www.wordpress.org) and Typepad (www.typepad.com).

What you write in your blog is entirely up to you. You can even make money out of problems that you have had. Perhaps you have just been made bankrupt and you are about to lose your house? Writing about the day-to-day reality of it can be helpful to you and to others who are going through the same thing or think they may be facing it soon. Or maybe you have a specialism – or even just a special interest in something – that you can write about on a regular basis. If you are knowledgeable and enthusiastic then over time your enthusiasm and knowledge will attract readers.

If you're interested in getting other people to read your blog (not everyone is) then make sure you let your friends know about it and get them to tell their friends too. You can also publish it on blog directories such as Technorati (www.technorati.com), so that people who are interested in reading blogs generally can find it. The more people who read your blog, the more are likely to click on the ads and make you some money (see below).

Once you have set up your blog, sign up to a service like Google Adsense (www.google.com/adsense) or Yahoo! Publisher Network (www.publisher.yahoo.com) that use search technology to target your site with relevant advertising. The way it works is that any time someone comes to your blog and clicks one or more of the ads, you get a share of the ad revenue.

The amount you can make very much depends on how much 'traffic' you are getting on your blog and how keen people are to click on the ads. Quite often the more informative your site is, the more people will click on relevant ads. These ads are unlikely to make you rich – you have to have a *lot* of clicks before you can make anything like sensible money – but they're a start and they don't cost you anything to be there.

There's nothing to stop you selling things via your blog too. Ramit Sethi, who writes a blog called Iwillteachyoutoberich.com, sells his own services as a speaker via his blog (and a very good blog it is too, I think). Another blog called Chromasia.com sells great photos.

There are various things you could sell or advertise on your blog. For example, you could set up a premium-rate helpline for people to call if they have problems that you could help with, thanks to your experiences. You could also set up an affiliate link with Amazon (affiliate-program.amazon.co.uk) and sell books that you recommend on your blog through them. There are also Text Link Ads (www.text-link-ads.com), which will put paid links behind key words in your text so that if a reader clicks on it you get a few pence, just like Google Adwords. Be careful with this option, though, because too many of these links can be annoying for your readers.

If you run your blog as a business you could set up an occasional newsletter that your readers can subscribe to. There are lots of services to help you send them out easily, including AWeber (www.aweber.com), Constant Contact (www.constantcontact.com) and iContact (www.icontact.com).

BIG-MONEY BLOGS

Belle de Jour (www.belledejour-uk.blogspot.com) is one of the most famous British examples of a blog making the writer wads of money. In 2003, the *Guardian* named it Blog of the Year. It was subsequently turned into two books: *The Intimate Adventures of a London Call Girl* (2005) and *Playing the Game* (2008), and a television series.

For other examples of books based on blogs, check out the 'Blooker Prize' (www.blookerprize.com). If you did really well with your blog, produced a book and won this prize, you could be up for a nice amount of prize money. The winner in each category (fiction, non-fiction and webcomic) gets $2,500, and the overall winner gets $7,500.

Making the Most of a Downturn

When money is tight, everyone is looking for cheap ways to get things done. If you can offer services locally at a much cheaper rate than proper businesses, you could get even more work than before:

- *Find out how much window cleaning companies in your area charge and offer your services for 20 per cent less.*
- *If you're at home looking after your children, register as a childminder. Many families who used to employ nannies or a private nursery will be looking for cheaper options now and there should be more of a demand for childminding.*
- *If you're a cleaner and you're worried about being dropped because of cost-cutting, offer extra services such as cooking and filling the freezer for your clients.*
- *If you have secretarial skills, offer your services to businesses around the world as a virtual assistant (see page 320). Learn book-keeping as well and you will have many more work opportunities.*

Here are a few more ideas:

- *Babysitting, especially if you're already looking after your own children.*
- *Home-tutoring – maths, science and English are particularly in demand. You will need a Criminal Records Bureau (CRB) check if you will be working with children under 18.*
- *Book-keeping.*
- *CV writing/consultation.*
- *Videoing/photographing weddings and other events.*

Earn Money While You Sleep

From a Money Magpie point of view, being truly 'rich' is about having quality of life. This means having quality free time, not just large quantities of money. That's why it's a good idea to consider setting up some passive income streams as part of your overall money plan. As the name suggests, a passive income stream is a business or other activity which, after an initial input of time, effort and carefully selected investment, will bring in an ongoing stream of income without you having to do very much.

INCOME FROM YOUR OWN WEBSITE

There are lots of ways of making money from websites (and lots of ways of losing it that way!) You could set up a site specifically to sell things (maybe hampers or children's toys or specialist books). Or you could set up an information website that people come to for help and you would make money from advertising and, perhaps, selling your services through it.

One way to make money from a website without having to put up much money at the start is to create a 'free guide' which you use to promote a website that carries useful information. You can use the guide to offer titbits of information and then offer the full story at a cost, or offer the full story for free and organise for adverts to appear alongside that will earn you money. This is a very simplistic description of a sophisticated business but, if you are determined, you can learn the process through testing and persistence.

Here are the basic steps:

1. Create a simple website using free Wordpress software on a cheap web hosting company such as Powweb (around $5 a month). Powweb will install Wordpress on your website for free. If you need more help they'll give you that too – for a price.
2. Populate the website with extremely valuable, insightful information about a skill that you have and enjoy finding out about – for example, gardening, match box collecting, throat singing or whatever you are passionate or knowledgeable about.
3. When you have between 20 and 40 pages of useful content insert Google Adwords on the site (http://adwords.google.com).
4. Produce a free guide (as a downloadable ebook, for example) of the top 10 tips you have learned in your given area of expertise and include the website name in the title of the guide. For example, 'The www.moneymagpie's-gardening-tips.com 10 must-have rules for growing your own vegetables'. For each step create an affiliate link in which you recommend a good product directly related to that step. This could be a book or a relevant tool (such as a particular trowel for gardening if that's your skill).

WHAT IS AN AFFILIATE LINK?

An affiliate is, in simple terms, a website that promotes a product. For example, www.good-gardening-tips.com might recommend the Greenstuff Trowel, giving a link to where a user can buy that trowel. If a user does look at www.good-gardening-tips.com, click on the trowel link and buy the trowel then the company selling the Greenstuff Trowel will pay www.good-gardening-tips.com a small commission fee.

There are affiliate links for pretty much every product you can think of. If you want to put affiliate links on your site then the best place to start is with affiliate networks – organisations that gather lots of companies selling all sorts of products online. You can join them for free and get relevant links for your site. Try www.buy.at, www.clickbank.com and www.omg.com.

5. Now you have to put the word out that your guide exists. Offer your 'free guide' to every relevant organisation you can think of. Join every relevant social website forum (such as Facebook) and blog in which you can offer *genuinely useful* advice. In your sign-off at the bottom of each post you make *do not* say 'find out more at my website' as that will get you banned from pretty much everywhere. Instead, just put your name and URL.
6. Keep on promoting your website. Get yourself in the local newspaper (perhaps starting with letters and then offering to contribute a column). Get on to local radio with the same purpose in mind. You might want to test spending

money on Google Adwords but this should be handled with great care as it can become extremely expensive extremely quickly. The premise of Google Adwords is that you pay when someone clicks through from Google from a set of words that you nominate.

7. At any stage in the process you can include products to sell on the website. For example, you could stock a manual on specifics such as 'how to grow vegetables indoors', 'how to make best use of a greenhouse' or 'how to make money from growing your own vegetables'. Alternatively, you could give a seminar talking about these ideas, have it recorded and then sell the full seminar as either a video or audio download or get it transcribed and sell it as a book. Install PayPal to take care of payments automatically. If you're not sure how to do this then do a quick search on Google, Yahoo or any other search engine asking for help – the answers are on the internet; you just have to look for them.

These steps are just a guide to making a passive income stream using the internet. They are not the only way to do it. Online marketing is a massive and constantly changing world. So be prepared to study online marketing and to apply what you learn to what you want to sell. As with everything else, nothing can beat a good helping of common sense applied to your own personal circumstances.

ONLINE COURSES

Online courses are another way of selling information on the web. Instead of packaging all your wit and wisdom in one ebook, some people reason that it makes more sense to divide each 'chapter' into a separate lesson and sell each one as an email or ebook, perhaps offering your customer a discount if they pay for the whole lot at once. There is more work involved in selling an online course than selling a single ebook, but the potential income is bigger too.

You could look into developing your own subscription site, although this is not simple or quick to do. You have to have some genuinely valuable information that is updated and embellished on a regular basis. It has to be proven and, ideally, from personal experience. Internet marketing constitutes a whole area of study in itself, but marketing gurus who have produced good materials include Dan Kennedy (www.dankennedy.com) and Yanik Silver (www.surefiremarketing.com).

NETWORK MARKETING

If you have a flair for selling, have lots of friends and enjoy meeting new people then network marketing may be for you.

Network marketing, which is also known as 'multi-level marketing' (MLM), first began in the USA. It is based on the simple concept that almost all of us are part of networks, whether it be our extended family, our friends, our work colleagues, our church or mosque, our book club. You may well be part of more than one network, and the chances are that every single person in each of your networks is part of a whole lot of networks too.

One of the earliest forms of network marketing involved just one person setting themselves up as distributor for items such as cosmetics or Tupperware. They would sell them to friends by hosting get-togethers, either in their own homes or by being invited to other friends' homes to hold parties there. These product parties are still going strong today (see page 318). Most of us are likely to consider paying for a product or service when it is recommended to us by someone we know and like. With this in mind, companies like Amway and Tiscali have been selling their wares through MLMs for some years.

The beauty of the MLM concept (when legitimate and operated through a reputable company with a good product range) is that it's based on mutual success. You sell the product and find other people who would also like to make extra money selling it. You are given incentives to help them succeed in the form of bonuses for the total sales revenue generated by your group of people – your network. So the people helping you have the incentive to ensure you make as much money as possible as well. This can keep going indefinitely so that after two to five years, *if* you have dedicated yourself to this business, you have a chance of being at the top of a network of people selling the product – a passive income stream. Take note of the 'two to five years' point though. Any promises of success within two years are probably bogus. And, in case you hadn't already decided this for yourself, this isn't for everyone!

BEWARE THE CURSE OF THE PYRAMID

Multi-level marketing can be controversial. This is because many people find it difficult to distinguish between a legitimate MLM and a purely fraudulent scheme known as 'pyramid selling'. Many people think they know what a pyramid scheme is ... until you ask them to define one! The best way to find out if you are looking at an MLM system or a pyramid scheme is to contact the Direct Marketing Association (www.the-dma.org). If they have not heard of the scheme then run a mile. Things that often give them away are wild claims that are too good to be true and carefully worded suggestions that you should recruit your friends in return for money. Keep away!

A genuine MLM system is essentially a small business. It requires a certain amount of investment up front – from a couple of hundred pounds upwards. There ought to be a training and support structure in place and a genuinely useful or desirable product or service being offered.

The final and critical ingredient for success is determination. You will need to work hard and be prepared to sell the concept and the product to other people. If you are offered an opportunity to join an MLM that denies that hard work and sacrifice are required then chances are it is not MLM but *fraud*. So if you are ambitious, determined and enjoy selling you might just be able to join the select group of people who have made a success of their MLM businesses.

- Get selling or renting anything you don't want any more.
- Think 'outside the box' if you need to make extra cash in hard times. There are always ways of getting through the tough times.
- Start thinking about something you could set up as a passive income stream.
- Don't rush into anything – start by thoroughly researching any ideas that look interesting to you.

conclusion

Bringing it All Together

Phew – you've nearly made it to the end of the book! What a lot of stuff you've learnt (I hope), and started to put into action. In this chapter, I thought I'd include a few helpful hints and some tools to keep your good work going year after year. There is also info about the Moneymagpie.com message boards, where you can chat with others about your progress and see how they're going. There's plenty of support and bags of ideas there if you need them. In this final section you will find out:

- *How to get good money habits (see opposite).*
- *How to get support from family and friends (page 354).*
- *Basic tips for keeping a balanced outlook (page 356).*

Let's take a step back and remember why you bought – or were given – this book. Maybe you were deep in debt and looking for a way out; or perhaps you were living way beyond your means and needed a reality check. Did you want quick suggestions for making money? Whatever the reason, once you've learnt new ways of living, spending and saving, make sure you don't go back to the old ones. Here are some ways you can keep the new habits fresh.

The Secret of Good Money Habits

One of the simplest ways to make a real change in your finances – and to teach your children positive ideas about money too – is to make good money management a habit. That's not to say you need to be constantly stressing about your incomings and outgoings but, now that you know the basics (and if you don't, get back to Chapter 1 and start reading again!), you can adopt them on a daily basis.

If you find it tough, why don't you imagine a little version of me sitting on your shoulder when you're heading down to the pub or to the shops? Imagine me saying, 'Why bother spending £100 tonight, when a couple of Saturday nights saving half of it will get you a great trip or that iPod you had your eye on? Or even better, pay off that £400 Sat Nav you bought on your credit card, which is costing you more than £600 as the interest adds up.' Or I could be saying, 'If you wait till next week, could you get that suit with 20 per cent off in a sale?' Or, 'Could you make a bit of extra money for your family by using your computer, DIY or baking skills?' Don't imagine it too much though. After a few days you will want to slap me down!

Get wise though. As you know, the shops are pretty crafty when it comes to getting you in to buy things you could probably do without. You need to keep an eye on that, especially if shopping is your weakness or 'comfort blanket'. It's fine to spend money in the shops, but it should be money that you have left over after you've paid off your debts and started saving for your other goals in life (such as a new car, a house or children).

Spending won't make you feel fulfilled and happy with your lot. Take a 2008 study by Selftrade – a company that sells SIPPs. It asked 2,000 British people over the age of 40 to think about the goals they set for themselves in their teens and twenties and then compare them with what they'd actually achieved. For more than four in ten (43 per cent), life hadn't turned out the way they hoped. More than 70 per cent of people surveyed simply wanted a life of health, happiness and financial stability, yet fewer than half of them (44 per cent) had achieved it. Makes you think, doesn't it?

A HOME TRUTH

The only person who's going to get you the life you want is you – one step at a time. You won't get it sitting on your hands.

10 STRAIGHTFORWARD GOOD MONEY HABITS

Here are 10 good money habits you can dip into throughout the year. You might like to jot them down on a calendar or on the fridge.

Weekly

1. Check your bank accounts and credit cards online, particularly if you make a lot of transactions. Checking

your statements regularly will help protect you from fraud because you'll see early on if someone is using your identity or your card. It can also mean that you can stop yourself going overdrawn and being charged through the nose for it!

2. Make a mental tally of how much you've spent this week (or have a look at your spending diary).
3. Cut out things you don't need and limit treats to once or twice a week. Treats don't have to cost money either; there are lots of fun things you can do for free.

Monthly

4. File your pay-slips, bills, statements and any information sent to you about tax or investments.
5. Keep a spending diary.

Twice a Year

6. Check the interest rates on your savings accounts. Are they as competitive as when you first opened them? If not, switch to better ones.

Annually

7. Check your major household bills and look for cheaper versions on comparison sites.
8. Shop around for a cheaper mortgage rather than taking the first offer you come across.
9. Go to a comparison site to find cheaper insurance (via Moneymagpie.com for a good one).
10. Find a better deal for your phone and internet. With such huge leaps in technology, there are a number of ways

you can now talk for free – including a video link over the internet. Check them out.

See Moneymagpie.com for other tips for cutting costs all round.

TIPS TO KEEP YOURSELF ON TRACK

- **Keep your goals in mind.** *If necessary, write them on a piece of paper and take them around with you. Start training yourself to think about the bigger picture and focus on the long-term rewards rather than being swayed by immediate potential purchases.*
- **Get into the fun of beating retailers at their own game.** *So, they want you to spend do they? Well, you can see how much better you are at not spending! Don't be mugged by them. Be your own person.*
- **Get into a habit of asking yourself whether you really *need* something or if you just *want* it.**
- **Give yourself the odd treat here and there.** *Controlling your money is about balance. You don't have to deny yourself everything and it's a good idea to have a treat every now and then. If possible, see if you can get that treat for free (like having a meal out for free through mystery shopping).*

Getting Support from Friends and Family

Sticking to your new habits will be a lot easier if you have lots of support from family and friends. There's nothing worse than having someone always on at you at home about buying non-branded alternatives; or friends who earn a lot insisting you split the bill at dinner when you're scrimping and they're having three courses and several bottles of wine.

Have a quick chat (one-to-one) with the people you think you'll struggle with and ask for their support. Explain what you're working towards (for instance, to pay off a very large debt), and say that it won't be possible if you don't cut back on groceries, drinking and so on. Ask explicitly for them to help by giving supportive comments, asking how you're doing and helping you celebrate milestones.

Your children can also help out in practical ways. When visiting the supermarket, for example, they can tally up your shopping for you and look for the best prices. Try these ideas once you've got there:

- *What fruit can we get this week for the best price?*
- *Can you collect all the ingredients from this list for less than £10 so that we have enough left over to get the ingredients to make biscuits at home?*

And for older children:

- *What healthy, good-value alternatives can we get for this bargain pizza?*
- *If I have £10 to spend on the family each night for dinner, what are some healthy options and what ingredients would you need for each?*

There are plenty of opportunities around the home for children and young people to help out too. What about keeping their rooms tidy for a little bit of pocket money, so mum or dad can have a couple of hours each week extra to maintain a budget?

If everyone has to cut back to afford things like family holidays, you might like to give your teenager the opportunity to manage their own clothing budget. You could agree to give them a set amount, say £150–200, for the year to spend on clothes (not including school uniform) and let them find the best deals. The key here is to make it 100 per cent clear that you will not be giving them extra money if they spend it all in the first few months. If you think there's really a chance they'll do that, you might like to give it to them in instalments. It could help them to realise the importance of valuing the money in their hands.

Spending time with positive people (especially when you're feeling a bit low about your progress) will really help. Just keep an eye on who you choose. If you know that you always spend a lot when you go to the pub or the shops with a particular friend, then suggest somewhere else to go with them – such as to the park, to see a free exhibition or to listen to some free music.

How to Keep a Healthy Outlook

THINK OF OTHERS

Give some serious thought to the people around you who are worse off. One of my Money Magpies had a birthday recently and the present that moved him the most was £30 given to a charity that supports children in the Philippines

TIPS FOR KEEPING IT REAL

- Need less. Spend less. Enjoy a simple life.
- Appreciate what you can get for free. Use what's around – sunshine, healthcare, free shows, free offers, a good night's sleep and so on.
- Acknowledge and be grateful for what you have – however little you might think it is to start with.
- Be generous with your time and your money. Life really is poorer if you try to grab everything for yourself.
- Work and invest for the future but remind yourself to live in the 'now'. Decide to be happy, whatever your circumstances.

who live – yes, live – on rubbish dumps. We tend to rate our level of happiness and wealth by comparing ourselves to others, so it's important to acknowledge what you have, and not listen to the constant chatter from society that you're not rich enough, tall enough, smart enough, beautiful enough … (you get the idea).

Volunteering with people whose lives are much more difficult than yours will help you appreciate things like your ability to go to work each day and earn a living, the roof over your head and the food on your table. There is also a high correlation between people who do voluntary work and those who are generally happier in life.

There's no objective measure of richness – it's entirely up to us whether we feel rich, poor or just about okay. It takes work to get some perspective on your situation and look ahead to the next steps. If you want to be richer, embrace the habit of gratitude; be thankful for the little things. Sounds very clichéd I know, but the more gratitude you actually feel, the 'richer' you will be.

I remember, a while ago, hearing that crooner Neil Sedaka talking about his song 'I miss the hungry years'. He said it was based on his own feelings about missing the tough times – the times when you look ahead and work towards something. Those times may seem tough while you're going through them but, looking back, you can often see that they were fun, exciting and genuinely happy. There is a level of money that we need to cover the basics, but other than that having money doesn't make you happy. Believe it or not – like Neil says – working hard for little bits of cash, particularly if you do it with someone else, can actually make you happy. Having loads of money can make you unhappy as you lose your reason for going on – everything is easy so nothing has value or interest.

> If (when) you have money, make sure that you use it well. Do good with it, invest it in others, give it away (wisely). Money is like manure – it needs to be spread around to do good things and to help others grow. If it is piled up it just sits there in a stinking, pointless mess. If you're going to give it away, do it thoughtfully, particularly when it comes to giving to your children.

Quiz: How Are Things Now?

In Chapter 1, there was a quiz to help you find out what sort of 'money type' you are (see page 8). Now, having read the book and, I hope, learnt something, how do you feel about money? I have kept in some of the original questions and added some new ones.

1. How would you describe your feelings about your money situation right now?
a. I feel a bit better but I'm still worried.
b. A lot more hopeful, almost excited!
c. Ready for more action.

2. Do you now have a financial plan?
a. Nearly … well no, but I now know that I should.
b. Yes, pretty much, although it's not quite finished.
c. Yes, and it's much clearer and more detailed now.

3. Are you feeling happier about numbers and how to deal with the basics of your own finances?
a. A bit. I still wish someone could come over to my house and go through it all with me though.
b. Yes, quite a bit. It's scary but I feel a lot more confident.
c. Oh yes. I really do think I'm the best at running my money. Who else cares as much as I do about achieving my goals?

4. What have you done with your bills and other expenses?
a. I've taken them out of the envelopes and looked at

them. Some of them are nasty but I've stopped some old direct debits so I'm already saving money!

b. I've filed them in some really nice, colourful files with labels on!

c. I've carried on filing them.

5. What about your debts? What's the situation now?

a. Still very much there but I've managed to pay a bit off because of some of the money I've saved.

b. On the way out – I just need to pay off the overdraft and I'll be in the black again. Have also started to make a bit of extra money.

c. I didn't have debts other than the mortgage.

6. Have you set up a savings account?

a. No, you said I had to get rid of my debts first (aargh!) I'm still trying to get my head around the idea that I can't have a savings account until I pay them off but I can see the point really. It's just a bit scary.

b. Yes, I'm about to set one up as soon as my overdraft is fully paid off. The first step is to save enough to cover myself for three months. It looks like a mammoth task but I've already saved loads using the tips in the book and I can see ways to make some extra cash.

c. Yes, I always have had but I'm earmarking one of them as my 'savings safety net'. Some of the other money I'll take out and put into long-term investments now. I feel more confident about my future plans.

7. Do you know what your monthly outgoings are?
a. Nearly. It's more than what I bring home each month, but I am going to do something about that.
b. Yes, and I'm bringing them down too. I've even been out getting great deals!
c. Yes, and they're now less than they were. I can't believe how much I wasted on coffees, lunches and take-aways!

8. Do you have any investments?
a. No. It'll take me a long time to get to that stage!
b. Not yet, other than the company pension. But I will be starting once I have the savings account sorted.
c. Oh yes, and I will be doing more as soon as I pay off my mortgage.

9. Have you found some good ways to make extra cash?
a. Yes – brilliant! I'll do some of those.
b. Yes, I have and I've already started some of them.
c. Yes, and I'm particularly interested in setting up passive streams of income. I love the idea of starting it now and then just sitting back.

10. Have you changed your home life at all?
a. Yes, I've stopped buying quite a few things that I didn't really need like bottled water.
b. Yes, I'm changing the way we live – no more wasting money on stupid things. We're going to save up for good holidays and nice big things.
c. No, I'm just a bit more focused.

11. How much money have you saved since reading this book?

a. It's got to be a few hundred.

b. Oh hundreds definitely, and I'm hoping to *make* more in the next few months.

c. By overpaying on my mortgage as well as the other savings I know I'll be saving thousands.

12. What do you think about the stock market?

a. Terrifying still, but maybe one day I'll be able to look at it.

b. Kind of interesting now. I'd like to invest for bigger money.

c. Even more interesting. I'm going to read up more about it.

13. Do you have any regrets?

a. I wish I'd known some of this stuff earlier.

b. I wish my parents had known this stuff then we would have had more money and I wouldn't have wasted so much for so long.

c. Yes, I wish I had invested earlier.

14. If you have, or want to have, children, what would you teach them about money?

a. Not to do what I did.

b. How to budget and live within their means.

c. How to budget and invest for the long term.

15. Do you have a five-year plan?
a. No, but I might do one day.
b. Sort of – at least a two-year one.
c. Yes, I'm looking at the long term and it includes plenty of things to make my life richer.

16. Have you been able to simplify your life since reading this book?
a. I did a car boot sale and made some cash. There's more to go too.
b. Yes, my papers are all filed now, I've got rid of some junk and I've closed down some savings accounts in order to pay off some of the overdraft.
c. Certainly, both in terms of home life and investments. I see that the simpler investments are usually the best in the long run.

17. If you have a mortgage, are you planning to pay it off quickly?
a. I don't have one.
b. Yes, as soon as I get the savings account together.
c. Oh definitely!

18. How long could you keep going if you suddenly lost your income?
a. Probably a few weeks now that my bills have gone down a bit.
b. A month or two but I hope to make that longer later by building up my savings safety net.
c. Six months. I have enough put by in savings to cover me in case I lose my job.

19. What advice would you give to someone in money troubles?

a. Read this book!

b. Read this book, go on money websites and talk to the free advice charities.

c. Read this book and let me know if you need any help.

20. What are your next steps going to be towards your goal of improving your finances and life?

a. I'm going to look for more ways of making money on the side.

b. I'm going to keep my spending diary going. I will set up a savings account and find more ways of making money on the side.

c. I'm going to look for new opportunities to build a richer life, including lots of ways to create a passive income stream.

HOW DID YOU GET ON?

Mostly 'a's: Beyond Beginner

It looks like you're on your way to getting a handle on your money situation. You've already made progress so pat yourself on the back for that. Go back and reread some of the chapters – particularly in the first part of the book – and work through the steps, incorporating them into your life one at a time. Don't worry if it takes a while – if you persist you will change your life.

Get busy on the Moneymagpie.com message boards. There you will find support and help with getting out of debt and making more money from some of the other people in that community. One day you will find, to your surprise, that you're giving your friends tips and advice about their money. Oh yes you will!

Mostly 'b's: Intermediate

You really have moved on a lot by reading this book. Keep up the good work! Put the tips into practice and continue to read the information on Moneymagpie.com and in the money sections of newspapers and other websites. Once you get more knowledge, and therefore more confidence, you will be able to be really clever with your spending and even smarter with your investing. You will certainly become a major Money Magpie.

Mostly 'c's: More Advanced

Awesome work; you're an inspiration! Please jump on the Moneymagpie.com message boards and share your top tips with the people who are working through the first two stages. Keep going with your plan to pay off your mortgage as soon as possible. Make sure you have a balance and live in the now, as well as thinking of the future. Well done!

What to do now ...

- If you haven't done so already, get yourself straight on to the Moneymagpie.com newsletter list; check out the updated tips in the special ebook on the site reserved for readers of this book (remember, it's at www.moneymagpie.com/bookgift) and initiate and take part in discussions on the Moneymagpie.com message boards. Keep saving and making money; use us as your support group and you will get there!

101 Ways to Get One-up on the World of Finance

25 Ways to be Clever with Your Finances

1. Do a budget and update it at least once a year.
2. Always pay your credit card off in full every month if at all possible. If you can do this every month then get a cashback or rewards card so that you get paid to spend (only on things you genuinely need of course!)
3. Pay off your mortgage as fast as possible. It's safe, secure, tax-free and will mean a big burden is lifted off your shoulders.
4. Get money-smart. Read one or two articles about money each week, either in a weekend newspaper or on a money website like Moneymagpie.com – my team of Money Magpies consists of real people facing the same sort of challenges that you do. We have a sense

of fun and of achieving things together with no complicated financial jargon.

5. Make a will, whatever age you are.
6. Give away as much as you can while you are alive. It's tax-efficient and you can enjoy the effects of your generosity. Also, it means that your descendants aren't hanging around waiting for you to die in order to inherit! They're around because they want to be.
7. Always check your receipts, and monitor your bank statements and bills weekly or monthly. You never know who has got hold of your details, or what automatic payment you've forgotten. So you need to keep tabs on what is going out and coming in.
8. Keep all your receipts and bank statements for at least five years.
9. Keep on top of your finances by filing important documents and sorting those files out once or twice a year.
10. If you have debt problems, seek help as early as possible. Contact your mortgage company and other lenders as soon as you think you might have problems paying the loan back. Get free help early on from agencies such as the Citizens Advice Bureau, CCCS, National Debtline or Shelter.
11. If you regularly have difficulty paying off your credit cards, either switch to a 0 per cent deal or, if you can, cut them up entirely and only use cash.
12. Read the small print in all contracts (including bank, credit card, loan and insurance contracts). It's a boring exercise but it can save you thousands.
13. Check your credit rating once a year. You can get it for

free if you sign up to Experian or Equifax's 24-hour credit-checking service, but make sure you cancel before the end of the first month or you will have to start paying.

14. Make sure you get all the benefits and tax credits you are entitled to.

15. Don't pay any more tax than you have to. Use up all your tax allowances including ISAs. Give money away each year to help with inheritance tax if you can afford it. Make sure you make use of any tax credits you are entitled to and share your investments with your spouse so that you cut down on your capital gains tax.

16. Check your council tax band. To find out if you are paying too much, check what your neighbours are paying at www.voa.gov.uk.

17. Make copies of your passport, your credit cards and any other important financial documents before you go abroad and leave the copies with a friend or family member.

18. Be aware that if you cohabit you do not have the rights that a married person has, even if you have children. Make sure your name is on any jointly owned property and keep your own investments if you don't have a ring on your finger.

19. Never invest in anything you don't understand. Ask, ask and ask again until you either understand how this thing makes money or you decide that it's all just smoke and mirrors.

20. Invest for your children's future – use the stock market for any investments that you want to make for longer than five years. Start moving money into more stable cash and bond investments five years before your child will cash in the investment.

21. Go against the crowd, particularly when it comes to investing. If you are investing for the long term, you should try to put your money into products you have researched and found to be intrinsically good when they are at their cheapest – that's usually when no one else wants them!

22. Be sensible about short-term finances but don't be too cautious about long-term investing. The longer your money is in something like a stock market fund, the safer it is and the more profit you are likely to make on it.

23. Only lend money to friends and family if you don't mind losing it. Relationships are more important than money so make sure the loan isn't something that could drive a wedge between you. Sometimes it's better just to give money than lend it and have the loan hanging over your heads.

24. Same with investing in businesses run by friends or family. Only put in money that you could afford to lose. Also, make sure that you have proper legal documents to show your investment and your percentage ownership of the business.

25. Set up passive streams of income. It may mean extra work at the start but setting up a small internet business that runs itself, for example, can bring in money each year without much effort.

25 Ways to Be a Smart Spender

1. Research big-ticket items before you buy them. Cars, beds, sofas and certainly houses should be researched on the internet, in magazines and newspapers and with friends and experts before they are bought.
2. Get the best deals. Don't be lazy and stick with your utility provider, bank or phone and broadband provider just because it's easy.
3. Compare prices to see if you're getting the best deal. Use the Moneymagpie.com comparison pages to search around for the best deals at www.moneymagpie.com/index.php?action=showComparisons.
4. Go electronic. Paying by direct debit and receiving electronic statements can save you money because paper bills now incur extra charges from some services.
5. Do a mortgage check. Some mortgage providers are loosening up and cutting their rates. Some are even willing to waive the arrangement fees, which makes remortgaging even easier. Moneymagpie.com has a guide to how to remortgage your home that will tell you exactly what you need to do.
6. Make as much as you can from your savings.
7. Consider using prepaid credit cards abroad. These are cards that you load up with money beforehand but you cannot borrow on them. If your prepaid card is stolen or 'skimmed', fraudsters cannot access your bank and borrowing details as they can with credit or debit cards. Also, it's a good way of budgeting when on holiday and stopping yourself overspending.

8. Get the best insurance deal. You should always be checking if you can get a better deal. With road tax on the rise, reducing the cost of your car insurance is a must. Lots of companies also offer 12 months' home insurance for the price of nine, or 25 per cent off when you buy online. Try the insurance comparison on Moneymagpie.com.
9. Watch what you spend in the supermarket. Keeping your wits about you when shopping can save you money. Look at the price per unit (usually per 100 grams or kg) to compare prices. Mysupermarket.com will do all the price comparison for you.
10. Go 'own brand' to make big household savings. Boots' own-brand shower gel starts from just 99p while the cheapest branded product is £1.49. That's a 34 per cent saving. The same goes for medication. Many 'own brand' products are made with exactly the same ingredients as the branded stuff but are a fraction of the price.
11. Make the most of good supermarket offers. The ultimate offers are 'buy one get one free'. If something you like and use frequently is on a two-for-one deal then pick up a load of them. Then you can store them and use them when you need them.
12. Make sure you're signed up to your supermarket's loyalty scheme and earning points. However, *don't* be tempted by the discount vouchers on specific products that they send you – most of these are trying to get you to buy things you normally would not. The 'money off whatever you buy' vouchers are a different matter – those are great! If they don't have a loyalty scheme (like Asda, Lidl and Aldi) don't worry about changing supermarket – as long as you are getting cheaper prices overall.

13. Give yourself a spending plan. Take control of your spending by sticking to it. Make a list of everything you spend on in a week and weed out all the little extras you don't need. Total up the costs of things you really have to buy and this is your budget.

14. Plan your weekly menus. Even if you're not a budding chef, planning meals is a great idea. Knowing exactly what you need helps focus your shopping list. This avoids any temptation if you have to pop to the shops to get a missing ingredient.

15. Buy seasonal fruit and veg. It's no longer trendy to eat peaches in the middle of winter. It's bad for the environment to ship them here from hotter destinations, plus it means they cost more. Root vegetables like carrots and swede are winter vegetables and are grown in the UK. You can also get squashes, cabbage and broccoli in winter. Blueberries and blackcurrants are also autumn/winter fruits, so steer clear of those out-of-season berries. You'll save money and help British producers.

16. Make a clothes shopping list. If you know you're a bit of a shopaholic, this is a really good tip to keep the habit under control. Make a list of all the clothing items you and your family need. Put it in your wallet. Then when you are out and do a bit of impromptu shopping, you know exactly what you should be looking for.

17. Charity shops are treasure troves and getting more and more popular. Get in on the game by visiting shops in affluent areas for clothes, toys, books and music.

18. Ditch the bottled water. Some bottled water is more expensive per litre than petrol. If you could get free petrol, would you continue to spend so much on it? I didn't think so.

19. Use your local library. Give up buying expensive DVDs, CDs or books. Your local library will let you rent them for a small fee or for nothing. It is free to register at all local libraries, and prices for DVD rental are usually more than 50 per cent cheaper than from your local Blockbuster. Plus, if you want to keep it for a bit longer, you can often just renew the item online, rather than paying hefty late fees.

20. Make your own fun. There are loads of ways to entertain the kids in the home for very little or even for free. Recycle old paper by letting them draw and make collages on the other side. Make anything you can out of leftover packaging. Add a little glue and paint to some cut-up cereal boxes and they can create some great 3D pictures. Make your own ice lollies and sweet treats. It's fun and a lot cheaper than buying them in the supermarket.

21. Don't pay out for an expensive television package. Have you got Sky? Do you really need it? If you can bear to part with it you should. The basic Sky package is very similar to the service you'd get with a Freeview box. You can get one of these for as little as £5, and there's no monthly fee.

22. Use your computer as a television. Instead of buying extra televisions, use screens you've already got. The major television channels now let you watch their programmes online, so if you have a computer in a room you don't really need an extra television in there.

23. Don't gamble away your money. Gambling might make you think of casinos or betting shops but it includes scratch cards and a weekly flutter on the lottery. You are more likely to be struck by lightning than you are to win the lottery. It's better to put that weekly couple of pounds into a high-interest savings account and make it your Christmas savings.

24. Drink less. I know – it seems like I'm taking away all your fun – but cutting down to just one pint instead of two after work can save you almost £20 a week. One bottle of wine every other night, instead of every night, will save at least £10.

25. Get rid of the ready meals. Even if you think you can't cook, there's no excuse for ready meals if you're trying to save money. They've got extra additives and preservatives that you can't control, plus they are far more expensive than it would be to make the same dish yourself. Cooking is not hard; you just need simple recipes and basic ingredients.

25 Ways to Make the Most of Your Money

1. Get as much as you can for free. There's a lot out there you can get, from free samples and free food and drink to free entertainment, free travel and free holidays. You can even get free money if you put a bit of effort into it!

2. Think about what you spend your money on and what you should sacrifice. Ask yourself each time you go to spend: 'Do I need this or would the money be better spent somewhere else?'

3. Don't forget to negotiate on the high street. At least ask for a discount or something thrown in for free. They can only say 'no'. If you are offering cash or the assistants are on commission then they are very likely to say 'yes'!

4. Never stop being generous. Just because you're cleverer with your money now it doesn't mean you should give less away. In fact, you should have more to give to those who need it. Cultivate generosity and unselfishness. Without those two qualities our lives are poorer, no matter what money is in the bank.
5. Make extra cash where you can. Think laterally. You could make money out of your space, your time, your skills and your computer. There are even ways of making extra cash while watching the television.
6. Go for value rather than the cheapest of everything, particularly in financial products like insurance.
7. Think about what you love and spend on that. Save on things that don't matter to you so much.
8. Buy quality, style and design that will last, where possible. Better to have a few items of good, well-designed and well-made furniture in your home than have it cluttered with tat. Same with your wardrobe: buy a few well-designed and well-made 'investment' items and update them each season with cheap fashion accessories. The main point here is to spend less – don't use this advice as an excuse to go and buy expensive things!
9. Pay for help with your chores if you think the time it frees up will help you make money.
10. If you are thinking of getting married make sure you are open about your money situation with your partner beforehand. Best for them to know about your debts and the way you want to organise your money before you start sharing finances.
11. If you are planning on having a baby, try to save up

enough money to cover your costs for at least six months. Children cost money and the more you have saved before you have them, the less strain you will feel as a family.

12. Teach your children how to manage their money as early as possible. Even if you don't have money to give them, helping them manage theirs will ensure that they are never poor.

13. Don't underestimate the value of points, reward schemes and vouchers. Don't buy things just to get points or rewards because they're not worth it, but if you are buying something anyway, you might as well get points that you can redeem for freebies later on.

14. Never let your credit card out of your sight when you use it to pay in restaurants, hotels or other retail outlets. If they cannot bring a machine to you, walk with them to where their till is so that you can watch what they do with your card. If you carry your driver's licence with you then don't sign the back of your credit card – instead write 'Photo ID required' so that if someone does steal your credit cards they will find it more difficult to pass themselves off as you.

15. Never invest in anything that you are told about by a salesperson ringing you up. If it were such a good investment, why wouldn't they keep it to themselves? Anyone who contacts you by phone, email, post or even pigeon about the latest 'amazing' investment is a con-artist.

16. Never open attachments to emails that you do not recognise.

17. Be very careful about emails that seem to be from your bank. If you are in doubt, phone your bank to see if it is a genuine email.

18. Get a shredder (you can get a good grade three shredder for under £20 now) and shred any official documents or letters with personal details that you are planning on throwing out. Don't give your identity away.

19. Cook for yourself and for others more. Take lessons if you don't know how to. Doing this cuts down on costs and keeps you healthier and happier, particularly when you cook for others.

20. Walk every day, to keep yourself healthy and able to work, even if it means walking round your dining room table for 10 minutes! Keep everything moving, especially when you would rather just sit.

21. Clear out your junk at least once every three months. Either sell it through the internet or a car boot sale or just take it round to your local charity shop. Clearing your clutter helps you to think more clearly and live more simply.

22. Have a present box and fill it through the year with unwanted gifts or cheap items you have picked up. When birthdays and Christmas come around you will have at least a few presents to start you off. It might be a good idea to also make a note on them about who they're from, so you don't give them back to the same person!

23. Always get at least three quotes for any work you have done in your house or your business. Remember, though, the cheapest is not always the best.

24. Recycle, recycle, recycle. Not only is reusing things in the home and business better for the environment, it's better for your wallet too. Reuse paper, including old envelopes and junk mail if it can be written on. Find new uses for empty bottles and packaging. Turn old clothes into rags or into new clothes. Think before you throw.

25. Write yourself a list of things you have right now, including friends and family, health, the trees outside your window, food in the fridge and so on. Do this any time you feel impoverished and low. Remember, a third of the world lives on less than a dollar a day. Whatever you make, you are better off than them.

25 Ways to Make Savings in Your Home

1. Embrace old-style cleaners. Forking out for 'miracle' cleaners that don't work is a pain but there's no need. White vinegar will unblock sinks, remove lime scale and clean your worktops. Bicarbonate of soda will descale teacups and teapots, get rid of smells in your fridge and clean the microwave. See www.goselfsufficient.co.uk for ideas.

2. Get a cheap lick of paint. Save money on sprucing up your house by checking out the 'oops' gallons at DIY stores. These are paint tins left over from when the mixer doesn't quite get the colour right.

3. Put the lid on. Never boil water (or heat anything, actually) in an uncovered pan. The lid will prevent heat escaping, the water will come to a boil faster and you'll use less energy.

4. Floors need a revamp? Replacing your carpets can cost a small fortune. However, giving them a good steam-clean can restore them to almost as good as new.

5. Do your own DIY. Save money by taking a local adult education course in DIY instead of hiring a handyman.

6. Reuse your old clothes and jewellery. For example, make old jeans into draught excluders by cutting the legs off, stuffing them and then sewing up the ends. Keep retro jewellery in a dressing-up box for your kids.
7. Have a 'use it up' week. This is where you don't buy anything new, but make yourself use up the odds and ends of things you have already bought. Whether it's a half-finished bottle of shampoo or open cereal packets, using everything up will save you money.
8. Buy cooking ingredients in bulk. Despite the bigger initial spend, you'll end up saving. Do the same with toilet paper, detergent and other household items. Buy in bulk from a wholesale supermarket or from your regular supermarket when there is a special offer.
9. Make your home more efficient. Losing heat and electricity is like throwing money away. According to the Energy Saving Trust (www.energysavingtrust.org.uk), the average household loses around 50 per cent of the heat generated from inside it. So you're paying for power you're not even getting the benefit from.
10. Block those draughts. Even small insulating measures like draught excluders or thicker curtains can really make a difference. You could get up to £2,700 in grants from the government to help. Find out more at Energysavingtrust.org.uk.
11. Turn your heating down. It's hard to do it when it's chilly, but turning the thermostat down a few degrees can save loads. According to the Energy Saving Trust, a reduction of just one degree can reduce bills by as much as 10 per cent. Even reducing dust on radiator surfaces can save

energy and money as dust and grime seriously impede the flow of heat in your house.

12. Switch everything off. We spend £1 billion every year on powering our electrical appliances while they are on standby. It's so easy just to turn them off at the mains and save money.

13. Save your hot water! The average bath uses about twice as much hot water as a five-minute shower.

14. Get rid of the tumble dryer. Tumble dryers are one of the most power-hungry appliances in the home. They take twice as much power to dry your clothes as it takes to wash them.

15. Wear your winter woollies. No, I'm not talking outside. Wearing your winter woollies indoors can save you big bucks. Wearing closely woven fabrics can help you retain an extra half degree in warmth, and a light long-sleeved sweater gives you another two degrees. Go for a big woolly jumper or hoody and you can gain up to 3.7 degrees more. Plus, the air between the layers serves as insulation to keep more body heat in.

16. Clear out your junk. You could have hundreds of pounds' worth of unused stuff lying around in your house. All you've got to do is gather up all the old junk that you don't need and sell it off at a car boot sale or on eBay.

17. Grow your own fruit and veg to reduce your food spend. The seeds cost as little as £1. You don't need a garden to grow stuff either – get things growing on your window-sills, balcony or just in the kitchen. You can even make money by selling on any extra plants. If you don't have a garden and your neighbour does, offer to take over a part of it in exchange for a share of some of your produce. You never know!

18. Make things last. Don't throw away a ketchup bottle with the dregs left in the bottom. Save money by draining it into the new bottle. This works for most condiments and it can be a bit of fun for the kids to get the bottles balancing. Other handy saving tips are to snap dish-washer tablets in half, water down beauty products, mix value products with more expensive stuff, turn stale bread into breadcrumbs and use scissors for cutting open old toothpaste tubes so you get everything out.
19. Say no to packaging. Buying loose items instead of those that are pre-packaged is cheaper and produces a lot less waste. You can also choose exactly how many items you want, rather than paying for items you don't need.
20. Don't spend more for the garden. Almost everything you need for the garden can be found from household products and waste. Don't buy new garden pots – reuse old colanders, teapots or even terracotta chimneys you find lying around. Great compost can be made from vegetable leftovers from your kitchen. You can also make your own weed killers from washing-up liquid, water and vinegar.
21. Use 75 per cent less washing powder. Among other genius inventions, Lakeland has come up with Dolly Washer balls. You pop them in your washing machine with your wash. They then use their scrubbing power to clean your clothes, reducing the need for so much detergent. This saves you money and there is less detergent residue on your clothes afterwards. Great.

22. Only run full washing machines and dishwashers. We know you're not supposed to overfill them, but running them half-empty defeats the purpose. Most dishwashers and washing machines use the same amount of water and heat, no matter how full they are.

23. Keep your freezer stocked. Freezers work far more efficiently when they are frost-free and full up. If you don't have enough to fill up your freezer, fill the gaps with ice cube trays.

24. Recycle old fabric and towels. Old curtains can be made into seat and cushion covers and cleaning rags. If your towels are going a bit grey, bring them back to life by dyeing them a new colour.

25. Don't shell out for new furniture. Give old chests of drawers, wardrobes and cupboards a new look instead of replacing them. All you need is a lick of paint and some new, inexpensive handles.

ONE FINAL TIP...

Sign up to the free newsletter at Moneymagpie.com! That way you get to hear about new top savings deals, the best credit cards around and the latest way to save and make money to put you ahead of the rest.

Glossary

Accountant: Professional number-cruncher. Traditionally much maligned for having about as much charisma as a dial-tone, but come tax return time they can be your best friend, taking the headache out of your financial form-filling and saving you serious amounts of money.

Additional voluntary contribution (AVC): Extra payments you can choose to make into your pension, on top of what your employer asks you to pay.

Annual equivalent rate: The amount of interest your money will earn in a savings account if you leave it alone for a year.

Annual percentage rate: A common way of expressing how much borrowing money will cost. It's the amount of interest you will be paying, over a year, on a sum you have borrowed.

Annuity: An income you're paid after you retire, until you die. You buy the annuity from a company, which then agrees to give you a fixed sum every year. Worth putting off pushing up the daisies for as long as possible or you'll lose out.

Bankruptcy: A way of dealing with debts you can't pay. Usually to be avoided. You can voluntarily declare yourself bankrupt, or you can be forced to by a creditor to whom you owe more than £750. You're then bankrupt for a certain amount of time (normally a couple of years, though this can vary), during which you lose control of your assets and are stopped from doing lots of things like getting much credit or acting as a company director.

Bond: Nothing to do with James. More like an IOU: lenders hand over their money to a business or the government and expect to get it back, plus interest, in the future. There are many different kinds of bonds – they may be short term or long term and interest may be paid at a fixed or variable rate.

Broker: So called because if you use one of the posh ones with expensive offices, you are. A broker is basically a middleman who brings together two parties for a financial transaction, such as selling customers insurance policies or shares. Now you can use much cheaper online brokers for buying and selling shares.

Capital: Ker-ching! A load of money or the value of your assets.

Capital gain: The profit you make when you sell an asset, such as the proceeds you get from selling shares, minus the cost of the shares. You have to pay capital gains tax on this profit if it goes above a certain threshold.

Compound interest: (See also 'Interest'.) Compound interest is a bigger version of interest as it is calculated both on the sum and on the interest that has accrued on the sum in previous periods. Basically, a get-rich-slow scheme.

Defined benefit scheme: An occupational pension scheme with no surprises. Rules specify what you'll get when you retire, depending, for example, on what your salary is or how many years you've worked there.

Defined contribution scheme: An occupational pension scheme with surprises. Your contributions are fixed, but the amount of pension you finally receive will depend on things like the size of the fund that you've built up.

Dividend: Money that companies give out to shareholders. British companies usually fork out a couple of dividends a year, one larger and one smaller. You usually get an amount for each share; the company can decide how much cash to share out and how much to keep in the business.

Endowment: A combination of life insurance policy and investment – you or your dependants are guaranteed a payout either on your death or on a fixed date, whichever is sooner. Generally expensive and poorly performing and a better money-maker for the person who sold it to you than for you.

Equity: A word for a plain old share in a company. Can also mean the amount of your house that you own (the value of the property minus any mortgage you still have to pay on it).

Exchange-traded funds (ETFs): A relatively new kind of investment fund which can be bought through most stockbrokers. They are similar to tracker funds as, effectively, they track the stock market. A cheap way to get into the stock market, as admin charges tend to be very low.

Final salary scheme: A rather nice little pension scheme where you get an annual payout of a percentage of whatever your salary was when you retired. Expensive for employers to run and consequently disappearing fast.

Financial Services Authority (FSA): The independent, non-governmental body that regulates the finance industry, including mortgages. (Not to be confused with the Food Standards Agency, which has the same acronym.)

Front-end loading: Nothing to do with washing machines,

or any kind of domestic appliance for that matter. A front-end load is the initial admin and/or commission charge made when you invest in a unit trust, life-assurance company or any other kind of investment fund.

FTSE All-share Index (pronounced 'Footsie'): Includes around 700 of the top companies in the UK.

FTSE 100 Index: A share index of the 100 biggest companies listed on the London Stock Exchange (LSE). The FTSE 250 tracks the big firms ranked at 101 to 350.

HM Revenue and Customs: Quite possibly the most exciting government department in the world. It has responsibility for all sorts of taxes: VAT, customs and excise, national insurance, tax credits, child benefit and child trust funds, among other things. Find out more at www.hmrc.gov.uk.

Independent financial adviser (IFA): Someone with a posh Merc and a second home in Marbella. IFAs are licensed to advise you on financial products offered by a range of different companies. Some earn commission for selling particular products, which might lead you to question just how independent they really are.

Index tracker: An index is, quite simply, a way of measuring how well a stock market is performing by comparing the performance of shares in a group of different companies. A tracker fund is basically a microcosm of the index – it has shares in the same companies and in the same proportions they are found in the index. The idea is that the tracker will emulate the performance of the index, and hopefully get bigger as the market goes up.

Individual savings account (ISA): A way of saving money without having to pay tax on it. You can put up to £7,200 per tax year (April to April) into an investment wrapped in an ISA. You can either put the full £7,200 in a shares-based ISA or up to £3,600 in a cash ISA and then the rest in a shares ISA.

Inflation: The tendency of prices to rise over time. This means the value of your money can drop if you don't keep up, such as by investing.

Inland Revenue: (See 'HM Revenue and Customs'.)

Interest: The charge you pay if you borrow money, and the income you receive if you lend it or invest it in a savings account or other interest-bearing product like gilts. For example if you borrow £1,000 at an interest rate of 10 per cent per year, the interest payable is £100 per year. Similarly, if you invest £1,000 in something that gives 10 per cent interest you will make £100 in that year.

Investment trust: A company that invests its shareholders' funds in the shares of other companies – it's up to you whether or not you trust them. This might sound a bit Kafkaesque, but it means people without a lot of money can invest in a wide range of companies without incurring massive trading fees.

Life assurance: A policy where you pay a premium in order to get a lump sum paid out in the event of your death. The stuff of a million murder mystery motives, this started off as a way to cover your funeral expenses, but these days can enable you to get some tax breaks on your savings.

Life insurance: The term is often used interchangeably with life assurance, although technically, insurance protects holders from events that might happen.

Mutual society: A company that has no issued stocks or shares. Instead, it is owned by its investors.

Negative equity: A nasty thing that can happen when

house prices crash. If the value of your house falls below the value of your mortgage, you are said to have negative equity.

Occupational pension scheme: A pension scheme for employees of a particular company, or possibly a trade.

Official receiver: A civil servant in the Insolvency Service and an officer of the court who is responsible for administering the first stages of an insolvency (bankruptcy) case. This includes collecting and protecting any assets and investigating the causes of the bankruptcy or winding up.

Open-ended investment company (OEIC): An American idea that came over to the UK in 1997. A bit of a hybrid between a unit trust and an investment trust, an OEIC sells shares in itself then uses that cash to invest in other companies. They usually operate as umbrella funds, often having a few different smaller funds. They're known as open-ended because, if demand for their shares rises, they simply issue more. Unlike a unit trust, OEICs tend to have just one share price, whether you're buying or selling.

Personal pension plan (PPP): A pension scheme for those without occupational pensions, such as the self-employed and people whose employers don't have a group pension scheme. An employer can contribute to your PPP, but there's nothing to say they have to. You can take a PPP with you when you change jobs. PPP contributions get tax relief, and you can buy life assurance, which may also be eligible for tax relief if it's bundled up with the pension. Apart from stakeholder pensions, though, PPPs tend to be expensive, opaque and badly performing.

Self-invested personal pension (SIPP): A kind of DIY personal pension for people who know a bit about the stock market themselves. Rather than letting an insurance company decide where to invest your cash, you can choose what to invest in – including shares, property, art and antiques. Fees and charges for a SIPP usually work out at about 2 per cent a year, though (they're capped at 1 per cent in a stakeholder pension), so they're best reserved for those with lots of money to invest.

Share: If you buy a share, then you own part of a company. Usually, people buy lots of shares in the hope that they'll go up and up in value – one on its own is unlikely to be much of an investment. Roughly speaking, a company's share price is determined by market forces: if a lot of people want to buy shares, their value will go up; if a lot of people want to sell shares, their value will fall. So in theory, there's a lot of money to be made, but it's always a risk, and if a company goes bust, shareholders are last in line to get any of the cash.

Shareholder: As the name suggests, anyone who holds shares in a company. Shareholders are also entitled to do stuff like receive the company's accounts and vote at their Annual General Meeting. Most companies pay regular dividends to their shareholders.

Stakeholder pension: A fairly new type of low-cost, flexible pension. Even if you're not earning you can pay in a limited amount each year, and get tax relief on this. Anyone in a company pension scheme earning less than a certain amount a year (set by the HMRC) can pay into a stakeholder pension as well, and employers with five or more employees must give them access to a stakeholder scheme if the company doesn't have any other kind of pension fund set up.

Stamp Duty: Another way the government punishes us for doing well. It's a fixed tax you pay when you buy shares (0.5 per cent) or property above a certain value (1–4 per cent, depending on the value of the property).

Stock: The basis of many a good soup. What Americans call shares. In the UK, a fixed-interest financial asset like a government bond. There is usually a redemption date and, in the meantime, they are traded on stock exchanges.

Stock exchange: A market in which securities are traded, such as the London Stock Exchange. The other big ones are in Tokyo and New York.

Stockbroker: An agent who does the trading on the stock exchange; usually far from broke.

Tax: Money you have to pay to the government which, in theory at least, is then used to pay for useful things like the nation's health and education. There are many different kinds, such as income tax that comes out of your pay packet and VAT which is charged on many goods you buy. Basically, if you make a bit of money out of anything the government wants a cut of it. Also known as 'daylight robbery'.

Tax credit: A well-intentioned but rather bureaucratic system of extra tax-free allowances. A tax credit is an amount taken off the tax bill of certain groups of people, such as some couples with children under 16, so the lucky souls don't have to pay as much.

Tax relief: A system whereby someone doesn't have to pay tax on part of their income. Always worth snapping up, if you qualify.

Yield: The annual income you get from an investment, expressed as a percentage of the value of that investment. The interest rate on a savings account, for example.

Resources

WEBSITES

Comparison Sites

Try these if you want to get the best deals on ...

Switching Your Bills

- *Moneymagpie.com*
- *Moneysupermarket.com*
- *Energyhelpline.com*
- *ConsumerChoices.co.uk*
- *SwitchwithWhich.co.uk*
- *Comparethemarket.com*
- *Gocompare.com*
- *Kwik-fitinsurance.com*
- *Moneyextra.com*
- *Fool.co.uk*

Purchases

- *Pricerunner.co.uk*
- *Kelkoo.co.uk*
- *Mysupermarket.co.uk*
- *Amazon.co.uk*
- *CDWow.com*

Useful Sites for Making Money

Go here if you want to ...

Make Some Quick Cash

- *Cashbackshopper.co.uk*
- *Adsoncars.com*
- *Envirofone.com*
- *Zubka.com*

Be in a Focus Group

- *Researchbox.co.uk*
- *SurveyShack.com*
- *Focus4people.co.uk*

Be a Mystery Shopper

- *TNSglobal.com*
- *Performanceinpeople.co.uk*
- *GfKNOP.com*

Find Ideas for the Over-60s

- *Homesitters.co.uk*
- *BritishDoulas.co.uk*
- *Nards.co.uk*
- *BarkingMad.uk.com*

Sell Your Stuff Online

- *Amazon.co.uk*
- *eBay.co.uk*
- *CQOut.com*
- *Ebid.net*

- *Tazbar.com*
- *Preloved.co.uk*
- *Auctionair.co.uk*
- *iBootSale.co.uk*
- *Greenmetropolis.com (books)*

Sell Your Stuff in Person

- *Carbootjunction.com*
- *Yourbooty.co.uk*
- *Farmersmarkets.net*
- *Country-markets.co.uk*
- *TheWI.org.uk*
- *LearnDirect.co.uk*

Be a Film/Television Extra

- *CastingCollective.co.uk*
- *RayKnight.co.uk*
- *2020casting.com*

Be a Market Researcher

- *RMLTD.net*
- *Research247.com*
- *NatCen.ac.uk*
- *Criteria.co.uk*
- *ACNielson.co.uk*
- *IMSHealth.com*
- *Fieldshare.net*
- *Ipsos-MORI.com*
- *RBG.org.uk*
- *AQR.org.uk*
- *RSS.org.uk*

Host a Product Party

- *VirginVieathome.com*
- *AnnSummers.com*
- *TheBodyShop.co.uk*
- *JustTrade.co.uk/party*
- *Shoes-Galore.co.uk*
- *IAmNatural.co.uk/party.html*

Be a Virtual Assistant

- *Allianceofukvirtualassistants.org.uk*
- *Societyofvirtualassistants.co.uk*
- *IAVA.org.uk*
- *VA4U.co.uk*

Do an Online Survey

- *Panelbase.net*
- *Toluna.com*
- *LightspeedPanel.com*
- *ValuedOpinions.co.uk*
- *MySurvey.co.uk*
- *Ciao-surveys.co.uk (surveys)*
- *Ciao.co.uk (product reviews)*

Earn Online

- *MyHPF.co.uk*
- *HTMail.com*
- *SendMoreInfo.com*
- *Yuwie.com*

Work for a Text Service

- *Ansanow.com*
- *Texperts.com*
- *63336.com (AQA)*

Sell Your Photos

- *Picturenation.co.uk*
- *Fotolia.co.uk*
- *Istockphoto.co.uk*
- *123RF.co.uk*

Sell Your Videos

- *Revver.com*
- *Spymac.com*
- *Tripr.tv*
- *Metacafe.com*

Rent Your Stuff

- *Rentrino.co.uk*
- *RentNotBuy.co.uk*

Rent Your Parking Space

- *Parklet.co.uk*
- *Parkatmyhouse.com*
- *Spareground.com*

Rent Your Rooms

- *Gumtree.com*
- *Easyroommate.com*
- *Roomsforlet.co.uk*

- *Torent.co.uk*
- *Letsdirect.co.uk*
- *Rentomatic.co.uk*

Rent Your House

- *Film-locations.co.uk*
- *LavishLocations.com*
- *LocationPartnership.com*
- *LocationWorks.com*
- *BBC.co.uk*
- *AmazingSpace.co.uk*
- *Locations-uk.com*

Useful Sites for Freebies and Bargains

Go here if you want …

Free Stuff

- *Snaffleup.co.uk*
- *Freecycle.org*
- *Gumtree.com*
- *Craigslist.co.uk*
- *Freebietown.co.uk*
- *Britishfreebies.co.uk*
- *Freestuffjunction.co.uk*
- *Free-stuff.co.uk*
- *Moneymagpie.com*

To Organise a House-swap

- *Holswop.com*
- *Digsville.com*
- *Homeexchange.com*

Discounts on Meals out and Entertainment

- *Toptable.co.uk*
- *5pm.co.uk*
- *Lastminute.com*

Cashback

- *Topcashback.co.uk*
- *WePromiseTo.co.uk*
- *FreeFivers.co.uk*
- *GiveorTake.com*
- *Rpoints.com*
- *Myshoppingrewards.com*

Useful Government Sites

- *Direct.gov.uk*
- *HMRC.gov.uk*
- *Thepensionservice.gov.uk*
- *OFT.gov.uk (Office of Fair Trading)*
- *Entitledto.co.uk*
- *Moneymadeclear.fsa.gov.uk*

Help if You Are in Debt

- *NationalDebtline.co.uk (0808 808 4000)*
- *Citizensadvice.org.uk (Citizens Advice Bureau)*
- *CCCS.co.uk (Consumer Credit Counselling Service, 0800 138 1111)*
- *Shelter.org.uk (0808 800 4444)*
- *Insolvency.gov.uk (run by the Department of Trade and Industry)*
- *R3.org.uk (insolvency practitioners)*
- *Bankruptcyadvisoryservice.co.uk*

Useful Sites for Saving and Investing

- *Moneymagpie.com*
- *Moneysupermarket.com*
- *Moneyfacts.co.uk*
- *Zopa.com*
- *Abcul.org.uk*
- *Nsandi.com*
- *Fool.co.uk*

Making a Will

- *Tenminutewill.co.uk*
- *Lawpack.co.uk*
- *Step.org*
- *Lawsociety.org.uk*
- *Lawscot.org.uk (Law Scotland)*
- *Lawsoc-ni.org (The Law Society of Northern Ireland)*

BOOKS

Birtles, Jasmine. *A Bit on the Side*, Piatkus, 2004.

Burns, Robbie. *The Naked Trader: How Anyone Can Make Money Trading Shares,* Harriman House Publishing, 2007.

Douglas, Mark. *The Disciplined Trader: Developing Winning Attitudes,* Prentice Hall Press, 1990.

Ferriss, Timothy. *The 4-Hour Work Week: Escape the 9-5, Live Anywhere and Join the New Rich*, Vermilion, 2008.

Koch, Richard. *Investor's Guide to Selecting Shares that Perform,* Financial Times Prentice Hall, 1994.

Levitt, S. and Dubner, S. *Freakonomics: A Rogue Economist Explores the Hidden Side of Everything*, Penguin, 2007.

Index